Fit**KIDS**

HEART
AND STROKE
FOUNDATION
OF CANADA

Fit KIDS

A practical guide to raising
active and healthy children
from birth to teens

KidsHealth®

Mary L. Gavin MD
Steven A. Dowshen MD
Neil Izenberg MD

DK

Project Editor Norma MacMillan
Senior Managing Editor Jemima Dunne
Design XAB Design
DTP Designer Julian Dams
Managing Art Editor Marianne Markham
Production Controller Louise Daly
Category Publishers Mary Thompson, Corinne Roberts
Art Director Bryn Walls
Editors, Canada Julia Roles, Ian Whitelaw

HEART AND STROKE FOUNDATION OF CANADA
Michael Sharratt, PhD
Alison M. Stephen, PhD

KIDSHEALTH
Editor Debra Moffitt
Medical Editors Sandra G. Hassink MD, Jessica Donze RD, MPH
Consulting Chef Niklaus Fuster

FIRST CANADIAN EDITION 2004
04 05 06 07 08 10 9 8 7 6 5 4 3 2

The Fit Kids Guide provides information on a wide range of health and medical topics.
The book is not a substitute for medical diagnosis, however, and you are advised always to consult your doctor for specific information on personal health matters.

Any recipes in this book are intended for people of generally good health, without specific food allergies.

Dorling Kindersley is represented in Canada by Tourmaline Editions Inc.,
662 King Street West, Suite 304, Toronto, Ontario M5V 1M7

National Library of Canada Cataloguing in Publication

Gavin, Mary L
    Fit kids : a practical guide to raising healthy and active children -
from birth to teens / Mary L. Gavin, Steven A. Dowshen and Neil
Izenberg. -- Canadian ed. / Heart & Stroke Foundation of Canada

Includes index.
ISBN 1-55363-039-4

    1. Physical fitness for children. 2. Children--Health and hygiene.
I. Dowshen, Steven A II. Izenberg, Neil III. Heart & Stroke
Foundation of Canada. IV. Title.

RJ133.G38 2004   613.7'042   C2004-900439-5

Colour reproduction by Colourscan, Singapore
Printed and bound in Singapore by Star Standard Industries (Pte.) Ltd.

Foreword

We are witnessing an alarming rise in obesity rates among Canada's children, a trend that we cannot afford to ignore. Since obesity is a major risk factor for cardiovascular disease and contributes to type 2 diabetes and high blood pressure—which are also cardiovascular disease risk factors—it is critical that we step in now to reverse the current trend in childhood obesity. Parents play an important role in shaping the habits and health of their children: encouraging them to make healthy food choices and to be physically active early in life will promote lifelong cardiovascular health.

While many young Canadians are already overweight, we need to pay equal attention to those who are not. Today's environment of physical inactivity and unhealthy food puts all children at risk of eventual weight problems, so parents, caregivers, and educators need to work together to ensure healthy kids stay that way. By reinforcing healthy habits, children's role models can help prevent potential health issues caused by inactivity and poor nutrition.

FitKids is a valuable parent resource that is full of new ideas to help kids grow up healthfully. From start to finish, FitKids offers tips for parents to become effective role models for their children. From first foods and first steps to school lunches and team sports, this book helps overcome the challenges of picky eaters and children who might not enjoy sports.

Parents who set a good example for their children hold the key to solving the growing childhood obesity problem. Small, everyday decisions at home, such as turning off the TV and going for a walk or eating more nutritious meals together, can go a long way toward widespread change. We owe it to our children to provide them with a lifetime of good health, and we have the power to give it to them—by introducing good habits now and reinforcing them every day.

Cleve Myers, CA
Chair
Heart and Stroke Foundation of Canada

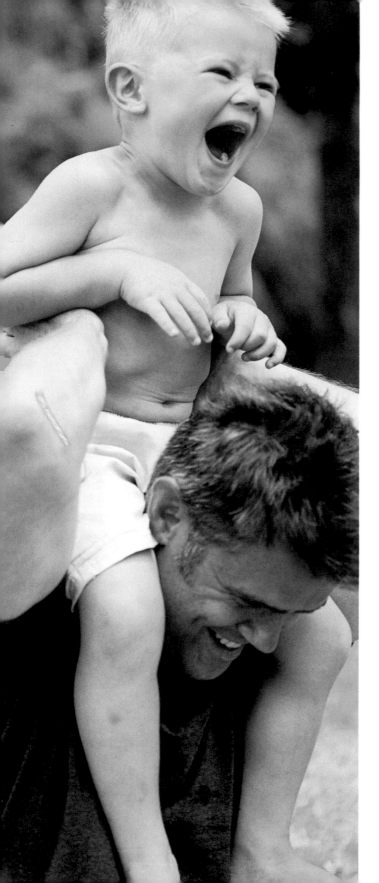

Introduction

We're living longer than any time in history. Children born today in this country have every hope of living to their 80s, 90s—or even beyond. The quality and availability of health care has improved dramatically in the last few decades. We now have year-round access to better, more plentiful foods than ever before. We know more about vitamins and nutrition, and that—amazingly—a proper diet can ward off serious medical conditions, including certain cancers, heart disease, and diabetes. More than ever, we are a nation that values exercise, respects both women's and men's athletics, and acknowledges the importance of maintaining lifelong fitness.

So, our children (and we parents) should be in the greatest physical shape ever, shouldn't we? Well…not exactly. It's true for some of us. But many parents and children are struggling. Despite the proliferation of diet foods, diet plans, and gyms, we're not in the shape we want to be. In fact, we could do a lot better.

More and more people are overweight

We are fatter than we were even a generation ago—and the rate of obesity is rising alarmingly. Movie theatres, buses, and sports arenas are being redesigned to make seats—well—wider, to accommodate our widening seats. But squeezing into our seats (or our pants) isn't the worst part. Our health—and the health of our kids—is at risk. Being overweight or out of shape also causes social and emotional pain—often in a big way.

The big problem is that food tastes great. Our exquisitely sensitive tastebuds let us revel in the pleasures of rich, chocolate ice cream and fries. Our refrigerators and pantries are usually well stocked.

Grocery shelves groan under unlimited choices, and packaged foods are brilliantly engineered to appeal to our eyes and our palates. Food tempts us everywhere —at home, in our workplaces, and in our schools. Who can resist? Even gas stations have become fast food markets, where you can grab a big bag of chips and an ultra-large, sugary drink. It may be second nature to slurp and munch on the road, but boy, does it all add up. Exceed your energy needs by just one extra pop a day and you can pack on 7kg in a year. You know what that means—another notch on your belt.

Food is not just fuel

It would be easier to resist if food were just about nutrition and getting "fuel" in our tanks. But food often means love, celebration, and family togetherness. Parents and grandparents have long rewarded kids with food. And whether we're kids or adults, the process of eating feels good, even when we're not hungry. Food can easily become a consolation when we're feeling lonely or down. We deserve a little treat (or two), don't we?

We can't blame food alone. Our expanding waistlines have as much to do with our output (activity) as our input (eating). Most of us aren't active enough and there are good excuses: too little time and a lethargic lifestyle built around sedentary activities. It's easy to sit at a work desk all day and watch TV all night. Yet being physically active is the key to good health.

Children mimic their parents

Kids learn from their parents' patterns and imitate us, so why not set the kind of example you know they need?

Maybe you were never good at sports and rarely exercise. Some kids are the same way and may not enjoy organized team sports. But that doesn't mean you and your kids can't be active, have fun, and stay in shape. It's not hard to achieve, and you can do it without clocking long hours in the gym or enduring a lot of sweat and pain.

With food, too, you can set the right example. Make healthy eating a fun and delicious way of life, steering your kids in the right direction, even as their needs change through the years. The aim is not to build elite athletes, or to put children on a fast-acting, cure-all diet. It's about getting kids—all sorts of kids— to adopt the lifelong habit of eating a healthy diet and being active.

There is no quick fix

If anyone tells you that it's easy to get kids to eat well and stay active, they're kidding you. But there's reason to invest the effort now. Many adult health problems start in childhood—though they may not be recognized until much later, when it's harder to undo them. We want today's children to avoid those problems, so they can enjoy many years of fun, activity, and good health.

As pediatricians and health educators, we feel for families trying to adopt healthy habits and fight the threat of overweight. We also celebrate (though not with a slice of pie) the successes of many who are already walking the walk. With reasonable effort, thoughtfulness, and some planning, you can make nutrition and exercise a natural part of your family's life. What you'll get in return will be priceless: fit and healthy kids.

1 CHILDREN'S WEIGHT
AND FITNESS

Eat well and be active—good advice that can be difficult to put into practice. But **you can help your children** do just that by setting a healthy table as well as **getting the whole family involved** in physical activity.

Healthy for life

It's a challenge to instill good eating and fitness habits into your kids, which you'll know if you've ever substituted carrots for potato chips as snacks or tried to ration computer time.

Creating the foundation

You want the best for your children, especially when it comes to their health and well-being. You know how important food and fitness are for good health, as study after study has shown. And, as parents, you realize that making decisions about exercise and nutrition is a weighty responsibility. Children need nutritious food and physical activity for optimal growth and development, so how can you encourage healthy habits in your family? If you aren't sure, you're not alone. As with all aspects of parenting, the aim is to create a foundation that will enable your children to make wise choices as they grow more independent.

The wrong signals

Some common strategies related to food, such as bribing kids with dessert or making them clean their plates, are easy options, but they send the wrong messages. They convey two incorrect ideas:

● Sweets are a reward.
● Hunger—or lack of it—has no bearing on the decision to keep eating or put down the fork.

A parent's attempts to get a child to exercise can backfire as well. For example, starting a child in team sports too young, or in a sport or activity that is beyond his or her ability, can lead to frustration and loss of interest.

Setting good examples

The family's daily habits and how parents live their own lives form a part of the child's landscape—what will be regarded as normal. Over time, the child will grow accustomed to the kinds of breakfast cereals that are in the cupboard, for example, and how Saturday mornings are spent, be it sleeping in or working out. No mom or dad will be perfect, but by making more good decisions than poor ones, parents can create an environment that supports the growth of a fit and healthy child.

This is by no means easy to do. Habits are ingrained and food is abundant. Modern lifestyles encourage eating on the run, as well as spending long hours sitting in cars, at computers, and in front of TVs. It can be tough to swim against this tide, but there are compelling reasons to do so: The number of overweight children—and adults—has risen dramatically and this trend upward shows no sign of stopping. Making changes in the way your family operates can be a lifelong gift you give to your children.

"I love apples"

Assessing your child's health

If you want to improve your child's health and well-being, it can be tough to know where to begin. Here's some useful advice about assessing how things stand right now. It will also be useful as you continue to monitor how nutritious your child's eating habits are and his or her fitness levels throughout childhood.

Look at eating habits

Answer "yes" or "no" to these statements to determine how healthy your child's eating habits are:

- My child eats fruit every day.
- My child eats vegetables every day.
- My child eats a variety of foods, including dairy, whole grains, fruits, vegetables, and healthy sources of protein.
- My child usually eats only when hungry, not to relieve stress or boredom.
- My child will try new foods.
- Our family rarely eats meals or snacks in front of the TV.
- Our family eats together at least five times a week.

Look at exercise habits

Answer "yes" or "no" to these statements to determine how active your child is:

- My child gets physical activity every day.
- My child seems to enjoy being active.
- My child likes his or her body.
- Our family exercises together, such as taking walks, swimming, playing tag, or doing outdoor chores.
- I make time to exercise on my own.
- I know how much physical activity is right for my child's age group.
- My child's favourite pastimes are active ones, such as sports, playing freely, or bike riding.
- My child has access at home to a variety of sports and activity equipment, such as balls, bicycles, jump ropes, and athletic shoes.

What were your answers?

If you answered "yes" to a statement, you and your family have already adopted that healthy habit. If you answered "no," you are now able to identify what you need to do to make improvements in your family's lifestyle. Tackle the areas one at a time, if necessary, and work on them until you can say "yes" to all the statements.

Some areas may be more of a struggle than others, or may grow in complexity as your son or daughter gets older. Also remember that you are an integral part of the picture. It might be illuminating to ask yourself the same assessment questions. Do you eat fruit every day, enjoy being active and like your body? If you come up short, resolve that you and your child will start making progress together.

What parents say...
about being a role model

"We are a very close family—three generations—and do lots of things together. My parents, now in their 70s, are extremely active. They cycle, walk, and do round and square dancing, which my daughter also loves. My mom always cooked from scratch, and I follow her example with my own family. I try to set good examples for my kids with exercise, too. I jog and do aerobics and weight training, and as a family we do some kind of physical activity on the weekends."

21st-century challenges

With our modern lifestyles, it can be tough to strike a healthy balance between energy consumed and energy expended through physical activity and exercise. There are many challenges for both parents and children.

Obstacles to overcome

Today, life has a one-two-three punch for anyone trying to maintain a healthy weight and lifestyle:

- a plentiful supply of food that's quick to buy or make and easy to overeat;
- sedentary routines, including long commutes, desk jobs, and free time spent in front of the TV or computer;
- daily schedules so jam-packed that it's difficult to find time to prepare wholesome family meals or exercise.

Even the most motivated parents, who take time to prepare a home-cooked meal, may find that their kids would rather eat a cupcake than a carrot, even with a delicious hummus dip. And they may resist trying new, healthy foods. Finding time for exercise also may seem impossible for working parents, especially if both of them work, as weekends are spent doing laundry and buying groceries, not hiking or playing soccer in the backyard. While parents try to tackle the household tasks, many kids may simply park themselves in front of the TV or computer, instead of being active.

Fast food

After long days at school and work, many families are too worn out to wait for a healthy meal to be prepared. Everyone is hungry, but there's homework to do and night is falling fast. As a result, convenience foods are staples in many households, despite their low nutrient value and high fat content. And, of course, fast food is in plentiful supply.

It's not just *what* kids are eating: it's *how much*. Portion sizes have increased over the last 20 years for all fast foods except pizza (see the chart below). In some cases, fast food restaurants are serving food and drink portions that are four, five, or six times the size that was offered in 1955.

Fast food portion sizes **on the rise**

Since 1955, the size of fast food portions has increased dramatically, resulting in mega-servings of calories, fat, and sugar. While a modest portion was once standard fare, hungry consumers can now buy extra-large meals that include a half-pound (225-g) burger and more than a litre of pop.

FAST FOOD SIZES THEN AND NOW

FAST FOOD	SIZE IN 1955	SUPER SIZE IN 2002
Pop	200mL	1.2L
Hamburger	45g	225g
Fries	70g	200g

INCREASED CALORIES, FAT, AND SUGAR

FAST FOOD	SIZE IN 1955	SUPER SIZE IN 2002
Fries	210 calories / 10g fat	610 calories / 29g fat
Cola	85 calories / 24g sugar	500 calories / 140g sugar

Empty-calorie drinks

High consumption of sugary, energy-dense beverages also contributes to weight gain among kids. Adolescents are drinking more soft drinks, replacing healthier beverages, such as milk, water, and fruit juice. The average teen drinks about two cans of pop a day. Pop isn't the only problem: Many juice "drinks" are heavily sweetened and contain only a small percentage of fruit juice. The calories from 100-percent juice can also add up quickly if consumed in large quantities, but fruit juice does contain more nutrients than juice drinks.

Drinking pop not only adds empty calories, it often goes hand in hand with snacking on energy-dense, high-fat foods. Soft drinks are often paired with fast food and salty snacks, so it's natural for kids to associate the two. When they're downing a cola, kids are more likely to reach for chips than a bowl of fresh fruit or vegetables, and they're already getting too little of these (see page 43).

A sedentary lifestyle

Before the conveniences of modern life—automobiles, washing machines, microwaves, televisions, computers, and so on—families spent more active time together doing household chores, walking to school and work, and playing outdoors. But today, daily life requires little physical activity.

As television viewing has increased, time spent in active work or play has decreased. Also, many kids snack in front of the TV, and research has shown a clear link between watching TV and being overweight. Many children can't, or aren't allowed to, walk or bike to school. And suburban neighbourhoods are often isolated and disconnected from the functional parts of towns, where a kid could once have walked on his or her own to go to the library.

Even children who have physical education classes at school and participate in team sports may not be getting enough exercise. One study found that gym classes offered third graders only 25 minutes of vigorous activity per week. Parents may overlook the value of free play, especially for pre-adolescent children. But simply letting a child do his or her own thing may be a welcome break from lessons and sports practices. It also may result in more sustained activity. As kids get older, they're even less likely to be physically active. By high school, nearly half don't play on any sports teams and 35 percent don't get regular physical activity of any kind. Changing that trend will mean changing the way parents and children think about sports and activity. Exercise is for everybody, not just the natural athletes among us. Later in the book, we'll talk about the value of an active lifestyle and introduce the concept of a "lifetime sport," which your child can enjoy for decades to come.

Time bind

Lengthy commutes, long work hours, and overscheduling leave little down time for parents. Meanwhile, they are getting up earlier in the morning in an attempt to accomplish even more before the sun rises on the day.

Modern families feel so crunched by the demands of jobs, children's activities, and running the household that, more often than not, they don't eat meals together. For some families, eating at the family table happens only at birthdays and holidays. That is unfortunate, because a meal shared by the whole family is more likely to be nutritious. And it gives parents a chance to introduce kids to new foods and to act as role models for healthy eating.

Computer games can take over
Kids younger than eight spend two and a half hours a day watching TV or playing video games, while kids older than eight spend four and a half hours doing the same. All children over two should be limited to two hours maximum.

Look at your child's development

Growth is one of the most important indicators of a child's health. But remember that children come in many sizes and shapes and there's no one perfect weight or ideal body type.

Is my child growing properly?

Normal children develop at different rates, so even kids the same age as your child may be bigger or smaller, or at a different stage of physical maturity. Your child will be weighed and measured during regular check-ups with the doctor. The readings will be plotted on a growth chart (see opposite) to follow your child's height and weight over time. You can plot your own chart at home, too.

Understanding growth charts

From the moment your child is born, the measurements start, with your child's doctor documenting growth at each regular check-up. Typically, infants are seen at two weeks, then at two, four, six, nine, and 12 months. During the second year, visits are less frequent. After two years, annual check-ups are recommended.

The curved lines on a growth chart represent percentiles. A percentile is based on a scale of 100. If your child is in the 50th percentile, half the kids his age are bigger and half are the same size or smaller. On a growth chart, these lines indicate expected patterns of weight gain and height growth. It's ideal when height and weight percentiles are about the same, but they may differ depending on your child's build.

Your child may be growing along a high, low, or middle percentile. It's not like a grade on a test—the 95th percentile is not better than the 50th. There can be some variation, but growth usually progresses along the same percentile. What you need to watch out for are sudden and major changes.

"I want to be this tall!"

Assessing **height and weight**

Height and weight are plotted on standardized charts. Charts make checking growth easy because you can see, at a glance, when a child who had been growing steadily veers off course. A single point on the chart provides a snapshot of how one child compares with other children who are the same age. But plotting your child's height and weight over time yields the most important information. This visual aid can offer reassurance that your child is growing properly, or spot trends that need attention. The charts shown here are based on North American data.

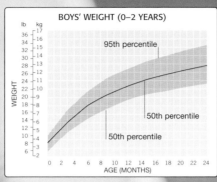

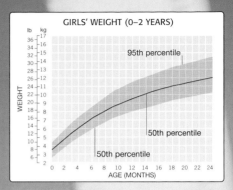

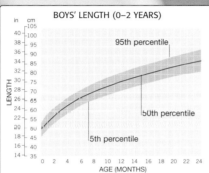

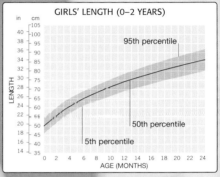

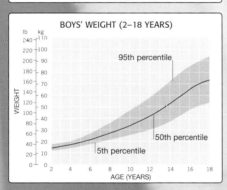

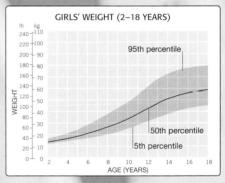

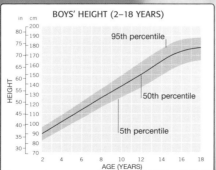

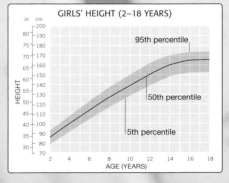

Is your child a healthy weight?

Although growth charts can be useful, Body Mass Index (BMI) charts are better for determining if a child is at a healthy weight. Using a formula, you can calculate your child's BMI, and your doctor can help you interpret the results.

BMI and what it means

This is a way of using height and weight measurements to estimate how much body fat a person has. After calculating BMI (see opposite), the resulting number can be plotted on the standard BMI chart just as your child's height and weight are plotted on growth charts (see page 17).

Most children fall into the "ideal" BMI category, which takes in a wide range of height and weight measurements. But BMI charts also can help doctors identify children and teens who are overweight or at risk for becoming overweight. If spotted early, doctors and parents can work together to prevent a child from becoming overweight by helping the child make changes in exercise and eating habits.

Because the number of overweight children is increasing, a new recommendation encourages doctors to calculate and plot BMI for all children at annual visits. As with height and weight percentiles, this allows parents and doctors to track the child's BMI over time.

Putting BMI in perspective

For most children BMI is a good indicator of body fat, but it is important to recognize that it is not a direct measurement of body fat. In fact, for some children and teens, BMI values can be misleading. Muscle is significantly heavier than fat, so more muscular children may have high BMI scores even though their percentage of body fat may be in the healthy range. A muscular teen could have a BMI in the overweight range, but probably does not have too much body fat.

On the other hand, a child with an ideal BMI can still have too much body fat. And kids in the ideal weight range can be at risk of becoming overweight. Risk factors include a low level of physical activity, a diet high in fatty, energy-dense foods, and a family history of weight problems.

BMI also may be difficult to interpret during puberty, when it's normal for girls and boys to gain weight rapidly and show dramatic increases in BMI. A parent may need a doctor or nutritionist's help to judge whether a child's rapid weight gain is a normal part of maturation, or if it warrants concern.

Some parents worry that their child is too thin, or doesn't eat enough. But few kids who are underweight on the growth charts turn out to have a health problem or other reason for concern. If you are worried about your child's low weight, talk with your child's doctor. Never start a thin child on a high-energy diet without consulting a doctor first. Unless the low weight is related to an eating disorder such as anorexia nervosa or bulimia (see page 147), regular exercise remains a healthy part of a child's routine.

What if my child is overweight?

When someone is overweight, genetic factors, lifestyle habits, or both are involved. Because both genes and habits can be passed down from one generation to the next, entire families may struggle with excess weight. You may be upset to learn that your child's BMI, weight, or the trend in weight gain is cause for concern. But identifying weight as a health concern can be the first step toward adopting new, healthier habits for your child and for the whole family.

For most overweight children, dieting is unnecessary and is not encouraged. You should never put your child on a diet without a doctor's or dietitian's okay. Drastically reducing calories or cutting out foods containing essential nutrients may be dangerous to your child's health or interfere with overall growth and development. The goal with children should never be hitting a specific mark on the scale. Instead, the aim should be to help your child get into a weight range that allows healthy growth and development.

It's important that children learn the importance of healthy eating and exercise—without taking it too far. Be on the lookout for signs that they are taking the initiative to diet on their own. Many adolescents, especially young girls, feel uncomfortable with the normal weight gain that occurs with the onset of puberty. Help them understand these changes and be willing to answer questions. Educate them about the dangers of fad diets, fasting, and other dietary restrictions that may hurt their health and growth. (To learn about the symptoms of eating disorders, see page 163.)

Assessing your child's **BMI**

To use this indicator, first calculate your child's BMI using the mathematical formula below. Now look for that number along the left side of the boys' or girls' chart, and then find your child's age along the bottom. Draw your finger along the lines from these two points. Where the lines intersect in the chart is your child's weight category. These charts are based on North American data.

BMI = [weight in kg ÷ height in cm ÷ height in cm] x 10,000

1 Divide your child's weight in kg (kilograms) by his height in cm (centimetres).

2 Divided the result by his height in cm.

3 Multiply the answer by 10,000. The result is your child's BMI.

THE WEIGHT CATEGORIES

Once you know your child's BMI you can find his or her weight category on the BMI chart. The four categories are:

- Underweight: less than the 5th percentile
- Ideal weight: between the 5th and the 85th percentiles
- At risk for overweight: between the 85th and 95th percentiles
- Overweight: BMI at the 95th percentile or greater

BMI is not a perfect measure and should be used in conjunction with other health measurements (skinfolds, activity/diet assessment, blood pressure etc.) to identify whether a child is truly at an increased health risk. Since children of different ethnic and social backgrounds differ in terms of fat distribution, and children are always changing in terms of growth spurts and sexual maturity, BMI does not always identify those children who are truly overweight.

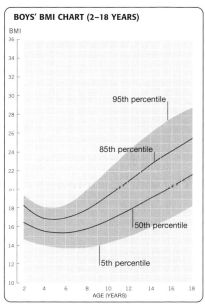

BOYS' BMI CHART (2–18 YEARS)

BMI

95th percentile

85th percentile

50th percentile

5th percentile

AGE (YEARS)

GIRLS' BMI CHART (2–18 YEARS)

BMI

95th percentile

85th percentile

50th percentile

5th percentile

AGE (YEARS)

"Sometimes I feel left out"

Overweight kids

Between 1981 and 1996, the number of children who are overweight doubled. Everyone wants to know why children are getting heavier and what needs to be done to stop this trend.

Problems ahead

Recent research in Canada found 37 percent of two- to eleven-year-olds to be overweight, and 18 percent of children in this age group to be obese. And in the US today, one in three kids is heavy enough to be considered at risk of developing a weight problem. That translates into a lot of kids and a lot of worried parents. The best advice is: Address the problem sooner rather than later. It's easier to help a four-year-old with a mild weight problem than a 12-year-old with a severe one. In fact, only 20 percent of overweight four-year-olds will become overweight adults, but 40 percent of older children and up to 80 percent of teenagers who are overweight will become overweight adults.

The good news is that kids have a few advantages over adults when it comes to reaching a healthy weight. One main advantage is you: a concerned parent who wants to help. Children, especially preteens and younger, can be positively influenced by parents who steer them in the right direction when it comes to food and fitness. On top of that, kids burn a lot of energy just being kids. Their bodies are working hard to grow and most kids are naturally very active.

Ignoring a child's weight problem can increase the risk of serious medical conditions (for information about this, see page 22). The social and emotional consequences also can be severe, and can multiply and worsen if a heavy child grows into an overweight adult.

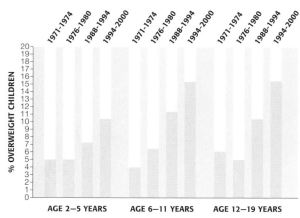

Rising number of overweight children
This North American data reveals that over the past 30 years, the percentage of overweight children has risen dramatically. This trend is worrisome because weight problems in childhood can set the stage for health problems in adulthood.

Emotional consequences

Overweight children often face social and emotional challenges. They may be ignored, teased, or viewed as unpopular by peers. As a result of social rejection, a child who is overweight may develop a negative self-image, which can undermine his or her feelings of self-worth and self-confidence. Social rejection based on weight becomes even more pronounced among adolescents. Exercise can help, but overweight kids may be reluctant to exercise because they can't keep up or are embarrassed about how they look in shorts or fearful of changing clothes in the crowded gym locker room. For some kids, the social difficulties caused by their weight may trigger additional problems. Children who are unhappy with their weight and appearance are more likely to skip meals or try dangerous diets. Overweight children also may be more prone to depression and risky behaviours such as drug and alcohol use.

Medical consequences

Pediatricians and family physicians now frequently must treat children who have weight-related health problems previously seen only in adults. High blood pressure, type 2 diabetes, and high cholesterol are now commonly diagnosed in overweight children. These are risk factors for cardiovascular disease in adults. But the seeds of these problems are often planted in childhood. In response, some doctors now take a more proactive approach with overweight children, including checking blood cholesterol levels for kids at higher risk for developing cardiovascular disease. Children who carry excess weight and resulting health problems into adulthood will be at increased risk of heart attack and stroke.

What is type 2 diabetes?

Diabetes is a disease caused by the body being unable to produce enough of the hormone insulin. Insulin is needed to move sugar, used as fuel, from the bloodstream into the body's cells.

There are two principal types of diabetes: type 1 and type 2. With type 1, the body is unable to produce any insulin at all, and regular injections of the hormone are needed to keep levels of blood sugar as normal as possible. The disease usually appears in young people, most commonly in young school-age kids and teens. The risk for getting it runs in families and it is not related to weight. (For more information about type 1 diabetes, see page 176.)

However, most people who get type 2 diabetes are overweight. A person with type 2 diabetes can continue to make insulin, but is unable to respond to it normally, a condition known as insulin resistance. As a result, oral medication and/or insulin injections may be needed.

Previously called adult-onset diabetes, type 2 diabetes was once considered rare in children. But researchers predict that if current trends continue, one in three North American children will develop type 2 diabetes during their lifetime. The estimated risk is even greater for aboriginal people, who will have a one-in-two chance of developing type 2 diabetes.

Diabetes and insulin resistance increase the risk of developing heart disease, stroke, and kidney failure later in life. In addition, new evidence suggests that having type 2 diabetes may increase the risk of developing Alzheimer's disease.

Common complaints

Although medical advances have improved children's health in many ways, there has been a rise in the number of overweight children showing up in the doctor's office. Overweight children often do not feel as well as their peers and there are many possible explanations. Here are some common complaints:

"I'm the tallest in my class." Overweight boys and girls tend to grow faster and may enter puberty at an earlier age, making them taller and more sexually mature than their peers. This can be a burden because they may be expected to act as old as they look, not as old as they are. Overweight kids who mature earlier, particularly girls, are more likely to carry their excess fat into adulthood.

"My knees hurt." Overweight kids may have trouble with their bones and joints. Knee pain is a common complaint and can deter a child from participating in gym class or other physical activities. Serious orthopedic problems that require surgical treatment can occur in overweight kids. Limping or complaints of pain in the knees, hips, or legs should be evaluated by a doctor.

"I'm so tired I fall asleep in class." Overweight contributes to restless or disordered sleep patterns including sleep apnea, an interruption in breathing that disrupts sleep. When a child doesn't get enough sleep at night, it makes it difficult to pay attention and learn during school hours. Sleep apnea also can lower oxygen levels in the bloodstream, straining the heart and increasing blood pressure.

"I skip a lot of periods." Though overweight girls tend to enter puberty early, they may have irregular menstrual cycles due to hormonal imbalances. These girls may have fertility problems later, when they reach adulthood.

"I'm out of breath in gym class." Exercise can make overweight children feel short of breath. For kids who have asthma, weight gain can make symptoms worse. A doctor should be consulted if a child has any breathing problems.

Health problems associated with **being overweight**

As more children become overweight, weight-related health problems are becoming more common. Some illnesses, such as type 2 diabetes, affect kids during childhood. Other problems don't occur until adulthood, but the seeds are often planted because a person was overweight as a child. Likewise, the risk of these health problems can be lowered if a child maintains a healthy weight.

CHILDHOOD

- exercise intolerance
- asthma and other breathing problems
- sleep apnea (pauses in breathing)
- high blood pressure
- type 2 diabetes
- slipped capital femoral epiphysis (causes pain and reduced function of hip joint)

- Blount disease (causes pain and reduced function of knee joint)
- menstrual irregularities
- high cholesterol
- liver disease
- gallstones and gall bladder disease
- depression

ADULT (LONG-TERM)

- high blood pressure
- high cholesterol
- type 2 diabetes
- cardiovascular problems (including heart attack and stroke)
- congestive heart failure
- respiratory problems, sleep apnea
- higher risk of certain cancers (breast, prostate, colon)

- higher risk of sudden death
- higher risk of complications from anesthesia and surgical procedures
- infertility and pregnancy complications
- arthritis
- liver disease
- gallstones and gall bladder disease
- gout
- depression

Getting help

Your child's doctor will evaluate the severity of any weight problem and may suggest a course of action. Options include a weight-management program or referral to a dietitian, who will be able to guide you and your child toward appropriate nutrition goals.

A change in lifestyle

Your child's doctor can recommend the steps you should take to help your overweight child. There are three possible approaches:

- slow the rate of weight gain;
- stop the weight gain;
- lose weight.

If related medical problems are severe, weight loss may be part of the treatment plan. Any weight-loss program should be supervised by a doctor and should emphasize long-term lifestyle changes, not quick, short-term weight loss. Commercial weight-loss programs intended for adults are not appropriate for children. Also be wary of any children's weight-loss program or camp that makes unrealistic promises or guarantees results. (See page 147 for more about weight-loss camps.)

Expert advice

The doctor may refer you to a registered dietitian or to a weight-management program at a children's hospital. Through these programs, overweight kids can get a medical assessment, which would include a complete history, physical, and lab tests. Some programs also include classes to teach kids and their families about adopting healthier habits. The programs often involve registered dietitians, who can be a great resource for your family. A dietitian will evaluate your child's medical history and physical condition, including growth (see page 16) and BMI measurements (see page 18). Using this information, the dietitian will help you and your child create nutrition goals. The dietitian also will offer personalized suggestions to help your family meet those goals, depending on your child's age, developmental stage, gender, and health status.

Work together

It's important to remember that helping your child with a weight problem is a family affair. Avoid laying down new food and fitness rules that apply only to the overweight child. Everyone will benefit from healthier habits, such as more nutritious meals, less TV time, and more exercise. Families who work together for healthier lifestyles have a better chance of success, so set achievable goals and celebrate the positive changes you're all making.

As you help your child, remember that it took time to gain weight, and it will take time for your child to make strides toward a healthier body. You can help your child most by setting a good example and, of course, by being a dependable source of encouragement, support, and love.

Consulting a dietitian

If your child's doctor suggests that you consult a registered dietitian, it's a good idea to ask the doctor for a recommendation. You also can find dietitians through the Dietitians of Canada (see page 202 for the website address) or you can look in your local yellow pages—dietitians will be listed under nutrition, dietitian, or weight loss.

You may want to interview several dietitians before selecting one. Choose one who has experience working with children and who understands your child's condition or weight problem. And, because nutritional counseling can be expensive, it's a good idea to investigate first whether it will be covered by your provincial health plan.

Take a family approach

It may seem like an impossible dream to change your family's daily routine, but it's not. You can succeed by starting with small steps, and everyone will benefit from adopting a healthier lifestyle.

"I love walking with mom"

Team spirit

If you set out to change the way your family eats and exercises, expect a challenge. The process may lead you to re-examine and change some of your own habits. Stay the course, even when the going gets tough. The lessons you impart today about nutrition and fitness may become the healthy principles your child practices for a lifetime.

Involving the whole family is the best way to promote better eating and activity habits for your children. A whole-family approach simply means that everyone—parents and kids alike—works together as a team to achieve good health and well-being. As with any team, there's a leader or coach, and that's where you, as a parent, come in.

Lead by example Adult family members are important healthy eating and exercise role models. Talk about why you eat fruit as a snack, take an exercise class, or go for walks.

Start 'em young Don't wait until your child is overweight to institute good eating and activity habits. It's much easier to maintain a healthy weight than to lose pounds later.

Be active together Make it usual for the family to be active, not sedentary. Being active as a family allows kids to expend energy in a positive way. Adults reap benefits, too.

Cook together It may be impractical to do it every day, but invite kids into the process of preparing food. Little kids can learn math skills by measuring and they'll begin to understand the chemistry of cooking. They'll also gain an understanding of healthy ingredients. Older kids will enjoy having the authority to select and prepare foods they like. It may even inspire them to eat healthy on their own.

Eat together Eating a meal as a family sends the right messages about nutrition. Kids will see their parents eating healthy food and may be inspired to try new foods. They will also come to see mealtime as a time for socializing and sharing. Parents get a chance to offer nutritious food, note their child's likes and dislikes, and tune into their child's triumphs and troubles through conversation.

Family **goal chart**

Keeping a chart can remind family members to pay attention to eating and exercise habits. Choose family goals, such as exercising every day and eating fruits and vegetables, then keep track of who meets those goals. Keeping a chart can remind family members to pay attention to eating and exercise habits.

DAY	EXERCISED TODAY					ATE FRUITS AND VEGGIES TODAY				
	MOM	DAD	JAKE	EMILY	MIKE	MOM	DAD	JAKE	EMILY	MIKE
Monday	✓	–	✓	✓	–	✓	–	✓	✓	✓
Tuesday	–	–	✓	–	✓	✓	✓	✓	–	✓
Wednesday	✓	✓	–	✓	✓	✓	✓	–	✓	✓
Thursday	–	✓	✓	✓	✓	–	✓	–	✓	✓
Friday	✓	–	–	✓	–	✓	✓	✓	–	✓
Saturday	–	–	✓	–	–	✓	–	✓	–	–
Sunday	✓	✓	✓	–	✓	✓	–	✓	✓	✓

tips

Family-friendly activities

If your family is prone to turning on the TV to relax, get out of your remote-control rut by trying these activities around the house:

Morning madness Does the sound of cartoons overwhelm your family breakfast? Instead of turning on the TV before you serve the toast, do some simple stretches or calisthenics with your child to get the blood flowing. Jumping jacks, push-ups, and running in place will wake you up.

Chore patrol All family members can participate in household tasks appropriate for their age. This not only results in more activity, your house will look better, too.

Rainy day resolutions When it's raining, it's all too easy to let the TV take over. Instead, plan ahead by creating a rainy-day box filled with toys, games, and activities that your kids can do only on those days filled with precipitation.

Blow off some steam Before settling in for evening activities or before dinner, take time to unwind together from a long day at school, home, or work. Play a quick game of soccer, tag, badminton, or catch in the backyard for an early evening boost.

Dance for your dinner While preparing dinner, put on some favourite tunes. Your child can dance along while you cook.

Jump on a hobby horse Do you enjoy woodworking or scrapbooking? Teach your child the basics of your favourite hobby, and work on simple projects together. They'll love the quality time spent with you.

Raising a healthy eater

Healthy, positive attitudes about nutrition can be a lifelong gift you give to your children—and yourself. Remember that your kids will be influenced by the choices you make when you shop for food, cook family meals, and eat out in restaurants.

A nutritious, varied diet

Good nutrition in childhood is essential for optimal growth and development. It also:

- helps kids maintain a healthy weight;
- provides fuel for learning and physical activity;
- encourages healthy eating habits that will serve kids well throughout their lives.

Some parents wonder if they need to give their child vitamins. For most children, vitamin supplements are not necessary if they eat a variety of foods. The quantities of vitamin-rich foods don't have to be huge: With just half an orange, a five-year-old can meet the daily requirement for vitamin C. For a ten-year-old, a few baby carrots can meet the daily need for vitamin A. (See page 39 for more about vitamins and what they do.)

myth: **Eating healthy means throwing away cherished family recipes.**

fact: You can lighten up your family's fare without fuss, using these food substitution ideas. Try a small amount of the substitute first, then gradually increase the amount to ensure that you maintain the consistency and texture of the original ingredient. Your family members will never know the difference!

- Replace cream in puddings, sauces, and casseroles with evaporated skim milk.
- Cut the amount of oil in half when sautéeing.
- Substitute applesauce or puréed prunes for oil and butter in baked goods.
- Try defatted chicken broth to moisten mashed potatoes rather than butter.
- Make salad dressings and marinades with fruit juice rather than oil.
- Use cocoa powder in place of unsweetened chocolate in brownie, cake, and fudge recipes.

Here are three simple guidelines for serving wholesome and nutritious food to your children:

- Offer plenty of fruits, vegetables, and whole-grain breads and cereals.
- Serve a variety of lower-fat protein foods, such as poultry, lean meat, tofu, fish, and eggs (see page 35 for more about protein).
- Encourage your children to drink water or milk, instead of fruit drinks and soft drinks.

In addition to offering healthy foods, parents can raise healthy eaters by teaching them to listen to their body's own hunger cues. This begins in infancy, believe it or not—even a baby will send signals that he or she is full by turning away from the bottle or breast.

As children get older, parents can continue to educate them about what their bodies are saying about feeling hungry or full. Responding to the body's hunger cues is a vital skill in maintaining a healthy weight.

Healthy shopping tips

You may think that it costs more to eat healthy foods, but, in fact, healthy, basic foods give you more bang for your buck than a cartful of unhealthy snacks.

- When you sit down to write your shopping list, focus your week's menus on wholesome, nutritious ingredients, such as fresh and frozen fruits and vegetables, lean meats and poultry, fresh fish, whole grains, and low-fat dairy products.
- To save cash, choose produce that's in season.
- Visit farmers' markets and produce stands in your area for the best that local growers have to offer.
- Shop the perimeter of the grocery store and avoid the inner aisles—the outer aisles usually contain the freshest foods and ingredients, whereas the inner aisles contain more expensive and less healthy prepared foods and snacks.

For more information about healthy food shopping, see pages 46–48.

Don't take the hard line

If you get completely swept up in your lifestyle overhaul, you might be tempted to declare a ban on all foods that contain sugar or chocolate, or that are high in fat. Don't do it. Completely eliminating sweets and favourite snacks can backfire if your child feels deprived. The result could be that your child overeats the off-limits food whenever given the opportunity outside the home.

Instead of taking the hard line or completely giving in, strive for moderation. Try not to talk about "bad foods." Don't be afraid to allow your child to choose a treat at the grocery store. You could even bake a special dessert together. But set limits. For example, fill a small bowl of tortilla chips to satisfy a snack craving, rather than leaving the whole bag out. This is enough to meet your child's desire for a sweet or crunchy snack food while still allowing room for healthier foods.

Dining out

With busy schedules, many families turn to restaurants for quick and easy meals. But it's no secret that restaurant portions are often enormous. When there's no time to cook at home, try to use restaurant food wisely.

At a full-service restaurant, don't limit your kids to the children's menu, which usually offers hot dogs and chicken nuggets. Instead, look for healthier choices on the adult menu and ask if you can get a child's portion of an adult meal. If not, given the size of most entrees, you might be able to split the meal between two kids, or you could share the meal with your child. If that meal includes a salad or vegetable, all the better. You also might consider getting take-out so you can order fewer entrees and serve the meal family-style at home.

If you find yourself at a drive-through window or lining up at a fast-food counter, you're not alone. Since 1971, Americans increased their spending on fast food from $6 billion a year to $110 billion in 2001. The consequences of this are obvious on the waistline.

But even fast food can be managed through moderation. For example, let your child have a burger and fries once in a while, instead of every day or every week. If fast food is the only option, be a role model with your own order. Fast food restaurants are expanding their menu of lower-fat alternatives, which means you can opt for grilled chicken, salad, yogurt, or soup. Your child might follow your lead next time.

tips

Dos and don'ts for healthy eating

- Do allow your children to eat according to their hunger signals. Listen to them when they say they're hungry, and allow them to stop eating when they indicate their hunger is satisfied.
- Do help your child cultivate an adventurous approach to different food tastes and textures.
- Do ensure your child eats plenty of whole grains, fruits, and vegetables to promote digestive health.
- Do provide structured eating and snacking times each day, based on regular meals and snacks.
- Do limit eating at fast-food restaurants.
- Do eat together as a family and offer nutritious choices.
- Do take your time at family meals. Eating slowly allows your child time to digest the food and register a sense of fullness.

- Don't offer dessert or any other sweet treat as a reward for finishing a meal (or to reward anything else).
- Don't use food as an incentive or for stress and boredom relief. Food is easily associated with soothing hurt feelings, nurturing, and comfort, but it's important to help children learn other ways of comforting themselves so that they do not become dependent on food for this.
- Don't force your child to eat everything that's served. Did your parents admonish you to "clean your plate" because "children are starving in other countries"? Past attitudes toward eating may have focused on reducing waste, but that may lead to unhealthy habits, because it puts kids out of touch with their hunger signals.
- Don't eat in front of the television.

Raising an active child

From an early age, children enjoy moving their bodies. The trick for parents is to foster and encourage that natural love of activity so children can reap the physical, emotional, and social benefits of regular exercise as they grow older.

Instill positive fitness habits

Active children develop self-confidence, feel more in control of their bodies, and are less likely to be overweight. Through activity, they learn balance and coordination, burn calories, and build muscle. And, just like adults, exercise allows children to relieve stress. So when children are young, start a routine of family-centred fitness. Initially, this may seem like an unproductive way to spend a few hours, but it's an excellent strategy for instilling positive fitness habits. Those habits may be very beneficial later on, when it's tempting for kids to drop exercise in favour of sedentary activities. The time you spend learning a new sport together or hiking in the woods is also an opportunity to connect with your child.

Many ways to be active

You'll want to select activities that are appropriate for your child's age. (Turn to the age-specific chapters for help with this.) It's not reasonable, for instance, to expect a three-year-old to complete a 20-kilometre bike ride. Also, if you have kids who span a range of ages, you'll need to find an activity that will work for everyone.

Let your children explore different ways of being active by taking classes to learn new sports, and join league teams to get regular practice sessions. Seek out noncompetitive leagues for young children and for kids who dislike the pressure of competition. Be sensitive to your child's likes and dislikes. Some kids may choose solitary pursuits, such as running or swimming, over team sports.

If a child doesn't want to do something or doesn't seem ready, it's best not to push too hard. Children develop skills at different ages (see more about this on page 54), and should be allowed to progress at their own pace. Also remember that a child's interests will grow and change over the years. A three-year-old may be happy to play catch in the backyard, but a school-age child might be more interested in a game of whiffleball. And in the teen years, whiffleball may seem too childish, so your adolescent may want to take a yoga class or join a basketball league.

Rationing the TV and computer

Regular physical activity is only one piece of the puzzle. Another key strategy is to limit the amount of time family members spend in sedentary activities. Experts say parents

A natural mood-lifter
Everyone can reap the benefits of getting exercise. And just like family meals, family exercise is a good chance for parents and children to connect with each other.

myth: **Your child needs at least an hour of vigorous exercise to reap any benefit.**

fact: The consensus is that your child doesn't need to run for an hour on the treadmill each night to be physically fit. But starting in the preschool years, children need 30–60 minutes of physical activity every day, such as playing backyard games or going for a walk. They also need an hour or more of free play every day. In addition to being active every day, teens need to get some vigorous physical activity.

should not allow children under age two to watch any TV or videos. All children over age two (and that includes teens) should spend no more than one to two hours a day watching TV and playing computer games.

Aside from being sedentary, watching TV can have other negative effects. Commercial TV allows advertisers to target kids' shows with commercials for snack foods—it's no coincidence that kids often snack in front of the TV. Try to offer them healthy snacks (or, better still, avoid associating TV-watching with eating altogether!).

Fitting in fitness

Though it may seem trivial, seize everyday opportunities to get a little more activity yourself. You may be surprised how easy it is to fit some simple exercise into your daily routine.

- Take the stairs, not the elevator or escalator.

- If it's feasible, walk, instead of driving, to a neighbour's home or a nearby store.
- On shopping trips, take an extra lap around the mall, walking briskly, to get the blood pumping.
- Instead of circling the parking lot looking for a close space, choose a spot farther away from the store or your office and get in a brief but brisk walk.
- If your child's school is close enough, walk or bike your child there and back.
- When doing household chores, get the whole family involved, and get everybody moving energetically.

Finally, don't neglect your own health. When you act as a positive role model for your child, it shows him or her that fitness isn't just for kids—it's about being healthy for life. Make time for exercise several times each week and let your child see that exercise is a priority for you, too.

Ideas for outings

Are you stumped as to what to do for your next family outing? Here are some tips for keeping your family interested in fitness:

Make it kid's choice Maybe your child is clamouring for a game of baseball at the park, even though you've planned a hike. Letting your child choose the family activity encourages physical fitness and helps him or her develop self-confidence.

Now we're getting somewhere Let your child research how many miles it is to a state or city she'd like to visit. Then, every time you walk a mile as a family, record it. When you've "walked" as far as the destination, reward your child with a special toy or activity.

Won't you be my neighbour? You don't have to drive to get active—organize a neighbourhood basketball, soccer, or softball game with the other families on your street or block.

Sign up the family for a fun run Or try training for a bike race. The thrill of competing together as a family is one of the best ways to cement everybody's commitment to fitness.

Give back Volunteering can be a great way to get out and get active. Look for local opportunities for your family to spend time outdoors—check with the local community centre or parks and recreation organization for ideas.

2
PRINCIPLES
OF NUTRITION

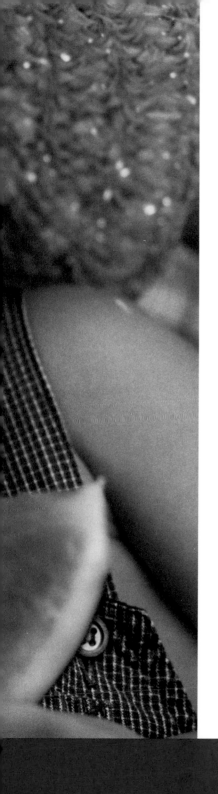

If you want to **help your child eat properly**, all you need to do is serve healthy foods that have the **nutrients kids need to grow** and develop. Don't argue with your child over food. **Be flexible**— but in a smart way.

"drink more milk..."

The vital components of food

Each family's diet will vary according to tradition and personal preferences, but the building blocks of a healthy and nutritious way of eating are the same for everyone.

What we need and how to get it

Our bodies—and especially the growing bodies of children—rely on carbohydrate, fibre, protein, fat, vitamins, and minerals, as well as water. We obtain these from the food we eat. In the right amounts, these nutrients provide the basis of good health and vitality.

It's easy to be confused about good nutrition for children and to get lost in all the recommended guidelines. It can be tough to understand why your infant needs almost half of his or her calories from fat while your six-year-old would be better off with only a third from fat and more from carbohydrate (see chart, opposite). Meanwhile, you have to ensure that your 11-year-old daughter has the calcium she

needs—which is more than her younger brother requires (see page 38). And if your child is a bit picky, you may be wondering how you can cover all the bases with only pizza and peanut butter sandwiches. Happily, you don't need a doctorate in nutrition science to feed your child a healthy diet. You just need to understand some basic principles and to adopt a few healthy habits—habits that will be good for the whole family.

The recommended daily allowances (RDAs) for individual nutrients, serving sizes, and grams per day are useful guidelines, but can be difficult to track. It's reassuring to know that you can achieve good results by striving for a diet full of variety, colour, and, of course, fun!

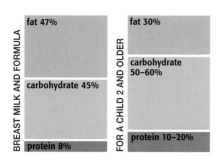

BREAST MILK AND FORMULA
fat 47%
carbohydrate 45%
protein 8%

FOR A CHILD 2 AND OLDER
fat 30%
carbohydrate 50–60%
protein 10–20%

Changing requirements
A diet of breast milk or formula gives a baby plenty of fat to fuel growth. Between 12 and 24 months, the diet should change gradually to include more protein and carbohydrate, and less fat.

Why variety?

Children who eat a wide assortment of foods increase their chances of meeting their nutritional requirements. Serve foods from all the food groups: grain products, milk products, meat and alternatives, vegetables and fruit (for more information about the food groups, see page 40).

Why colour?

A colourful plate typically contains a good range of nutrients and also looks very appetizing. Here's a tempting example: red salsa and green guacamole alongside a fajita filled with chicken, red onion, green bell pepper, and yellow squash. This provides protein, carbohydrate, fat, vitamins A and C, folate, potassium, and calcium.

Why fun?

Whether your child is seven months, seven years, or 17, food should be a shared source of enjoyment. It's important that kids see food as a pleasure, so don't force them to clean their plates or eat foods they dislike. This doesn't mean they should get to pick alternative meals or alternative mealtimes. It just means letting them choose how much to eat from the variety of healthy foods you make available. Let toddlers feed themselves, even if they get messy. Tempt preschoolers with a sandwich cut into a fun shape or a vegetable smile atop a pizza. Encourage older kids to select and help prepare dishes. And congratulate all kids when they try new foods.

It averages out

Nutrition is all about averages. Not getting enough of one nutrient on one day isn't a problem if your child gets enough on most days—it all balances out. In fact, meeting daily nutritional requirements is easier than you might think. With just ½ cup (75g) of cooked broccoli, a four- to eight-year-old child would get 25 percent of daily fibre needs, 15 percent of the recommended vitamin A, 10 percent of iron, 5 percent of calcium, and more than 100 percent of vitamin C.

Some of you may be thinking, "My child won't touch broccoli!" It is true that the child who will eat only a few foods does create a challenge. But even picky eaters can meet their nutritional requirements without parents pleading or yelling about their eating habits. The good news is that pickiness can be just a phase.

The best ways to make children eat well—whether they are picky or easy-going about eating—are to have plenty of healthy food choices available and to be a good role model by eating them yourself. By doing this, you'll increase the chances that when hunger strikes, your child will reach for something nutritious, even if you're not there.

info

Calories in, energy out

A calorie is a unit of energy, and the number of calories in a serving of food indicates how much energy that food gives the body. The components of food contain differing amounts of calories:
- 1 gram of fat provides 9 calories.
- 1 gram of carbohydrate provides 4 calories.
- 1 gram of protein provides 4 calories.
Naturally, children's energy requirements vary with weight, age, and activity level. Requirements increase as kids grow older, and especially as they enter puberty.

These figures for calorie requirements per day assume normal activity:
- Toddlers: 1,000–1,200 calories
- Preschoolers: 1,200–1,600 calories
- School-age kids: 1,600–2,500 calories
- Adolescent girls: 2,200 calories
- Adolescent boys: 2,500–3,000 calories
As adults, we are conditioned to try to avoid calories, to prevent weight gain, but they are necessary for the body to function and grow. Calories become a problem only when people take in more calories than they are able to burn off.

Carbohydrate

Both adults and children need carbohydrate, which is the body's most important and readily available source of energy. (See the age-specific chapters for carbohydrate needs.)

Most foods contain carbohydrate. The two major forms that provide energy are simple sugars, and starch, which is broken down to simple sugars when digested. Fibre is also a carbohydrate and is present in foods alongside starch in grains and some fruits and vegetables (bananas, potatoes), and alongside sugars, especially in fruits. Foods containing carbohydrate are not bad for you. But some carbohydrate foods are healthier choices than others.

● Unrefined grains, brown rice, and whole-grain breads and cereals, are packed with nutrients. They're broken down more slowly in the body and are high in fibre, so are filling enough to discourage overeating. Whole fruits contain simple sugars and have the added benefit of vitamins and fibre.

● Refined sugars and more refined grains, like white rice and white flour, are stripped of fibre, minerals, and vitamins when they are refined. However, many minerals and vitamins are added back or "enriched" to flour and other grain products, to make sure intakes remain adequate. With less fibre, these carbohydrates are easier to overeat because they are less filling.

When carbohydrate is eaten, the simple sugars released during digestion are absorbed into the blood stream. As the sugar level rises, the pancreas releases the hormone insulin, which is necessary for moving sugar from the blood into the cells where the sugar can be used as a source of energy.

For decades, scientists have known that different foods, even if they contain the same amount of carbohydrate, don't cause the same rise in blood sugar (and insulin level). This is related to the specific types of carbohydrate in the food, the fibre content, and other factors that affect the way carbohydrate is digested and absorbed. To measure these differences, foods can be analyzed in terms of their glycemic index (see below).

Scientists have been investigating the possible relationship between carbohydrate and the risk of developing diseases such as diabetes and heart disease. Some studies suggest there is an increased risk among people who eat a diet high in foods that cause a greater rise in blood sugar. It's thought that the higher insulin levels in the blood triggered by these foods may play a key role in the increased risk of disease.

Fibre

Everyone needs fibre, which moves food through the digestive system, fighting constipation. Most fibre adds no calories, yet makes us feel full. Some types may lower LDL-cholesterol ("bad" cholesterol) levels and help prevent heart disease.

Fibre is found in plants—fruits, vegetables, and grains. Food made from plant products, such as breads and cereals, as well as fruits and vegetables, provide fibre. Whole-grain breads and cereals contain more fibre than white bread and white rice. Some of the best fruit and vegetable sources are apples, oranges, berries, prunes, broccoli, carrots, peas, and beans.

There's a simple rule for figuring out how many grams of fibre your child needs per day: Just add five to the child's age. So a five-year-old would need 10g. After the age of 15, children (and adults) need about 20–25g of fibre per day.

Q: What is the glycemic index?

A: Over the past 20 years, researchers have developed a standardized method of evaluating how the body handles the carbohydrates in different foods. Called the glycemic index (GI), this measure compares the rise in blood sugar that occurs after eating a particular food with the rise in blood sugar that occurs after eating the same amount of carbohydrate in a standard food (usually white bread). The higher the spike in blood sugar, compared to the bread, the higher the food's glycemic index.

Because foods with a low GI are thought to be healthier, magazines and books are now promoting the virtues of a low-glycemic-index diet. But the findings of scientific studies, which have been done mostly on adults, are still being hotly debated and everyone agrees that more research is needed. What does all this mean when deciding what to feed your child? You're already on safe ground if you're limiting simple sugars and foods made from refined flours and grains. These are also the ones with the highest GI. Opt instead for more high-fibre, nutrient-rich carbohydrate foods, such as fresh fruits, nonstarchy vegetables, and whole grains. These foods have health benefits for children—and most have a low GI.

tips

Easy ways to get more fibre

● Leave skins on fruits and vegetables.
● Sprinkle wheat germ on breakfast cereal or yogurt.
● Add some bran to the mixture for a meatloaf.
● Offer raisins as snacks or add them to salads.
● Serve brown rice and whole-grain spaghetti and other pasta.
● Substitute whole-wheat flour for some of the white flour when baking bread, cakes, and so on.

A good source of fibre is one that provides 2.5g or more per serving. Bran cereals provide 4g or more. A medium pear with skin (4g fibre), 1/2 cup (125g) baked beans (3g fibre), and 1/4 cup (40g) raisins (3g fibre) are also good sources.

Protein

While carbohydrate provides fuel, protein helps build and repair essential parts of the body. Protein is found in red meat, poultry, fish, eggs, dairy products, nuts, seeds, legumes, and grains. The body breaks protein down into components called amino acids, which are used to build and maintain muscles, bones, body organs, the blood, and the immune system.

Protein is key to healthy growth, so it's important for children to eat enough on a regular basis. Fortunately, in Canada, few people get too little protein. You can figure out how much protein your child needs based on how much he or she weighs: The formula is 0.88 grams of protein for every kilogram of the child's weight, with a maximum of about 60g. So a 28-kg child should have about 25g protein every day. These foods together would satisfy that daily requirement:

● 1 tablespoon peanut butter (4g protein);
● 1 cup (250mL) low-fat milk (9g protein);
● 30g or two domino-size-pieces of Cheddar cheese (7g protein);
● 30g or a matchbook-size-piece baked chicken breast (8g protein).

Protein from animal sources, including milk products, is called "complete," because it contains all nine of the essential amino acids. Vegetable protein is considered "incomplete," because it lacks one or more of the essential amino acids. This can be a concern for someone following a vegetarian diet, but you can create a complete protein by combining different proteins that together provide all nine essential amino acids. This isn't hard to do: peanut butter with whole-grain bread, and red beans with rice are just two examples. And you don't have to make the right combinations at every meal as long as you eat a variety of foods throughout the day.

Fat

An adequate fat intake is essential to growth and development. Fat fuels the body and aids in the absorption of some vitamins. Fat provides the building blocks for hormones and is necessary for insulating all nervous system tissue in the body.

There is disagreement among nutrition experts about the amount of fat that should be in a healthy diet, for both kids and adults. It is true that fat has more than twice as many calories as protein or carbohydrate (see page 33), but some experts think the low-fat revolution has gone too far, overlooking the complex nature of fat and how it works in the body. For one thing, eating fat in a meal helps us feel more satisfied, so we may be less likely to overeat. And replacing fat calories with simple sugars in a low-fat diet can have negative effects on health as well.

info

What's the story on cholesterol?

Cholesterol has a negative image, but it's a necessary component of cells. There are two sources:

- foods such as meat, whole milk, and egg yolks (dietary cholesterol);
- cholesterol manufactured by the body in the liver.

Blood cholesterol exists in two major forms: HDL (the "good" type) and LDL (the "bad" one). Too much LDL in the bloodstream increases the risk of heart disease, as it can collect in the arteries and block them. HDL gets carried out of the bloodstream to be recycled and used elsewhere in the body.

Genes play an important role in how the body handles cholesterol and dietary fat. When children inherit a tendency to produce too much LDL and/or too little HDL, they have a higher risk of developing heart disease as they grow older. Eating the right balance of dietary fats is thought to be important for helping reduce this risk.

It used to be thought that avoiding foods high in dietary cholesterol was the answer, but the quantity of cholesterol you eat is not a major factor in determining how much ends up in your bloodstream: Now it is known that saturated fat and trans fats tend to raise the levels of LDL in the blood. This is true for children as well as for adults, so it's wise to begin watching your child's intake of saturated and trans fats after age two. Serve whole milk and meat with fat only occasionally. Instead opt for chicken, nuts, and other foods that contain the healthier unsaturated fats.

There are different types of fat

"Adequate" fat doesn't mean unlimited—too much can be a problem, as can the kind of fat you eat. The major types are:

Unsaturated fats: found in plant foods and fish. These fats are seen as neutral or even beneficial to heart health. Some of the healthiest include monounsaturated fats (found in olive, peanut, and canola oils and in avocados), polyunsaturated fats (found in most vegetable oils), and omega-3 fatty acids (from oily fish, such as albacore tuna and salmon).

Saturated fat: found in animal products including meat, lard, butter, cheese, and milk (except skim or nonfat milk), as well as in palm and coconut oils. A high intake of saturated fat raises blood cholesterol levels in some people and is a risk factor for heart disease (see above).

Trans fats: found in hard margarine, commercial snack foods and baked goods, and some commercial fried foods. Trans fats are created when vegetable oils are hydrogenated, so that they remain solid at room temperature. A high intake can pose the same risks to health as saturated fats. By 2006, manufacturers must list trans fats on food labels. Until then, some labels may not list trans fats. In this case, check the ingredients list for the word "hydrogenated." (See page 48.)

Water

Kids—and adults—need water, but as water is found in foods, such as fruits, and drinks other than water, like milk and juice, there's no guideline for how much water kids should drink. A healthy child's body does a good job of regulating fluid and kids tend to drink when they're thirsty. But what about kids who are too young to tell you they're thirsty?

Under normal circumstances, infants don't need water. Giving them water may diminish their hunger and keep them from getting the nutrients provided by breast milk or formula. But older kids can and should drink water, particularly as an alternative to pop and juice drinks.

When children are out in hot weather, offer extra fluids. Be sure they get a drink before, during, and after exercising, too. (See page 67 for information about dehydration.) The availability of bottled water makes this easy, but a sports bottle you can refill is a cheaper option—wash it with hot soapy water or put it in the dishwasher between uses.

The best drink
If offered water—or diluted fruit juice—from a young age, kids are more likely to keep drinking water as they get older, rather than sugary, empty-calorie drinks.

Vitamins and minerals

These substances serve critical functions in a child's growing body. Among their many roles, vitamins help with growth and development, and aid the functioning of organs and cells in normal metabolic processes.

Vitamins are found naturally in foods from animal or plant sources. In addition, children may get vitamins through vitamin-enriched foods, such as cereals or juices. Because different vitamins act on different parts and processes of the body, a healthy diet includes all the essential vitamins, from A to K. Each one offers its own benefits.

Minerals, such as calcium, potassium, and zinc, fulfill a wide range of vital needs. Unlike vitamins, minerals are inorganic—they are not produced in plants or animals. Instead, plants and animals pick up minerals through what they absorb or eat, and we get them from the plants and animal products that we eat.

Deficiencies

Deficiencies of most vitamins and minerals are uncommon in Canada, because most people eat a varied diet and many foods are enriched with nutrients. Two deficiencies that are prevalent are iron and calcium. Iron deficiency can lead to anemia (when the iron-containing pigment hemoglobin, which is found in red blood cells and carries oxygen, is low), as well as behavioural and learning problems in young children. Lack of calcium increases the risk of osteoporosis, or brittle bone disease, in adulthood.

Iron requirements vary by age, with menstruating girls needing the most. Here are the daily recommendations:

- six to 12 months: 11mg
- one to three years: 7mg
- four to eight years: 10mg
- nine to 12 years: 8mg
- girls 13–18 years: 15mg
- boys 13–18 years: 12mg

These are the calcium requirements:

- birth to five months: 210mg
- six to 12 months: 270mg
- one to three years: 500mg
- four to eight years: 800mg
- nine and older: 1,300mg

Certain diets can put a child at increased risk of deficiency. For example, a vegetarian, who doesn't eat meat, poultry, or fish, may not get enough iron. A very low-fat diet may prevent absorption of fat-soluble vitamins, such as vitamin A.

One vitamin deficiency has less to do with the foods you eat than with how much time you spend outdoors: When the skin is exposed to sun, the body makes vitamin D. You can also get vitamin D in foods such as fish and fortified milk.

Too much sodium

Sodium, a component of table salt, is essential for life. It plays an important role in maintaining water balance in the body and is needed to send nerve signals and contract muscles, including the heart. But Canadians are getting too much sodium in their diets—on average almost twice the daily recommended value of 2,400mg—a factor contributing to the development of high blood pressure. Although doctors may suggest a low-sodium diet for adults with high blood pressure, sodium should not be restricted in children.

Instead, the best approach is moderation. Read food labels and shy away from highly processed foods, such as salty snacks and soups, which tend to have a lot of sodium. Limit the amount of salt that is added when cooking and at the table. If you are serving your family a diet that is rich in whole grains, fresh fruits, and vegetables, you are already choosing foods that are naturally low in sodium.

Q: Does my child need vitamin supplements?

A: In general, children who eat a balanced diet and do not have special health concerns do not need vitamin or mineral supplements. There are a couple of instances, however, when a doctor may suggest supplements:

- Babies who are breastfed are often prescribed drops with iron and fluoride supplements, and sometimes vitamins A, C, and D as well.
- Adolescents who don't drink milk may need calcium supplements to promote the growth of strong bones.
- Though picky eaters usually get enough nutrients, giving a child a daily multivitamin may reassure some parents.

If you think your child needs a vitamin or mineral supplement, talk with your doctor. The safest supplements are multivitamins formulated for kids. Giving doses of individual vitamins and minerals can be very dangerous and lead to fatal overdoses.

Vitamins and minerals, and what they do

VITAMIN OR MINERAL	ESSENTIAL FOR	FOUND IN
Vitamin A (retinol)	healthy eyes, skin, teeth, bones	eggs, milk products, liver; carotenoids, which the body converts into vitamin A, are found in fruits and vegetables, including carrots, sweet potatoes, cantaloupe, dark green vegetables such as spinach
Vitamins B$_1$ (thiamine), B$_2$ (riboflavin), B$_3$ (niacin), and B$_6$	turning food into energy; maintaining nerves, muscles, skin, the digestive system, other structures; formation of red blood cells	whole grains, fish, beans, nuts, eggs, enriched cereals, meats
Vitamin B$_9$ (folate, the naturally occurring form of folic acid)	formation of red blood cells and DNA, which contains the building plans for all cells	whole grains, green leafy vegetables, beans and peas, citrus fruits, poultry, pork, enriched breads, pasta, and cereals
Vitamin B$_{12}$	central nervous system; formation of red blood cells	poultry, eggs, meat, seafood, milk products
Vitamin C (ascorbic acid)	absorption of iron; sustaining healthy tissues; helping heal wounds	citrus fruits, cantaloupe, strawberries, tomatoes, broccoli, cabbage
Vitamin D	calcium absorption; normal bone growth and maintenance	fortified milk products, fish, egg yolks
Vitamin E	formation of red blood cells; maintenance of body tissues	whole grains, wheat germ, leafy green vegetables, sardines, egg yolks, nuts
Vitamin K	blood clotting	leafy green vegetables, liver, pork, dairy products
Calcium	teeth and bones; transmission of nerve signals; muscle contraction; control of hormone secretion	milk products, canned salmon and sardines (with bones), green leafy vegetables such as broccoli, collard greens, bok choy, kale
Iron	formation of hemoglobin, which carries oxygen to tissues throughout the body	red meat, dark poultry, tuna, salmon, eggs, dried beans, dried fruits, leafy green vegetables, whole grains
Potassium	muscle and nervous system function; maintaining the balance of water in the blood and body tissues	broccoli, potatoes (with skins), leafy green vegetables, citrus fruits, bananas, dried fruits, legumes such as peas and lima beans
Zinc	immune system function; cell growth; wound healing	beef, pork, lamb, peanuts and other legumes

"Crunch on a carrot"

A healthy diet for children

Nutrition seems awash in numbers—percentages of this, milligrams of that. Fortunately, good nutrition still comes down to the basic food groups. A varied diet includes each one in the right amount.

The four food groups

Canada's Food Guide to Healthy Eating divides foods into the following four categories:

Grain products (breads, cereals, rice, and pasta) provide carbohydrates, fibre, various vitamins, and some minerals.

Milk products (milk, yogourt, cheese, and other dairy foods) provide protein, vitamins, and minerals, especially calcium.

Meat and alternatives (meat, fish, poultry, eggs, legumes, seeds, and nuts) provide protein and fat, as well as vitamins, and minerals such as iron and zinc.

Vegetables and fruit provide carbohydrate, fibre, vitamins, and minerals.

Canada's Food Guide to Healthy Eating is the current model for explaining the composition of a healthy diet. It's a subject of some debate: Critics say it fails to recognize that some fats are healthy and that all carbohydrates are not equally good for you. Health Canada is currently reviewing Canada's Food Guide to Healthy Eating, as well as Canada's Guidelines for Healthy Eating and Nutrition Recommendations for Canadians.

Servings are a simple way of assessing a child's (or adult's) diet. Health Canada created Canada's Food Guide to Healthy Eating to recommend the number of daily servings we should eat from each food group, for all Canadians over the age of four years. The number of servings of milk products varies with age, with those aged 10-16 years recommended to consume more than younger children or adults.

Making sense of **servings and portions**

Servings are a standard size for everyone except in the case of preschoolers, for whom "child-sized portions" have been estimated. These vary from one half to the full size of the servings in each food group. The number of servings per day varies with age, body size, activity level, and gender. Portions are not the same thing as servings—a portion can be a fraction of a serving, a few servings, or many servings. As children get older they eat larger portions—and thus more servings.

- A boy age nine may eat ½–1 cup (125–250g) spaghetti with sauce, which is one to two servings.
- A boy age 14 may eat 2–3 cups (500–750g) spaghetti with sauce, which is four to six servings.

RECOMMENDED DAILY SERVINGS

Canada's Food Guide to Healthy Eating suggests ranges for the number of servings people should eat daily, but only the low end of those ranges applies to children aged two to six. For instance, older kids and adults are urged to eat five to ten servings of vegetables and fruit, but the recommendation for younger children is only five servings.

FOOD GROUP	2- TO 6-YEAR-OLDS	OLDER THAN 6, INCLUDING TEENS AND ADULTS
Grain products	5 servings	5–12 servings
Milk products	2 servings	2–4 servings
Meat and alternatives	2 servings	2–3 servings
Vegetables and fruit	5 servings	5–10 servings

SIZING UP SERVINGS

Although standard servings are of a specified size, they vary depending on the type of food, even in the same food group (see below). For example, ½ cup (60g) fresh raspberries is a serving, but so is ¼ cup (40g) dried fruit such as raisins. For two- to three-year-olds, the serving size is about two-thirds of the standard one.

FOOD GROUP	STANDARD SERVING	SIZE COMPARISON (IF ANY)
Grain products	1 slice of bread	
	½–¾ cup (70–120g) cooked cereal, rice, or pasta	ice cream scoop
	30g ready-to-eat cereal	
Milk products	1 cup (250mL) milk	
	¾ cup (185mL) yogourt	
	50g cheese	3 dominoes
Meat and alternatives	50–100g cooked lean meat	deck of cards
	1–2 eggs	
	2 tablespoons (30mL) peanut butter	ping pong ball
	½–1 cup (125–250mL) baked beans	
Vegetables and fruit	1 medium vegetable or fruit	tennis ball
	½ cup (60–75g) berries/cooked vegetables	
	1 cup (100g) raw leafy vegetables/salad	
	½ cup (125mL) vegetable/fruit juice	

Once-in-a-while foods

Eating can be an emotionally charged issue and certain foods can really get a parent's dander up, especially if you're trying to encourage healthy habits. But attempting to ban your child's favourite foods is unlikely to be successful.

Limiting snacks and treats

If your son has a soft spot for cheesies, and he regularly overindulges, your impulse may be to forbid them. But it's wiser to allow him cheesies—as long as it's once in a while and in controlled portions. Snack foods have their place, but the trick is to limit them so they do not crowd out healthier fare.

The same goes for fast food, sweets, or other treats. Many snack and convenience foods are high in calories and fat, particularly saturated fat, and low in nutrients. A recent look at the typical deep-fried chicken nugget found it contained nearly 60 percent fat, which is more than a regular fast-food burger.

Another way to deal with snacking is to offer alternatives that are just as appealing but more nutritious. Here are some delicious substitutes to try:

- Instead of a bag of chips, try air-popped popcorn sprinkled with Parmesan cheese.
- Instead of ice cream, try fruit juice or a favourite flavour pudding frozen into popsicles.
- Instead of candy, try apple or orange slices dipped into vanilla or fruit-flavoured yogourt.

Dilution is another smart strategy for parents. If your child likes chips, occasionally buy a small bag and use them in a snack mix that contains mostly healthier foods, such as popcorn, pretzels, and peanuts. If your child yearns for a sugary cereal, let him or her mix a small amount into a lower-sugar cereal, as a compromise.

Also keep an eye on what's in your child's glass. Avoid pop and other sugary drinks or offer them only occasionally. Dilution works with drinks too, so cut juice with water or soda water to reduce the calories. More often, serve your children milk or water to drink instead.

How much is enough?

Many parents wonder if their children get what they need for good health when their eating patterns seem erratic or picky. Keeping a food log will help you understand your child's eating habits. If you record the type of food and amount your child eats for meals and snacks throughout each day over the course of a week, you will be able to make an accurate assessment of his or her diet.

Paying attention to the amount of food your child eats and understanding serving sizes may help when assessing your child's diet. (For information on recommended daily servings and serving sizes, see page 41.) You may realize that, more often than not, your child gets the recommended number of servings.

What's in their **favourites?**

Most kids, particularly teenagers, love fast food, snacks, and sweetened drinks. But most of their favourite treats offer only "empty" calories (without many nutrients)—and plenty of those calories. These snacks and fast foods are also a source of unhealthy amounts of fats, sugar, and salt, so it's worth trying to limit them in your child's diet.

FOOD	CALORIES	TOTAL FAT/SATURATED FAT	SODIUM
Ice cream (½ cup/70g, chocolate)	140	7g/4g	20mg
Regular cola (1 can, 340ml)	140	0g	50mg
Potato chips (30g)	150	10g/3g	180mg
Chocolate (1 bar, 45g)	230	13g/9g	40mg
Pizza (1 large slice)	258	8g/3g	540mg
Chicken nuggets (6 pieces)	300	18g/4g	530mg

Once you know what your child is eating, you can analyze it in several different ways:

- total energy intake in a day;
- nutrient intake, including carbohydrate, protein, fat, and fibre;
- number of servings of vegetables and fruit, and other food groups.

You also can use the food log to look for other patterns, such as variety in food choices, number of meals and snacks eaten each day, and possible excesses, such as too many empty-calorie snacks or drinks. Nutritional requirements vary by age. To check those for your child, see the appropriate age-specific chapter.

Working on the food log will help your child see what he or she is eating and how this compares to the actual daily requirements. Depending on their age, kids can "score" themselves. To provide even more incentive, you might consider awarding stars on the chart for achieving specific goals, such as eating the minimum number of servings of food from the grain or milk products groups every day or trying some new foods. Your food log can be as simple as hand-written comments in a small notebook, or as elaborate as a colour-coded chart studded with special stickers.

Five-a-day veggies and fruits

Only about one in five children eats the recommended five daily servings of vegetables and fruit. They miss out on important nutrients as well as another component of a healthy diet: fibre. Monitor what your child eats for a week or so and you may realize that a couple additional pieces of fruit and another serving of vegetables every day are in order. Any kid who can count up to five can start tracking progress toward the five-a-day goal.

Five-a-day may sound like a lot, especially if your family doesn't eat many vegetables or fruits, but the servings are small. These would satisfy the requirement for one day:

- ½ cup (75g) fresh strawberries on cereal
- 10 baby carrots
- 2 large broccoli spears
- ½ cup (125mL) fruit juice
- ¼ cup (40g) raisins.

Should kids eat a low-fat diet?

Restrictive diets aren't recommended for kids, and fat, despite the bad press, is not The Enemy. In fact, for young children, fat and cholesterol play important roles in brain development. For children younger than two, fat intake should not be restricted. From age two, children should move to a varied diet with about 30 percent of calories from fat. It's true that most kids eat too much fat, so here are some ways to keep your child's fat intake around 30 percent.

- Offer naturally low-fat foods, such as fruits and vegetables, whole grains, and lean meats, as well as lower-fat milk products.
- When cooking meat, opt for broiling, grilling, or roasting (on a rack). These methods allow fat to drip away during cooking, cutting down on calories, too. Frying keeps food in its own fat or requires added fat.
- Resist low-fat crackers, cookies, and other snacks. They may be high in calories and easy to overeat. Check for calorie levels per serving on the box and the number of servings in a box.

tips

How to be a role model

- Make time for your meals, even if it's just 15 minutes for a sandwich and a piece of fruit.
- Sit down to eat—it doesn't take much more time.
- Put your work or book away and concentrate on your meal. You'll be able to return to your project soon enough, with renewed energy from a healthy meal.

- Choose a nutritious snack, such as yogourt with a few slivered almonds sprinkled on top.
- Don't skip meals.
- Don't eat on the run, such as in the car, rushing off somewhere.
- Don't eat quickly while standing over the sink or at the refrigerator.
- Don't "graze" or snack all day instead of eating meals.

How to help kids eat healthily

It's all well and good to know what your child should eat, but getting the food from the plate to the stomach can be a challenge. It may seem wrong, but letting kids have some control is the way to go.

"I'm making muffins"

No prodding or pleading

Nutritionist Ellyn Satter puts forth a simple rule for parents: You decide what foods are available and the child decides what to eat and even whether to eat at all. Yes, this means they can walk away from the dinner table. But, because you control the food, it also means that they won't have the option of opening a bag of chips and using snacks to fill the dinner void.

Giving kids this kind of control might go against the parental grain. We may want efficient eating and clean plates, but this is not how kids operate. And that's actually a good thing. Kids, especially younger ones, respond to their own hunger cues. If you can respect those cues, too, your child may be on the way to a healthy and pleasurable relationship with food.

The challenge of picky eaters

Some kids may get on a food jag and refuse to eat anything but, say, grilled cheese sandwiches for weeks on end. This is obviously not ideal, but the parent who responds by forcing the child to eat other foods is not solving the problem. A better course is to continue offering a range of foods and hope that this phase will pass, which it inevitably does.

When trying to introduce healthy foods to infants and picky toddlers, don't give up too easily. It could take as many as ten tries before a child accepts a new food. Keep offering, without forcing, and your kid may end up liking squash after all.

Sometimes what seems like pickiness is actually just preference, so it pays to know what your child likes and dislikes. Just like you, they're going to favour some kinds of foods. One nine-year-old girl, to her mother's dismay, refused to eat breakfast, heading into her school day with an empty tank. But after talking it over, it turned out that it wasn't breakfast that the girl disliked. It was the kinds of foods that her mother offered—typical fare including toasted bagels and waffles. The girl preferred smooth textures in the morning, such as yogourt. Problem solved.

It's true, however, that parents may face disappointment when they set out to instill healthy eating habits. Kids like what they like and, sometimes, no amount of choices or vegetables cut into fancy shapes can change that. If this is the case, try not to dig in your heels, since that can make mealtimes tense instead of relaxed and enjoyable.

Have a realistic attitude

Food can become linked to negative feelings early on. If parents repeatedly grow frustrated when introducing an infant or young child to new foods, the child picks up on the mood. And if parents use dessert as a reward, the sweet treat can become the goal, making dinner just something to get through on the way to the finish line. These practices can create unhealthy eating patterns instead of resolving them.

Anyone who's ever fed an infant knows that food and comfort are intrinsically linked, and that food can be a way to show love and care. But be wary of using food to praise or reward a child, punish a child, soothe hurt feelings, or as the sole expression of love. Consistently using food in this way can build a dependence on food for support or even happiness. Having a child skip a meal as a punishment can tie food to disapproval. Once such connections have been forged, they can last a lifetime.

Children also pick up on adults' attitudes about food, so be aware of your approaches to eating, too. Don't expect a child to want to try a variety of foods if you regularly eat popcorn for dinner. If you view food as a collection of unwanted calories, your child may adopt a similar outlook. Instead, turn mealtimes into pleasurable, social events. Use them to your advantage by:

- eating together as a family;
- offering a selection of fruits and vegetables;
- modeling good habits by eating healthy foods;
- encouraging small, "try it" portions of a tablespoon or two;
- turning off the TV while you eat.

Kids in the kitchen

Try turning the tables and get kids involved in the selection of menus and the preparation of meals. This will do more than just expand your child's repertoire as far as eating: A kid who's at home in the kitchen feels empowered about food and gains first-hand knowledge of nutrition. This lays the groundwork for making healthy food choices later on.

If your kids are very young, give them empty pots, spoons, and other safe utensils so they can pretend to cook along with you. For younger school-age kids, let them prepare recipes involving five or fewer ingredients and where everything is mixed and cooked in the same container. If your child can read, let him or her read out the recipe—a great way to practice reading skills. Older kids can take over the creation of a meal if they're interested. Let them be completely in charge of dinner occasionally, from selecting recipes and shopping with you for ingredients to cooking and serving.

tips

Kids and food: 10 tips for parents

1 Parents control the supply lines: You decide which foods to buy and when to serve them.

2 Kids decide if and what to eat: From the foods you offer, kids get to choose what they eat or whether to eat at all.

3 Quit the "clean plate club": Let your children stop eating when they feel they've had enough.

4 Start them young: Food preferences are developed early in life, so offer a variety of foods.

5 Rewrite the kids' menu: Who says kids only want to eat hot dogs, pizza, burgers, and macaroni and cheese?

Let your children try new foods and they might surprise you with their willingness to experiment.

6 Drink calories count: Pop and other sweetened drinks add extra calories and get in the way of good nutrition.

7 Put sweets in their place: Occasional sweets are fine, but don't turn dessert into the main reason for eating dinner.

8 Food is not love: Find better ways to say I love you.

9 Kids do as you do: Be a role model and eat healthy yourself

10 Turn off the TV: You'll also turn off the advertising and mindless snacking.

"choose your own veggies..."

Be an informed food shopper

Learning to shop wisely will help you put the best foods on your family's table. Find out what to look for at the store or market, whether you're buying fresh, frozen, or canned products.

When fresh is best

It's no surprise that fine restaurants use the freshest fruits and vegetables. Their appearance and taste speak for themselves. But it can be challenging to buy and serve fresh produce. For a start, it's not always easy to find, and it can be expensive. Also, it can easily spoil before you get a chance to eat it. The secrets lie in knowing where to shop, how to choose excellent produce, and how to store it until you're ready to serve it.

Choose stores that feature fresh produce and turn over their stocks regularly. It's also worth trying farmers' markets and farm stands to see what's available locally. Wherever you choose to shop, it pays to know the time of year that your favourite fruits and vegetables are in season. Buying in-season produce is often a bargain, but don't buy more than you can store or use before it spoils. A good way to teach your children about seasonal fruit is by visiting an orchard or berry patch, so they can pick the fresh fruit themselves.

When you don't pick it off the vine yourself, how do you know produce is fresh? Whether it's cantaloupe or green beans, all fruits and vegetables give hints about their ripeness and freshness.

- Choose vegetables that look fresh and colourful. Most should be crisp and firm: With vegetables such as green beans, for example, don't buy them if they are limp or showing signs of decay.

myth: **Organic food is healthier than conventionally grown products.**

fact: Organic foods are produced by growers or suppliers who emphasize environmental protection and resource conservation. In general, organic growers don't use most pesticides, synthetic fertilizer, or other processes, such as ionizing radiation. With animal products, antibiotics and growth hormones are not used in production. In North America, an inspector visits the farm or factory where the food is produced, to certify that it deserves the organic label.

Organic products are typically more expensive, but are attractive to consumers seeking the most natural foods available. And organic produce is often grown locally, which ensures that it reaches the market at its freshest, but there is no guarantee that organic foods are any healthier than those grown conventionally.

- When choosing fruit, avoid bruised pieces, but remember that a perfect exterior doesn't necessarily mean the best quality: If it's cantaloupe you're after, for example, the best will have a yellowish cast and may be misshapen, but it will smell pleasantly sweet.

Careful storage will help you ensure that fresh produce lasts longer. Keep most fruits and vegetables in the refrigerator at a temperature of 5°C.

Vegetables will keep in the refrigerator for two to five days; root vegetables, such as carrots, will keep even longer. Store potatoes and onions in a cool, dark place for maximum freshness.

The merits of frozen and canned

For convenience, you can't beat frozen and canned fruits and vegetables, the best of which rival fresh when it comes to taste and nutrition.

Used in a recipe, your family may not be able to tell the difference between fresh and frozen fruit and vegetables or those from a can. A recent study of 1,500 people found that dishes prepared with canned ingredients were just as appealing as ones that contained fresh or frozen produce.

Whether fresh or frozen, you'll want to check the label to see what you're buying. Some frozen vegetables, for instance, are packaged with extra salt and fat. Instead, choose products that are packaged without any sauces or additives. With canned fruits, look for varieties that pack the fruit in juice, not syrup.

- Don't buy a package of frozen vegetables if the bag is ripped or the box is soggy or torn.
- With canned products, watch out for any can that has a large dent or a swollen appearance, or one from which some of the juices are leaking out.

When you bring cans of food home, store them at a temperature of no more than 24°C. They will keep their quality for about a year. If there isn't a sell-by or use-by date on a can, it's a good idea to label it with the date of purchase. Frozen food will keep best if stored in a freezer that stays at -18°C.

Other convenience foods

If you often have to prepare quick meals, you may rely on the convenient short-cuts that are readily available in the grocery aisles. Macaroni and cheese in a box, spaghetti in a can, and frozen entrees fall into this category, as do pre-seasoned raw chicken breasts and pre-boxed lunches for kids.

There's such a range of convenience foods that consumers need to consider what each one has to offer. Experts suggest looking carefully at the cost of the food and its convenience, as well as its nutritional value, before making a decision about whether or not to buy it.

Often, convenience foods are more expensive than cooking a meal from scratch. And, unlike cooking from scratch, the preparer has little or no control over how the dish is made or what's in it. Sometimes, of course, just the fact that it is quick and easy makes it worth its price. Just be sure that it has something to offer in terms of nutrition.

Try to avoid convenience foods that are high in sugar, salt, or fat, particularly saturated or trans fats. A quick scan of the ingredients list can be very telling.

You should always think twice about buying foods if any of the following ingredients appear as one of the top three in the list: fructose, honey, glucose, dextrose, maltose, sucrose, corn syrup (all of which are types of sugar), sugar, hydrogenated vegetable oil, coconut oil, lard, palm kernel oil, beef tallow, or shortening.

Reading labels

Labels on bags, boxes, bottles, and cans of food are there to help you decide how a food can fit into your family's diet. Find out how to scan these labels for the information you need, whether you're buying frozen green peas or oatmeal cookies.

Look for the label

For nearly 100 years, food labels have been growing increasingly comprehensive. Time was, you might have been lucky to learn what was in the box you were buying, but today, labeling is accurate and easy to read, to protect consumers. For example, terms such as "low-fat" are defined and regulated by Health Canada and the Canadian Food Inspection Agency (CFIA). If a food contains more than one ingredient, a complete list of ingredients is required. Manufacturers also must tell consumers how the food stacks up against guidelines for the number of calories, fat grams, vitamins, and other nutrients a person should get each day.

Nutrition Facts
Per bar (37 g)

Amount	% Daily Value
Calories 140	
Fat 3.0 g	4%
Saturated 0 g + Trans 0.5 g	3%
Cholesterol 0 mg	
Sodium 90 mg	4%
Carbohydrate 25 g	8%
Fibre less than 1 g	3%
Sugars 15 g	
Protein 1 g	
Vitamin A 15%	Vitamin C 0%
Calcium 0%	Iron 10%

The ingredients list does not form part of the Nutrition Facts, but will appear elsewhere on the packaging:

INGREDIENTS: FILLING [HIGH FRUCTOSE CORN SYRUP, STRAWBERRIES, GLYCERIN, MODIFIED FOOD STARCH (CORN, TAPIOCA), NATURAL FLAVOURS, CITRIC ACID, SALT], WHEAT FLOUR, SUGAR, DEXTROSE, PARTIALLY HYDROGENATED VEGETABLE OIL (SOYBEAN, COTTONSEED), NONFAT MILK, OATS, MOLASSES, CORN OIL, EGG WHITES, HIGH FRUCTOSE CORN SYRUP, WHEAT BRAN, THIAMINE, RIBOFLAVIN, VITAMIN A, VITAMIN B6, LECITHIN

Percent daily values These can help you determine if the food is a good or poor source of certain nutrients.

Fat The fat content is broken down to show how much of it is saturated and how much is trans fat.

Cholesterol This is not the same as fat, and even low cholesterol items may contain some saturated fat.

Sugars This will not distinguish between added sugar and naturally occurring sugars.

Protein The protein content must be shown, but the percent daily value is not required.

Ingredients All ingredients must be listed in descending order of weight.

Label lingo
It's worth the effort it takes to become a savvy label-reader so you can assess a food's nutritional value.

When deciding whether to buy something or not, it's important to understand the information on the label.

Serving size: This provides the size of one serving. From this you can calculate how many servings are in that package. Pay attention to serving size, because it's common to eat more than one serving.

Calories: This line will tell you the number of calories that the food contains per serving.

% Daily Value: This can be tricky when it comes to kids, because the daily values, which show how a food's nutritional content compares to the recommended daily allowances (RDAs), are based on 2,000 calories a day. So the amounts may not be on target for children. However, you can still use this information to determine if something is a rich or poor source of assorted vitamins and minerals, as well as fibre. For instance, a food supplying only one percent of daily fibre is not a rich source, either for an adult or child.

Fat: Measured in grams, this will tell you how much fat is in a serving of food. Look for the breakdown (mandatory as from 2006) showing how much of the fat is saturated and how much is trans (see page 36). These two types of fat are known to raise blood cholesterol levels and be a risk factor for heart disease. They are combined because the risk they pose is similar. A 10% Daily Value or less for saturated and trans fats in a food would be considered a low amount.

Cholesterol and sodium: These lines will show, in milligrams, how much cholesterol and sodium are in a serving of the food.

Carbohydrate: This section includes three numbers—one for total carbohydrate, another for fibre, and a third for sugars. These are all measured in grams. There is no % Daily Value given for sugars as there is no generally accepted recommendation.

Protein: This number is measured in grams.

Vitamins A and C: These two vitamins are always listed, but the manufacturer may list others as well.

Calcium and iron: It's helpful that these two minerals are listed on the label, because they're essential for kids.

Storing and preparing food

Providing nutritious meals for your family goes well beyond buying the food. Those who prepare food need to know the basics about kitchen hygiene and how to prevent food-borne illnesses. Uncooked foods—even raw cookie dough—should be off-limits for kids.

Good kitchen practice

- Check the temperature of your refrigerator to ensure that it is 5°C and your freezer is -18°C or less. Cool temperatures keep bacteria in foods from multiplying.
- Don't keep or buy fruit with broken skin because the opening creates an avenue for bacteria.
- Keep raw fish, meat, and poultry and their juices away from other foods in the refrigerator and on countertops. Store meat and poultry in the bottom of the fridge.
- Wash hands, cutting boards, counters, and knives or other utensils thoroughly after preparing raw foods, especially meats and eggs. Wash cutting boards separately from other dishes and utensils.
- Use separate utensils and plates for cooking and serving meat, poultry, fish, or eggs (or wash the utensils in hot, soapy water before using them to serve).
- Cook meats thoroughly, using a meat thermometer to check. Ground beef, especially, must be cooked until it is brown inside, not red or pink.

- Refrigerate any leftovers as soon as possible after cooking. If left to sit at room temperature, bacteria in the food will multiply quickly.
- Scrub all fruits and vegetables with water to remove pesticide residue, bacteria, and dirt.
- Some foods (such as Caesar salad dressing, cookie dough, homemade ice cream, and chocolate mousse) may contain raw eggs or unspecified raw food products and could be contaminated with salmonella, so they should not be given to children. Find out whether raw eggs are used and, if so, avoid them. Unpasteurized milk and milk products, and unpasteurized ciders or juices also could cause food-borne illness.
- Children whose immunity is weakened by diseases such as cancer or AIDS should avoid uncooked foods that could carry listeriosis bacteria, such as soft cheeses like feta, Brie, and Camembert, and blue-veined cheeses. Although precooked, deli meats and cold cuts must be cooked again before serving to kill any bacteria.

info

Teaching kids about kitchen safety

Any time you have kids in the kitchen, you'll need to think about safety issues. Younger children should be closely supervised, so they don't burn or cut themselves. But there are plenty of safe tasks that they will enjoy. Here are some ideas:
- washing vegetables
- mixing pancake batter
- sprinkling on spices and herbs.
In between tasks, let them set the table, take everyone's drink order, or pretend to cook alongside you.

Care needs to be taken with older children, too, as they may be overconfident in their abilities. Ensure that you:
- monitor their use of stoves, ranges, and other kitchen appliances;

- teach them the proper way to use knives and other sharp kitchen tools.
But don't let your safety concerns make them feel unwelcome in the kitchen. Invite your kids to pick new dishes to try and encourage them to pack their lunches.

Good hygiene
Kids also need to learn about another kind of kitchen safety—preventing food-borne illnesses, such as E coli, salmonellosis, campylobacter infections, and listeriosis (see above). Even the youngest child can learn to wash up before getting involved in a cooking project. As kids get older you can educate them about proper food storage, preparation, and cleanup.

3

PRINCIPLES OF FITNESS

Most young children are **naturally physically active** and love to move around. But **older kids may slow down**. Fight the couch potato trend and **help your child** cultivate a love of activity that will last a lifetime.

Fit and healthy for life

To many people, "fitness" is something that requires hours in the gym. But fitness can simply mean being healthy and having a body that's strong enough to do everything you want and need it to do.

A love of physical activity

Nearly all children start out fit and eager to be active. Just consider the unstoppable force that is the average preschooler, who runs, spins, leaps, and climbs at every opportunity. But as children get older, they encounter obstacles that may make it difficult to be active. There are plenty of explanations:

- the increasing demands of school;
- a feeling among some kids that they aren't good at sports;
- concerns about safety that prevent children from having the freedom to roam their own neighborhoods.

Despite these barriers, parents can help their children develop a love of physical activity at a young age, which, if encouraged, can be carried with them throughout their lives.

The many benefits of exercise

There are many health benefits for kids who are physically active. A child who is active will:

- have stronger muscles and stronger bones;
- have a leaner body because exercise helps control body fat;
- be less likely to become overweight;
- decrease the risk of developing type 2 diabetes;
- possibly lower blood pressure and blood cholesterol levels;
- have a better outlook on life.

Regular exercise also strengthens the heart muscle, which improves its effectiveness. A stronger heart pumps more blood with each beat, which means it is able to deliver oxygen throughout the body more efficiently.

All children can be fit

For the more athletic child, physical training can improve performance so the child may be able to run faster, jump higher, or throw a ball farther. But fitness is not an exclusive

"boing! boing! boing!"

club limited only to children who are gifted at sports or who have an athletic body type. All children can be physically fit, whatever their abilities and interests. Parents can influence their child's fitness habits—positively or negatively. A child who has active parents is six times more likely to be physically active. And it's not just what you do and say about exercise, but the way you deliver the message. Don't let your child view physical activity as a burden or another boring chore. Help your child see exercise as a broad category that includes a wide range of physical activities to choose from.

As the parent, it's your job to help your child discover which activities or sports he or she most enjoys. Then, find ways for your child to participate in them. This can sometimes be problematic, as a recent study of the U. S. Centers for Disease Control and Prevention (CDC) showed. In the survey, parents of nine- to 13-year-olds acknowledged the following obstacles to getting their kids physically fit:

- expense
- transportation problems
- parents' lack of time
- lack of opportunities in the area
- lack of neighborhood safety.

Expense and transportation problems were considered the top two issues. These problems were most acute in lower-income households, but also mentioned by middle- and upper-income parents. It's true that sports programs can be expensive, but it's also true that low cost alternatives are often available. To get your child involved at little or no expense, contact your child's school, the local government recreation department, and community organizations, such as the Boys and Girls Clubs of America or the YMCA.

If transportation is a problem, look for after-school programs to alleviate one leg of the journey. Also consider car-pooling with other parents, and, when a child is old enough, whether public transportation is an option.

But, most importantly, teach your child that physical activity doesn't have to come as part of an organized sport or program. Lead an active lifestyle together, running errands on foot instead of by car and spending free time at local parks. Also invest in balls, jump ropes, and sidewalk chalk.

Of the 3,800 children surveyed in the CDC study, 77 percent said they had participated in free-play physical activity during the last week while only about 39 percent said they had participated in an organized physical activity, like a team sport. A mix of both types of activity is ideal, especially as a child reaches school age. Being part of a team is a way to make friends and teaches a child about teamwork and following rules. The balance between free play and organized activities is your call, and your child's, but make sure your child gets enough regular physical activity. (For specific recommendations, see page 54.) If your child took this survey, what would he or she have said?

Why kids need physical activity

Children need to be fit for the same reasons adults do: to improve their health and ensure that they can perform normal daily tasks and activities. People who are fit sleep better and are better able to handle the challenges that a typical day presents.

Developing skills and fitness

Regular exercise helps children to grow, to build strong muscles and bones, and to develop important motor skills. Even the older child, who seems very capable, is learning new skills, and regular physical activity helps strengthen his or her developing body. Repetition leads to mastery of the basic skills, from throwing and catching and skipping to more precise movements, such as turning a pirouette in ballet or deftly placing a shot in tennis.

Depending on their age and development, children need different amounts of activity and types of exercise. For example, young children (one to five years) shouldn't be inactive for more than 60 minutes unless they're sleeping, and kids up to the age of 12 should get at least 60 minutes of free play time every day. Babies and toddlers get much of the activity they need through interaction and play with their parents. As children get older, their readiness to participate in different types of physical activity depends on age, development, and individual likes and dislikes. There's no point forcing a child to play a sport if it's not fun for them.

The suggestions and recommendations in the table below are those of the authors, but they reflect similar goals to the activity guidelines that are issued by Health Canada (see pages 63 and 203).

How much is **enough?**

AGE	DEVELOPMENT	DAILY ACTIVITY	SUGGESTED ACTIVITIES	WHAT PARENTS SHOULD DO
Infant	learning to roll over, sit, stand, walk	no specific recommendations	physical activity should encourage motor development; no formal programs necessary	provide a safe play space; avoid walkers; limit time in car seats, swings, and strollers
Toddler (1–3 years)	walking, running, climbing, kicking, jumping	1½ hours	play (especially outdoors), smaller scale playground equipment, pull and push toys, ride-on vehicles, balls	ensure 30 minutes structured activity daily with games, plus at least 60 minutes of unstructured play time
Preschooler (3–5 years)	hopping, balancing on one foot, throwing and catching, pedaling, skipping	1½–2 hours	catch, tag, playground time, trikes and bikes, wagons, bats and balls, tumbling and dance	provide 30–60 minutes of structured activity daily, plus at least 60 minutes of unstructured play time
School-age (6–12 years)	building more complex movements; developing hand-eye coordination; starting to understand rules	1½–2 hours	jump-rope, swimming, bike riding, team sports (non-competitive during earlier years), outdoor play	provide home play equipment; be sure kids get 30–60 minutes physical activity daily, as well as at least 60 minutes unstructured play time
Adolescent (13 and older)	body changes in puberty, growing taller and stronger	30–60 minutes	choose according to interests and age—competitive sports, classes, jogging, swimming, cycling	provide equipment and/or transportation; ensure at least three 20-minute sessions of more vigorous exercise weekly

info

Motivating overweight kids

Exercise offers tremendous benefits for overweight children, but it may be tough for many of them to get started. Be sensitive to reasons why an overweight child may not want to exercise, such as embarrassment over wearing a swimsuit or shorts or changing in front of other kids before gym class.

- Find activities that interest your child—some suit overweight children better than others. For example, swimming and walking are ideal choices because they are easier on the joints.
- If your child is more comfortable exercising at home, try an age-appropriate exercise video. Older children may be interested in using home gym equipment, such as a treadmill or stationary bike.

- Let them shop for workout clothes and sneakers that they like wearing and that offer adequate support.

Overweight children may be in poor physical condition, but, as long as the doctor approves, encourage them to get moving. Your child can start by walking five minutes a day and add a minute each day until they reach their exercise goal of at least 30 minutes every day.

An overweight child who has little experience with exercise is at risk of injury. Teach your child to warm up, and cool down afterward. Overweight kids are at increased risk of dehydration, too, so be sure they drink plenty of water.

Never criticize your child for being inactive, but praise kids who make even modest efforts to get moving. Also offer to exercise together.

Preschool kids don't have the skills that older kids have mastered, such as throwing and running at the same time. But a child as young as four or five may enjoy learning basic skills through tumbling, a dance class, or learning to throw a ball in the backyard. Preteens and teens can be left more in charge of choosing the kind of exercise they want to do—as long as they get enough. So find out what your child's interests are and work together to help him or her get enough physical activity. (For information about how to choose an activity that suits your child, see page 137.)

Organized sports

You may wonder when your child can start organized sports. Although some programs are designed for younger kids, six is a good age for most—any class or league for children younger than this should stress development of basic skills and having fun. By six or seven, though, children are more physically ready, they have a longer attention span, and they can begin to grasp simple rules.

As children get older, they can handle more competition, such as keeping score and keeping track of wins and losses for the season. But be cautious about leagues that require

tryouts, many hours of practice, and a lot of traveling, or that emphasize winning championships. While some children are motivated by competitive play, the average child may not be ready for the increased pressure of this kind of sport until he or she is 11 or 12 years old. Remember, too, that even with the more competitive leagues, the atmosphere should remain positive and supportive for all the participants.

Free play

In addition to sports, parents should encourage free play. Unlike organized activities, such as gymnastics or playing on a soccer or volleyball team, free play allows your child to choose how to be active.

- For younger kids, free play might include imaginative play, action songs, such as "Simon Says" and "I'm a Little Teapot," or dancing.
- As kids get older, hopscotch, tag, or "monkey in the middle" may be more fun.
- Free play for preteens and teens might mean skateboarding, inline skating, or going for a bike ride.

(For more advice on activities for different age groups, see the age-specific chapters.)

How to get physically fit

Though heredity and home environment affect a child's ability to get fit, almost all children—and adults—can enjoy the sense of well-being that comes with regular physical activity.

"go, go, go!"

What is fitness?

Physical activity is any movement of the large muscles of the body that results in burning more calories (see page 33) than would be used while resting. Physical fitness can be achieved through regular physical activity.

Fitness can be divided into two types: health-related and performance or skill-related. Health-related fitness improves heart and muscle function, strengthens bones, and increases well-being. An active child is more likely to be active into adulthood when health-related fitness has important long-term benefits. These benefits include improved quality of life and a reduced risk of developing certain diseases, such as type 2 diabetes and heart disease.

Performance fitness includes improvement in speed, balance, agility, and coordination—the types of activities that help people excel at sports. Some children may focus on improving performance just because they like the tangible results of being faster, stronger, or more capable. Usually, while focusing on gains in performance fitness, children are helping themselves achieve health-related fitness as well.

The three elements

If you've ever watched children on a playground, you know that they love to move their bodies, whether it's climbing to the top of the slide, or swinging from the monkey bars. Without thinking about it, they are developing the three elements of fitness: endurance, strength, and flexibility. While different kids will have different abilities, all children should regularly be doing activities that involve all three elements.

Endurance is developed when you move your body in a way that increases your heart rate and quickens your breathing in a sustained way. Described as aerobic exercise ("with air"), this improves the body's ability to deliver oxygen to all its cells, thus increasing the aerobic capacity and, with it, cardiorespiratory endurance. Kids get this kind of exercise when they run or jog, skip, jump, and play.

Exercises **for flexibility**

Body flexibility comes in handy all the time, even when you're doing something as simple as tying your shoes. Being flexible means that your muscles and joints stretch and bend easily, so your limbs can move through their full range of motion. With activities such as practicing a split or touching their toes, or stretching exercises like these, children develop flexibility.

Sit and twist
Sit with legs straight. Bend left leg and cross it over right leg so left foot is alongside right knee. Bring right arm across body and hold outer side of left leg near knee. Slowly twist body and look over left shoulder. Hold stretch for 10–30 seconds. Repeat on other side.

Thigh stretch
Standing up straight, bend one knee and bring ankle up behind body. Grasp ankle in hand on same side. Keep bent leg beside other leg. Pull ankle up until you feel tension in front of thigh. Hold for 15–20 seconds. Repeat twice for each leg.

Calf stretch
Place hands against wall with arms and back straight. Bend one knee slightly and extend other leg backward, keeping foot flat on floor. You should feel tension in back of extended leg. Hold stretch for 15–20 seconds. Repeat twice with each leg.

Overhead stretch
Clasp hands together and raise them, palms upward, above head, stretching your arms. Hold stretch for 20 seconds.

Resistance band exercises **for strength**

Some people think that strength training means lifting weights to get big muscles. But strength training offers a range of benefits for children. They will have improved muscle tone, their muscles will better support their joints, and weight-bearing exercise, such as running or jumping, builds stronger bones. (To find out more about weight training for kids, see below.) Resistance bands, which are strong elastic tubes or bands, can be a safe alternative to free weights or weight machines. Start with a set of ten of the exercises below and add additional sets as your child's fitness level improves.

Pull out
Stand with feet shoulder width apart, shoulders down. Hold handles in front of chest, palms facing in. Inhale. Stretch band out, straight across in front of body, keeping elbows slightly bent. (Children under ten should start out pulling only halfway.) Exhale. Hold for two counts, then control band back to starting position. Repeat.

Rowing
Put one handle of band under arch of foot. With feet together, hold other handle with both hands, palms in. Inhale. Raise hands no higher than chin, lifting elbows to side. Exhale. Lower band slowly. Repeat.

Arm curl
Place one handle of band under arch of foot. Slightly separate feet. Inhale. Draw band up toward shoulder, keeping back straight and holding upper arm against body. Exhale. Lower band slowly. Repeat.

Q: **Is weight training safe for my 12-year-old son?**

A: Some boys at this age are interested in lifting weights because they want to build muscles, especially if they see their peers maturing. Strength training, under the right conditions, can increase muscle tone and may help your son feel better about his body, but it won't build muscle until he has hit puberty.

Talk to your son's doctor about his interest in strength training. With the doctor's approval, seek out a certified athletic trainer, physical therapist, or coach who has experience training children. That person can help your son start a safe and appropriate program, ensuring that he won't be lifting heavy weights and will be supervised during the workout. Be sure your son uses light weights and does several repetitions.

Floor exercises **for strength**

If a muscle is strong, it can exert a lot of force. For instance, a strong arm can curl a heavy barbell. But kids don't need to lift weights to be strong. The simplest way for children to improve muscle strength is to use their own body weight as resistance during strengthening exercises. Doing repetitions of these sorts of exercises builds both muscle strength and endurance. Of course, kids also work on their muscles by crossing the monkey bars in the playground or learning to hold a handstand. Have your child begin with a set of ten of the exercises below and add additional sets as your child's fitness improves.

Push up
Lie flat on floor, face down, hands under shoulders, fingers straight. Bend knees and bring feet up at 90° angle to body. Lift body off floor by straightening arms; keep back straight and knees bent. Lower body until you have a 90° angle at elbows. Repeat.

Seat drop
With back to heavy block or sturdy chair and straight arms kept a shoulder width apart, place hands on front edge of block or chair. Stretch out legs straight in front, feet together and heels on floor. Lower body until arms are bent 90°, then straighten arms to pull yourself up.

Curl up
Lie on floor on back, legs bent and feet flat. Cross arms on chest. Lift chest toward knees until shoulders come off floor. Lie back down.

Leg lift
Lie on side with knee of bottom leg bent forward at 30–40° angle. Have ankle/foot of upper leg in a neutral position. Lift upper leg straight up to shoulder height. Hold for five seconds, then lower leg back down.

How to help kids get fit

The best way for children to get physical activity is by incorporating regular exercise into their daily routine, whether it be involvement in organized sports or enjoying free play. It's an excellent fitness strategy for the whole family to adopt.

Motivating your child

This is the $64,000 question: What will motivate children and teens to get fit? The answers can be found in the positive experience of kids who are fit and who enjoy physical activity. These children feel they are good at whatever activity they're doing, they feel accepted by their peers and important adults, and—most importantly—they have fun.

Here's how those good feelings about activity are built:

- Children enjoy activity because it's fun.
- Because they're active, they improve their skills.
- Because their skills improve, they get praise from peers, parents, and adults.
- Because of that praise, they gain self-confidence.
- And as a result, they enjoy physical activity even more.

Though it may be easiest with a child who's naturally interested in sports and athletically gifted, any child can be motivated. Start by finding something your child enjoys doing, or is interested in. Then, be sure the coaching staff or teacher is trained and knows the importance of praise and support. As a parent, you should also be supportive about the child's performance, while at the same time keeping expectations realistic. The goal is to help your child feel that he or she is succeeding.

You'll want to keep your child's age in mind because kids need different kinds of positive reinforcement as they grow from babies to teens. Infants and toddlers need attention, stimulation, and encouragement. School-age children feel competent when they master simple tasks, try hard, like

tips

Getting kids to commit

Here are some good ways to work with your child and encourage a commitment to regular physical activity.

Create an activity menu Younger children especially enjoy making an activity menu and using the menu options to plan a calendar of activities. Work with your child to draw up a list of favourite activities. Post this list where the child can see it and refer to it often. You can then let your child use the activity menu to create a calendar of planned activities. It also might be a good source of ideas for those moments when your child says, "I'm bored."

- Everyday activities: walking the dog, helping clean the house, and walking to school.
- Indoor activities: using an exercise video, dancing, playing games with soft sports balls, and having a game of "Simon Says."

- Outdoor activities: going to the playground, riding bikes, inline skating, and playing hopscotch.
- Special occasion activities: playing miniature golf, visiting a water park or amusement park, and going for a hike in the woods.

Keep an activity log Make a record of your child's activity for a week. You and your child can work on this together, noting what he or she likes to do, as well as how often they're done and how much time is spent in each active pursuit. This will enable you to track how much exercise your child gets.

Make a fitness contract This is one way to get an inactive teen moving (see page 167). Through a contract, parent and teen can set goals and develop strategies for how to reach them, with both parties working on them together.

What's your child's fitness personality?

Personality traits and athletic ability combine to influence a child's attitude toward participation in sports and other physical activities. When children are very young, most tend to move around a lot and don't need to be reminded to exercise. But this may change as kids get older. Which of these three types best describes your child?

- The nonathlete: this child may lack athletic ability, lack interest in physical activity, or both.
- The casual athlete: this child, who is not a star player, is interested in being active, but is at risk of getting discouraged in a competitive athletic environment.
- The athlete: this child has athletic ability, is committed to a sport or activity, and likely to ramp up practice time and intensity of competition.

The nonathletic child may need to limit sedentary activities, such as watching TV, using the computer, or playing video games. For the very athletic child, the difficulty may be finding more free time and rest time. If you understand the concepts of temperament and fitness type, you'll be better able to help your child find the right activities and get enough exercise — and find enjoyment in physical activity. For more discussion of this topic, see pages 143–145.

---

what they're doing, and get positive feedback from parents. Older kids want to know they compare well to their peers, so getting a compliment from a coach in front of the entire team can make a big difference. Older teens also get a boost from coach or teacher compliments, but as they near adulthood, they begin to set their own goals and work to achieve them.

One way kids can track their own success is to use a pedometer. This small device attaches at the waist and counts each step the child takes. A pedometer can be calibrated to properly measure the distance the child travels, as well.

Make sure it's fun

Can you create fun? It may sound odd, but researchers have come up with a list of factors that make physical activity fun for kids. Some of them are:

- having positive interactions with peers and coaches, who offer praise and support;
- feeling proud of mastering a skill and feeling good because others have noticed;
- loving the way it feels to do the activity—to glide through the water while swimming or somersault through the air in gymnastics.

Finding that special "fun" activity can be the catalyst for a lifetime of physical fitness. Your child will simply want to keep doing it. Parents need to have fun, too—for good reason: Research has found that parents who themselves enjoy physical activity are more likely to encourage activity in their children. So don't just walk the walk—make sure you enjoy the walk, too! See page 63 to learn about building up levels of activity throughout the day, and about planning activity goals for the whole family.

All kinds of activity

Including a variety of physical activities in a typical week—for example, walking to a friend's house, enjoying free play, and attending sports practices or classes—ensures a child has an active and healthy lifestyle. To get your child to commit to this, you might try setting up an activity schedule, and monitoring results with an activity log, or, for older kids, drawing up a fitness contract (see left).

Couch potatoes

In tracking activity, don't forget to note sedentary time, which can be the arch enemy of an active lifestyle. To encourage your child to increase his or her activity level, you may have to limit your child's "screen time"—the amount of time your child spends watching TV, using the computer, or playing computer and video games. The average child watches three hours of TV a day and spends as much as two more hours using the computer or playing computer games. Add to that the time children spend reading or studying, and it totals up to a lot of inactivity.

Here are some guidelines to follow:

- Children under two shouldn't watch any TV. Even the most educational show isn't as beneficial as exploring and interacting with the world around them.
- Children older than two should be limited to one to two hours of "screen time" per day.

Of course, quality counts as well as quantity, so parents need to be aware of their children's favourite TV programs and computer games. Monitor what your child watches on TV, including DVDs and videos. Also be informed about which computer software your child is using and which Internet sites are most often visited.

How to gauge fitness

Fitness is hard to measure, but the best way to start is by paying attention to how active your child is on a typical day. From toddlers to teens, children should be active every day, getting a mixture of structured activity and free play time. (See page 54 for recommendations.)

If you are keeping an activity log (see page 60), you have an easy way of checking to see if your child is getting enough exercise. The total can include any kind of activity, from mowing the lawn to running around a track. If your child is getting less than the recommended amount, talk with your child's doctor about starting a program to boost the active time.

Inactive children and youth should increase the amount of time they currently spend being physically active each day by at least 30 minutes and decrease the time they spend on TV or playing on computers each day by at least 30 minutes. Over a period of several months, children and youth should try to accumulate at least 90 minutes more physical activity per day and decrease by at least 90 minutes per day the amount of time spent on sedentary activities such as watching videos and sitting at a computer. The table opposite shows how this can be done.

tips

Get them away from the TV

If you're finding it tough to pry your kids away from the tube, here are some ways to gradually decrease the time they spend watching TV.

- Provide the weekly TV schedule for your children and encourage them to choose the programs they want to watch.
- Turn on the TV when the show starts, and turn it off when it's over.
- Provide alternatives, such as playing games or arts and crafts projects.
- Keep an ample supply of bats, balls, jump ropes, and other equipment on hand so that kids have easy access to them whenever they feel like playing.
- And no matter how much they beg for one, do not put a TV in your child's bedroom.

Dare to be **active**

Canada's Physical Activity Guides for Children and Youth, published by Health Canada, recommend that children and adolescents should increase the time currently spent on physical activity, starting with 30 minutes more per day in periods of at least 5 to 10 minutes. The Guides also recommend a corresponding decrease in the amount of "non-active" time spent on TV, video, computer games, and surfing the Internet. A schedule for achieving this is set out below. (To obtain copies of Canada's Physical Activity Guides, see page 203.)

Endurance, flexibility, and strength all contribute to a healthy body, and all three types of physical activity should be combined for best results. Endurance activities are those that make you breathe more deeply and make your heart beat faster, making you feel warm. These activities, such as running, jumping, and swimming, strengthen the heart and lungs. Flexibility activities encourage bending, stretching, and reaching, keeping the joints moving. Gymnastics and dancing are good examples. Strength-building activities, such as climbing and swinging by your arms, help to build strong muscles and bones.

MONTH–BY–MONTH INCREASED ACTIVITY SCHEDULE

	Daily INCREASE in moderate* physical activity (minutes)		Daily INCREASE in vigorous** physical activity (minutes)		Total daily INCREASE in physical activity (minutes)	Total daily DECREASE in non-active time (minutes)
Month 1	at least 20	+	10	=	30	30
Month 2	at least 30	+	15	=	45	45
Month 3	at least 40	+	20	=	60	60
Month 4	at least 50	+	25	=	75	75
Month 5	at least 60	+	30	=	90	90

Examples of moderate physical activity include:
- brisk walking • swimming • skating
- playing outdoors • bike riding

** *Examples of vigorous physical activity include:*
- running • soccer • basketball
- supervised weight training

GOAL PLANNING

Goals give you something to work toward–and they tell you how you are doing. Family physical activity goals help you and your family enjoy life and health together. Think about how physical activity goals fit into the rest of your life. Choose goals that you can do along with other activities. A more active life should not add stress, but create a sense of well-being. Remember to make staying healthy and keeping active as important as the other parts of your life.

- Involve the whole family. Get together and talk about the physical activities that you enjoy.
- Start simple. Your goal can be as simple as taking a family swim once a week, or walking the dog three nights a week.
- Be realistic. Start with goals you can achieve with a little effort.
- Write down your goals in clear terms. Say how often and when you will do an activity–for example, play catch together for 20 minutes on Sunday mornings.

- Keep your goals flexible. Allow yourself to make adjustments, but make up for any time you lose.
- Try something more challenging. Once you have achieved your goal, add some vigorous activities, or increase the time.
- Reward yourself for achieving your goals–with a healthy reward. Maybe a new game or CD, or just setting time aside to relax, is the reward you need.

For your own health, and for your children's health, have fun and live an active life.

"Snug fit"

Playing safe

No matter how a child chooses to be active—or how old the child is—a parent needs to take the lead when it comes to sensible safety precautions and preventing injuries.

A sensible exercise program

The principles of physical training are the same whether your child has ambitions to run a faster mile or just wants to start a gentle program of daily walking. An exercise program should include these four elements:

- a regular schedule of physical activity that's consistent from week to week;
- the right level of intensity, so the child's body is working harder than it does when at rest, but without overdoing it, particularly if the child is normally inactive;
- a variety of activities, so the child gets a good mixture of exercises and physical activities that improve endurance, strength, and flexibility;

- a gradual increase in the number of repetitions or in the amount of time spent exercising. Your child should make slow and steady progress toward a goal. Trying to go too fast can lead to injuries.

Good practice

Teach your child to exercise properly, from warm up to cool down. Before starting to exercise, have your child warm up with five to ten minutes of brisk walking, slow jogging, or jumping jacks. Start slowly and gradually increase the pace. Warm-up exercises can help reduce muscle strain and prevent injuries. After exercise, cool down by stretching, which relaxes muscle groups and increases flexibility.

Take this same measured approach to help improve your child's fitness level. A very sedentary child might start slowly, with just one ten-minute walk a day. Add extra minutes each day or week, perhaps offering a pedometer as an extra incentive. You can also keep an activity chart for your child and use it to set a baseline and choose a reasonable goal.

Some appealing activities are considered too dangerous for younger children because they lack the skills and judgment to do them safely. The following recommendations are generally considered to be helpful guidelines:

- Skateboards shouldn't be used by children under ten.
- Scooters shouldn't be used by children under eight.
- Trampolines should never be used at home.

The right gear

Protective equipment helps reduce the risk of injury by absorbing some of the blows that the body would otherwise take. An advantage of organized sports and league play is that most require appropriate protective gear and adult supervision. At home, parents should provide the right protective equipment for their children's activities (see the list of commonly used types of protective gear, below). Parents also need to be vigilant to ensure that children always wear the protective gear when playing or exercising, and know how to use it properly.

This may be easier to require of younger children, but don't give up on the older ones. Playing tackle football without pads or helmets is just asking for a trip to the emergency room. And remember that mouth guards not only protect the teeth but also help absorb the impact of hits to the mouth and jaw.

Older kids may cast aside bike helmets, believing they aren't cool or will muss their hair. Parents must enforce the helmet rule regardless—and wear bike helmets themselves. (For information about choosing a sports helmet, to be sure that it fits well, see page 66.)

The sports gear **your child should be using**

Helmets protect the head when bicycling, inline skating, skateboarding, and playing various team sports. They are also recommended for skiing and snowboarding. Pads and guards protect specific parts of the body that are vulnerable to knocks and blows in sports such as basketball, football, hockey, lacrosse, and soccer. Use other protective sports equipment as described below.

SPORT	EQUIPMENT
Baseball, softball	while batting and running the bases, a helmet with polycarbonate face guard and eye protection; if playing catcher, a face mask, throat guard, chest protector, and shin guards; if male, an athletic supporter and protective cup
Basketball	mouth guard
Football	helmet with attached mouth guard; shoulder, hip, thigh, and tail pads; thigh guards; athletic supporter and protective cup; padded pants
Hockey	helmet/face mask; shoulder pads, shin pads, elbow pads, hip pads, and tendon pads; padded hockey pants; gloves; mouth guard; athletic supporter
Inline skating, skateboarding	helmet; wrist, knee, and elbow pads
Lacrosse	helmet with attached mouth guard; rib, shoulder, and elbow pads; gloves; athletic supporter and protective cup; protective eyewear. For the goalie: chest protection; arm and leg pads
Soccer	shin guards; mouth guard

Be street smart

Parents should supervise young children whenever they are outdoors and be extra careful when children are playing near the street. Young children should be taught to ask for an adult's help to retrieve balls and to stay under control when riding bikes, trikes, or wagons so they don't drift into oncoming traffic. Consider getting together with your neighbours to install signs in the street alerting drivers to children playing and invest in temporary net fencing that can block toys from rolling out of the driveway. Use extra caution if kids are playing outside at dusk, when it's difficult for drivers to see them.

Fun as it may be, it's best to discourage older kids from skating, scootering, and playing street hockey or any other game in the street. Instead, provide them with transportation to parks or fields where they can have plenty of space.

While you're discouraging your child from playing in or near streets, you'll want to offer alternatives. Recreation trails and exercise tracks provide a safe environment for kids to walk, skate, or ride bikes without worrying about traffic.

Water safety

Children of all ages love the water, but water play and swimming can be dangerous: Drowning is one of the leading causes of accidental deaths in children younger than 14.

Children between the ages of one and four are most at risk of drowning. Close and constant supervision is essential, because so many drownings occur in home swimming pools and involve children who were out of their parents' sight for less than five minutes.

Swimming lessons are a good idea, though they are not a substitute for adult supervision.

- A child older than four is usually ready to learn how to swim. It's wise to use flotation devices—not water wings—to keep young children afloat in the water before they are able to swim on their own.
- Older children should be taught never to swim alone and that they should swim near lifeguards at parks, beaches, and lakes.
- If someone other than a lifeguard is monitoring the kids, that person must know how to swim. This sounds obvious, but you'll want to be sure that babysitters, neighbours, and grandparents are capable of rescuing a child, if necessary.

Swimming goes hand in hand with bright, sunny days, so you'll want to take sun-safety precautions as well. Insist that children wear sunblock and reapply it after swimming to ensure that it's still doing its job. Also encourage kids—especially those who are prone to burn—to wear hats to shield their heads and sunglasses to shield their eyes.

tips

The perfect fit

All sports helmets must fit well to protect your child in a fall. Make sure the helmet has a CSPC, Snell, or CSA sticker, which indicates that it meets current safety standards. When choosing a helmet:

- Pick one that fits snugly but comfortably on your child's head. The helmet should rest level on your child's head, not tilted forward or backward. Remove any hats or caps before putting the helmet on.
- Look for strong, wide straps that fasten snugly under the chin—no more than a finger's width should be able to fit beneath the strap when it is fastened correctly. Straps should be tight enough so that sudden pulling or twisting does not cause the helmet to move around on the child's head.
- If your child takes a significant fall, replace the helmet! It may have lost its effectiveness after taking a hit. Even if the helmet looks fine, it may be cracked inside, so throw it away and buy a new one.

Drink for sport

It's important to be sure your child drinks enough before, during, and after exercise. A child needs water, or other fluids such as juice mixed with water, to prevent dehydration as well as heat-related illnesses like heat stroke and heat exhaustion.

Provide lots of liquid

Parents can help prevent injury in kids of all ages by being on the lookout for dehydration. A child who is becoming dehydrated cannot perform at his or her best and is at greater risk of injury because energy, strength, and coordination may diminish.

Thirst is the first sign of dehydration, so offer your child some water to drink. But even if kids satisfy their thirst, it may not be enough to replace all the fluid lost on a hot day. Other signs of dehydration include feeling lightheaded, rapid heartbeat, and dry mouth and lips.

Decreased frequency of urination is another sign of dehydration, as is urine colour. If your child is adequately hydrated, the urine should be a pale yellow colour. If your child's urine is dark or strong smelling, it could be a sign of dehydration. But this isn't the most practical way to monitor your child during sports practice on a hot day, so frequent water breaks are important.

Heat-related illness

Children may be at greater risk than adults for heat-related illnesses such as heat exhaustion (fatigue, weakness, and discomfort when overheated) and heat stroke (when the body becomes dangerously overheated). This is because children's bodies are less efficient at cooling down.

Look for these early signs of heat illness, which, if untreated, can progress to shock and loss of consciousness:

- pale skin
- headache
- rapid heartbeat
- nausea or vomiting
- muscle cramps
- goosebumps or excessive sweating
- fatigue, weakness, or dizziness.

Quenching thirst
Children of all ages need to drink plenty of fluids when playing or exercising—even more when it is hot. Water is the best choice to keep kids hydrated.

To prevent heat-related illness, schedule breaks during exercise sessions and encourage your child to drink plenty of fluids; limit activity during the hottest time of the day (usually 10 a.m. to 4 p.m.); and be sure your child wears lightweight, loose-fitting clothing.

Anyone who cares for your child also should take steps to avoid putting your child at risk. This could include relatives, childcare workers, summer camp counselors, and coaches. In addition, be sure to teach your child to tell an adult if he or she starts to feel overheated and ill when playing or exercising. It's fine to work up a little sweat, but it's not okay to "play through" overexertion that could lead to illness.

4

THE **FIRST YEAR**

It all starts here.
In these twelve months you can start **building a foundation of good health** for your baby. Learn how to provide **proper nutrition and the right activities** during this important first year.

Making a good start

Your baby begins life completely dependent on you, but in just 12 months' time, that swaddled infant becomes a separate little person able to feed himself or herself and maybe even walk.

Do what comes naturally

Progress can be seen almost weekly as babies learn to lift their heads, roll over, sit up, crawl, cruise, and stand alone. Healthy eating and activity help a baby develop at this phenomenal rate, so parents often want to know exactly what to do and when to do it:

- How do I know the baby is eating enough?
- When do I introduce solid food?
- How can I encourage my child to crawl?

Though there are guidelines about feeding and activity that parents should know, much of what a baby needs parents do naturally as they love their child and begin a relationship with this fascinating new member of the family. A parent learns to respond to a child's needs, whether the baby is wet, in need of a cuddle, or hungry. This responsiveness helps the child feel secure.

Feeding your baby

When a baby cries, a parent's first thought may be to offer food. The trouble is, babies can't say whether they're hungry or not. But during a feeding, a baby might turn his or her head away—a sign that he or she may have eaten enough. "Enough" changes dramatically during the first 12 months of life. Newborns start out needing only 300–350 calories per day, but that requirement grows to about 1,000 calories by the end of the first year.

With time, parents can learn to spot cues that their baby is satisfied and even to distinguish a hungry cry from a tired one. By picking up your baby's cues—and responding in a sensitive way—you can help your child begin a healthy relationship with food. You may be concerned that you are underfeeding or overfeeding your baby. But, in fact, most babies take just what they need. Let your child use his or her innate ability to regulate food intake.

You can confirm that your baby is getting the right amount by watching his or her growth. At regular visits, your child's doctor will monitor weight and length to see that the baby is growing as expected. Following an initial weight loss that occurs in the first week of life, healthy babies quickly regain this weight and gain 140–200g a week until four to six months of age, doubling their birth weight in this time. By 12 months, a child may weigh 9kg or more.

Physical achievements to celebrate

Year one is a wondrous time as babies become more active. Your child grows from a curled-up infant into a baby who can sit unassisted, pull to a stand, cruise, and then walk.

To make tracks as they do, babies need stimulation and the opportunity to be active, but they don't "exercise." Watch for cues that your baby is ready to try new skills, so you can offer encouragement.

- If your five-month-old now can hold his or her head up and grasp objects, put a toy just out of reach, to challenge the baby.
- When you find your nine-month-old standing up in the crib, the child is showing you he or she is ready to take the next step. In a child-proofed living room, let the child stand holding onto the couch to practice standing and cruising along the furniture.

For older kids, it's important that parents are positive role models when it comes to physical activity. You may think this doesn't matter for your baby, and that he or she won't know whether you're snoozing on the couch or out for a walk, with the baby in a stroller, introducing him or her to the birds, squirrels, and big blue sky. At first your baby may seem oblivious to it all, but before long, he or she will adjust to the pattern of the family routine. If that routine is an active one, everyone—parents and baby alike—will benefit.

info

The overweight baby

Everyone loves a chubby baby, but if your doctor has told you your child is gaining too much weight, there's good reason to pay attention. Overweight babies are more likely to become overweight later in life, so consider whether a pattern of inactivity and overeating may have already begun. If you think this may be the case, never skip feedings or restrict your baby's feedings on your own. Seek advice from your child's doctor instead.

Feeding too much?

Start by considering whether you could be overfeeding your baby. It can happen even to the best of parents, often because they are simply worried the baby is hungry or isn't eating enough. The trick is knowing when to stop. Be alert to cues that your baby is full, such

as slowing down and sucking with less enthusiasm, stopping, or turning away from the breast or bottle. If your baby is eating solid food, spitting it out may indicate he or she has had enough. (For feeding guidelines, see the chart on page 73.) And consider whether your baby may be getting excess calories from juices or desserts.

Not active enough?

An overweight baby might be getting too little activity. Be aware of how much time your child is spending in the crib, swing, playpen, high chair, car seat, or any other place that restricts movement. Even young babies need to move around and explore. When babies are overweight, it can make it more difficult for them to reach milestones, such as sitting up and pulling to a stand.

"The best choice…"

Nutrition in the first year of life

From birth, parents and babies bond during feeding, which may have been first attempted minutes after delivery or not long after. It's about nutrition, but it's also a source of comfort and contentment.

What foods when?

The first decision parents need to make regarding nutrition is whether to breastfeed or use formula. Breast milk is the ideal choice. If the mother can't breastfeed or chooses not to, babies who are fed formula can grow up healthy, too.

You'll begin introducing solid foods around six months and may start table food around nine months (see the feeding chart opposite). But even when your baby starts solid foods, breast milk or formula remain the most important source of nutrition throughout the first year.

The method of feeding changes dramatically during the first year. Babies learn to accept cereal and other food from a spoon and then endeavour to feed themselves, raking a hand across the tray to scoop up some vittles. And they'll play with food, getting it all over themselves in the process—as well as the floor, wall, and anywhere else in close enough proximity to the highchair.

But before you know it, your baby's accuracy will improve and he or she will become skilled enough to pick up a piece of dry cereal between forefinger and thumb, and pop it in their mouth. At this point, babies are also deft enough to pick up things they shouldn't eat, so watch out!

By the time the family gathers to sing "Happy Birthday" to your one-year-old, he or she will be drinking from a sippy cup—though probably not without a few spills—and gamely eating a piece of their very first birthday cake.

sample **feeding schedule**

Use this chart as a guideline—consult your doctor for recommendations based on your child's individual needs. A baby's first solid food should be rice cereal. Introduce cow's milk and whole eggs at 12 months.

AGE IN MONTHS	BREAST MILK	FORMULA	IRON-FORTIFIED INFANT CEREAL (mixed with liquid)	VEGETABLES	FRUIT	MEAT, POULTRY	POTATOES, PASTA, RICE, NOODLES
1	on demand	420–600mL	none	none	none	none	none
2	on demand	600–840mL	none	none	none	none	none
3	on demand	780–960mL	none	none	none	none	none
4	on demand	840–960mL	none	none	none	none	none
5	on demand	840–960mL	none	none	none	none	none
6	on demand	840–960mL	1–2 tbsp twice a day (rice cereal to start)	small amounts: about 1–2 tbsp puréed	small amounts: about 1–2 tbsp puréed	none	none
7	on demand	870–930mL	2–3 tbsp twice a day	2–4 tbsp, puréed	2–4 tbsp, puréed	none	none
8	on demand	780–930mL	2–3 tbsp twice a day	6–8 tbsp, puréed	2–4 tbsp, puréed	none	none
9	on demand	720–900mL	3–4 tbsp twice a day	½ cup (125mL), puréed	4–6 tbsp, puréed	1–2 tbsp	none
10	on demand	660–900mL	3–4 tbsp twice a day	½ cup (125mL), puréed, mashed, or finely chopped	½ cup (125mL), puréed, chopped fresh, or cooked	2–4 tbsp	¼ cup (60mL)
11	on demand	600–840mL	4 tbsp twice a day	½ cup (125mL), puréed, mashed, or finely chopped	½ cup (125mL), puréed, chopped fresh, or cooked	30–55g ground or shredded	¼ cup (60mL)
12	on demand	480–720mL	4 tbsp twice a day	½ cup (125mL), chopped	½ cup (125mL), chopped fresh or cooked	30–55g ground or shredded	½ cup (125mL)

Feeding your baby in the early months

The menu is short for a newborn baby: Breast milk or formula are the only choices, because during these first six months, babies usually don't need and shouldn't have anything else—no water, no juice, no regular milk, and no solid food.

Breastfeeding

Through breast milk, a baby gets necessary vitamins and minerals and the amounts of other nutrients that nature intended. Breast milk also benefits a baby's immune system and may help reduce the risk of obesity later in life. While breastfeeding is the best nutritional choice for your baby, some supplements may be necessary, including vitamin D, fluoride, and iron. Talk with your doctor about these.

Breastfed babies should eat when they're hungry, which may be often because breast milk is so easily digested. Early on, a baby might want to eat every hour for periods, but in general, feedings will be two to three hours apart. Even if a baby is feeding often, a parent may wonder if the child is getting enough. The number of wet and soiled diapers is a helpful indicator. Expect five or more wet diapers and two to five soiled ones every day during the first few weeks of life.

Overcoming any difficulties

While breastfeeding can be relaxing and become second nature over time, the early weeks can be difficult. Mothers may encounter problems, including breast soreness and inadequate milk production, or the baby may have trouble latching onto the breast. To ease sore nipples, squeeze out a few drops of milk and spread it on the nipple as a protective coating, or try a medical-grade purified lanolin ointment. Breast pain can be a sign of infection, so contact your doctor if you are concerned.

Sucking is the best way to rev up milk production, so frequent feedings, or pumping between feeds, will help. Adjusting the way the baby latches on can help improve the milk supply and allow the baby to become a more efficient feeder. It can also make breastfeeding more comfortable. Be sure your baby takes the whole nipple into his or her mouth and begins sucking rhythmically.

Contact your child's doctor if your baby is not latching on successfully or not wetting diapers, or you have other concerns. Instead of just giving up and switching to formula, get some professional guidance first.

Establishing closeness
For babies, breast milk is simply the perfect food, strategically packaged to require a lot of close, warm, snuggling time with mom.

info

Comparing the benefits of breastfeeding and bottle-feeding

Breastfeeding
- requires no preparation or refrigeration
- costs little
- provides milk that is easily digested
- decreases baby's risk of allergy and protects against infection and other illnesses
- may reduce the risk of weight problems in future
- promotes bonding between mother and baby

Bottle-feeding
- offers more freedom and flexibility for the mother
- makes it easier to know how much the baby is getting
- may require fewer feedings as formula is digested more slowly than breast milk
- may make it easier to feed the baby in public places
- lets dad and other family members help feed the baby

It's recommended that babies are breastfed until they are at least one year old. If your child stops breastfeeding before then, switch to iron-fortified formula. Never give regular cow's milk to a child under 12 months. Talk to your doctor about making the transition from breast milk to formula.

The needs of breastfeeding moms

In the midst of all the attention being showered on the new baby, breastfeeding moms also need to remember to take care of themselves.

- To meet her own nutritional needs as well as her baby's, a mom generally needs an additional 300–500 calories every day, for a total of 2,200–2,700 (depending on the mother's activity level and pre-pregnancy needs).
- A breastfeeding mom is the baby's source of vitamins and minerals, so it's crucial that she eat plenty of fruits and vegetables, and calcium-rich foods (to get at least 1,200mg of calcium a day). She also should continue to take a prenatal vitamin that includes iron.
- While breastfeeding, a mom needs to drink lots of water and other fluids—especially before and after nursing.

Formula feeding

If you've chosen to feed your baby formula, you can be confident about meeting your infant's nutritional needs. Improvements in formulas have made them very close in nutritional value to breast milk. The two major types of infant formula are cow's-milk-based and soy-based. Your doctor will probably recommend which one to give your infant.

Most babies will do well on a cow's-milk-based formula, but talk with your doctor if your child develops rashes or digestive problems that you think could be related to the formula. A lactose-free or soy-based formula may be recommended if lactose intolerance is suspected. There are also hypoallergenic formulas available for babies who are allergic to cow's milk. Be sure to consult your doctor before switching formulas.

In the past, low-iron formula was recommended for some infants who were fussy or constipated. This kind of formula is no longer recommended as it lacks the amount of iron babies need. Iron is critical to brain development. Research has failed to show any connection between iron in formula and other problems, such as constipation. If constipation is a problem, consult your doctor about how to treat it.

Formula based on cow's milk does, of course, contain cow's milk, but it has been modified to be more easily digested and nutrionally complete. Babies should not drink the cow's milk you buy in the grocery store until they are at least one year old because it lacks the vitamins and nutrients babies need to grow. It also has too much protein for babies to digest, and too little of the fat a baby needs for normal growth and development.

tips

Burping a baby

Babies often swallow air while feeding, especially the very hungry ones who were crying beforehand. Because of this it's a good idea to stop during a feeding to burp your child, even before he or she starts fussing. A fussing baby will end up swallowing more air, which may make the child feel even more uncomfortable. Burping your baby regularly should also reduce the amount of spitting up.

Use gentle taps on the baby's back or slowly rock your upright baby's body forward and back to encourage a burp. Another option is to lay your baby across your lap, face down and gently pat his or her back. If your baby doesn't burp, don't worry. Just go back to feeding if he or she is still hungry, and try again at the end of the feeding.

- For breastfeeding moms, take some time to burp your baby when you switch breasts.
- If bottle-feeding, burp your baby once or twice during each feeding session, stopping to do so after about 60–90mL formula is taken, or as needed.

Don't be overzealous about burping your baby. It may backfire and lead to more spitting up. Air that is not burped out will pass through the baby's intestinal tract and come out the other end.

Formulas are designed to meet a baby's nutritional needs and should not be diluted with anything else, or replaced by any other liquid, unless the doctor has told you to do so.

What kind of formula?

You can buy formula "ready to feed" or as a powder or concentrate that needs to be mixed with water. They are similar in nutritional value, as long as they are prepared according to the manufacturer's directions. Be sure to check the labels to avoid mistaking "ready to feed" for the formula that needs to be mixed with water. Improperly prepared formula can interfere with growth and endanger health.

Once you have chosen a formula, you'll need a delivery system—a bottle and nipple. You have a variety to choose from, and you may have to try several before you find one that's right for your baby. Ask your doctor about sterilizing the bottles and nipples, as well as the water you use to make the formula. Some will say to sterilize the water for the first three months, while others will say it's unnecessary if you use water from a municipal system. Municipal water is likely to contain some fluoride, which is good for the baby's teeth.

How much to feed, and when

Though formula milk is digested more slowly than breast milk, bottle-fed babies still eat frequently, usually every two to three hours in the early months. Like breastfed babies, bottle-fed babies should be fed on demand. Newborns generally drink a little more than 60mL of formula a day for each 450g of body weight. A 3.6-kg baby will drink 480–600mL a day, or 60–90mL about six times a day. Babies who drink smaller amounts tend to feed more frequently. As they get older, babies will eat larger amounts and may feed less frequently.

Because it's less work to get the milk from a bottle, it's easier to overfeed a formula-fed baby. Be cautious of nipples that flow too quickly, and take breaks during feeding so your baby has a chance to sense being full. You might try filling the bottle 30mL beyond the normal feed so you are able to offer the extra if the child wants more.

Make the most of feeding time. Find a comfortable spot and nestle your baby's head on the inside of your bent elbow. Never use a bottle prop—it carries the risk of choking and encourages your child to sleep with a bottle in the mouth. Avoid putting a child to sleep with a bottle, even when he or she can hold it unassisted. It can cause serious tooth decay.

Getting it right

Eating patterns will vary from baby to baby, so it's important to be flexible and responsive to your child. Growth spurts also occur, triggering periods of increased appetite. During these times, a baby may go off his or her normal schedule to keep up with the demands of this growth. Even a small baby will let you know when he or she is hungry and when they've had enough. The trick is paying attention to the cues and not forcing a baby to eat beyond his or her hunger.

Babies who are getting enough seem satisfied after a feeding. A baby might show he or she is full by slowing down, stopping, or turning away from the breast or bottle. Pay attention to how your baby tries to get this message across. Some babies continue to suck after they are full, but usually with less enthusiasm. Particularly for a baby who is bottle-fed, this could lead to overfeeding. Most babies are comforted by sucking, so a parent may want to encourage thumb-sucking or try a pacifier. But don't use a pacifier as a substitute for feeding a hungry baby.

The baby who spits up a lot

Spitting up is an expected (but yucky!) part of an infant's early eating life. This usually becomes less frequent by six months and is nearly gone by nine or ten months. Spitting up a small amount (less than 30mL) isn't cause for concern as long as it occurs within an hour of feeding and doesn't bother the baby, who is growing normally. Minimize spitting up by:

- feeding the baby before he or she gets very hungry (a hungry baby is likely to swallow air and overfeed);
- keeping the baby in a semi-upright position (head raised) during the feeding and for an hour after eating;
- burping the baby regularly;
- avoiding overfeeding;
- checking the flow of liquid from the bottle's nipple to make sure the hole is not too large or too small; the liquid should drip slowly, not pour out of the hole;
- not jostling or playing vigorously with the baby right after a feeding.

Sometimes, spitting up can be a sign of another problem. Talk with the doctor if your child is frequently irritable, spitting up large amounts, or spitting up forcefully (projectile vomiting), as well as if your child seems to be losing weight or not gaining weight as expected. Also get medical attention without delay if your child has a fever or shows any signs of dehydration (such as not wetting diapers).

Introducing solid foods

"When are you going to give that baby some real food?" That's what well-meaning relatives and friends want to know. But young babies simply aren't ready to eat solid foods. And giving them solids too soon can increase the risk of food allergies.

The right time for solids

When you were a child, the doctor may have told your mother to give you cereal at two months—maybe even mixing it in with your bottle of formula. Today, most experts recommend waiting until six months to offer cereal or any other solid food. Here's why: To eat solid food, an infant needs good head and neck control and should be able to sit up. Your baby may not be able to do these things until four to six months. Before then, babies will push food out of their mouths just as quickly as you put it in. This is a natural reflex that is lost by about six months, after which it becomes easier for them to start eating solid foods.

By taking it slowly with solid foods, you'll also reduce the risk of your baby developing food allergies, especially if allergies run in your family. (See opposite for more about allergenic foods and when to introduce them.) A baby's developing immune system will be better able to handle new foods after the age of six months.

Infant cereal

Iron-fortified rice cereal is usually given first because it's less likely to cause an allergic reaction. Initially it is mixed with breast milk or formula so it's more of a liquid than a paste. Talk with your child's doctor about the right age to begin solid foods and how to phase them in. (See page 73 for a feeding guide.)

After your baby has tried rice cereal, other iron-fortified cereals, such as infant oatmeal or barley cereals, may be introduced one at a time. Hold off on mixed-grain cereals until the child is older.

Though your mother and grandmother may swear by it, never give infant cereal in a bottle unless a medical condition requires it. Babies who are fed this way may get too many calories and become overweight. Eating cereal

Feeding infant cereal
Use a spoon and offer small quantities, so your baby can learn the mechanics of moving food to the back of the mouth and coordinating swallowing.

Allergenic foods

Some foods can cause allergic reactions and should not be introduced to young children. A child is at higher risk for food allergies if one or more close family members have allergies or allergy-related conditions, especially food allergies, eczema, or asthma. (For more information about food allergies, see page 174.) Waiting until the child is a little older to introduce these foods may help prevent lifelong allergies, so talk with your child's doctor about this.

Here are recommended ages for introducing allergenic foods to children at normal risk of developing an allergy and those at higher risk.

FOOD	NORMAL RISK	HIGHER RISK
Eggs	12 months	24 months
Citrus fruits	12 months	24 months
Fish and seafood	24 months	36 months
Peanuts and peanut butter	24 months	36 months
Tree nuts	24 months	36 months

from the bottle also can interfere with the transition to other solid foods. Introduce infant cereal by feeding your baby with a small spoon, and be sure to take it slow. Never force food into a baby's mouth.

Babies won't be very efficient eaters when they first start eating infant cereal. In fact, they may eat as little as a tablespoonful. It takes time for a baby to learn how to take food from a spoon and you may need to experiment with the cereal's consistency. Strive to keep the experience calm and pleasant by choosing a good time of day when the baby is alert, interested, and not overly hungry.

When starting infant cereal, you may notice a change in your child's bowel movements. It's okay if the baby doesn't have a bowel movement every day as long as stools are soft. If the baby's stools are hard, dry, or difficult to pass, talk with your child's doctor.

One new food at a time

When introducing new foods to your baby, it is important to give him or her one food at a time, and to wait several days before trying something else new. This can get confusing, so you may want to introduce one new food a week and select a day of the week as "new food day." If your baby doesn't seem to like a particular food, reintroduce it at subsequent meals. It may take several tries before your child warms up to a particular food, so don't give up after the first attempt.

Introducing new foods one at a time also gives you an opportunity to see if your baby is allergic to it. If your baby is allergic, you may notice one of the following:

- a rash
- diarrhea
- excess gas
- fussiness after eating.

For more severe allergic symptoms, such as hives or breathing difficulty, get medical attention right away. (For more information about food allergies, see page 174.) Whether the reaction is mild or severe, don't try the offending food again until you talk with your doctor.

Some experts suggest that vegetables should be the first foods offered because they fear babies won't like vegetables if they've already enjoyed sweet fruits. But there's no evidence that giving vegetables first produces veggie-loving kids, so parents are free to start with a fruit, if they choose. That's not to say you should neglect vegetables. One approach is to alternate fruits and vegetables. If your baby tries bananas one week, you might offer carrots the next week. In this way, you'll be working toward introducing a wide variety of fruits and vegetables.

These first forays into the eating world begin to establish food preferences—your child's likes and dislikes—for years to come. Using a patient, gentle approach, you can help your baby develop a taste for many nutritious foods.

When should my baby have juice?

Juice can be given after six months of age, but remember that it adds extra calories without the balanced nutrition found in formula and breast milk. Also, drinking too much juice may contribute to overweight or cause diarrhea in infants. Later, it can contribute to tooth decay. When you introduce juice, follow these recommendations:

- Offer juice in a sippy cup or regular cup, not in a bottle.
- Limit the quantity of juice to 120mL per day.
- Start with juices of the fruits your child has already tried and tolerated.
- Serve only 100-percent fruit juice, not juice drinks or powdered drink mixes (which are sweetened).

Baby food

Parents can buy jarred baby foods or make their own, using a food mill or food processor. Commercial baby food has some advantages, especially if you choose brands that avoid fillers. Commercially jarred baby foods also don't need refrigeration and are easy to take with you. Processing reduces the likelihood of exposure to pesticides, but if you are concerned, consider organic alternatives, although they cost more. (For more information about organic foods, see page 47.) When preparing your own baby foods, be sure to follow the guidelines below.

Whichever type of baby food you choose, texture and consistency are important considerations. At first, babies need to eat finely puréed single foods (for example, just applesauce, not apples and pears mixed together). Later,

after they've had a variety of foods, they can have two foods mixed together, but still puréed. Around nine months, many babies are ready for coarser, chunkier textures, including more table food, but the transition should be gradual. Just as babies develop other skills, they need time to work on the various skills related to eating: accepting a bite of food, controlling food in the mouth, using the jaws to chew, and coordinating their swallow.

Certain foods, such as mashed potatoes or mashed, cooked carrots, are often the first table food a baby is offered. But don't give heavily seasoned foods to a baby, or dishes that contain foods the baby hasn't already tried. Also avoid those foods that are likely to cause allergic reactions (see the list of these on page 79).

What's my baby's temperament?

Even as a baby, a child has a unique personality that will become more fully developed over the months and years to come. An infant or child may be described as easy-going or difficult, or, more often, somewhere in between. Your child's temperament—the inherent way he or she interacts with the world—will influence mealtime.

By understanding your infant's temperament, you can avoid conflict and help him or her adapt to changes, such as learning to eat solid food or trying new foods. For example, an infant who is sensitive to the texture of food may initially reject a new fruit. Don't give up. Offer the new fruit in small amounts or mix the new fruit with an accepted cereal. Alternatively, simply try introducing it on another day.

info

Homemade baby purées

If you want to make your own baby purées, be sure to follow these guidelines:

- Freeze portions that you aren't going to use right away, rather than canning them yourself.
- Avoid home-prepared beets, collard greens, spinach, and turnips because they contain high levels of nitrates, which can cause anemia in infants. Serve jarred varieties of those vegetables.
- Adhere to food safety rules, such as frequent hand-washing, keeping utensils clean, and keeping hot foods hot and cold foods cold.
- Steam or bake fruits or vegetables instead of boiling, which washes away nutrients.

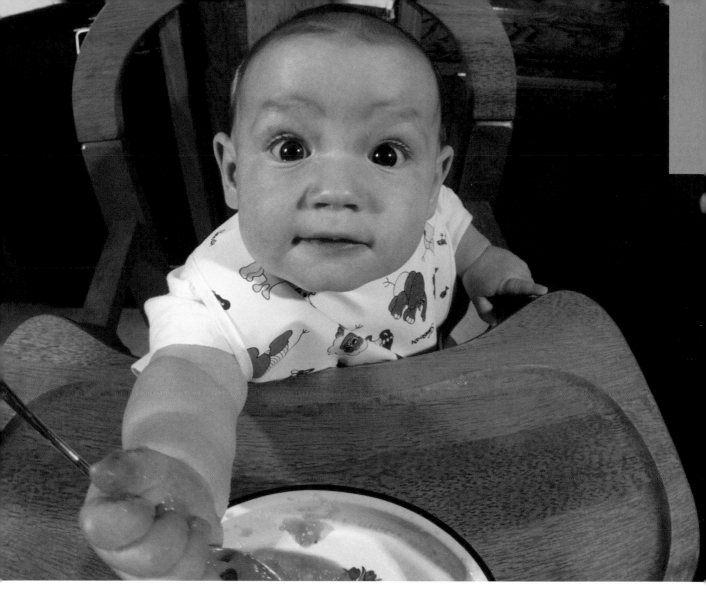

To learn more about your baby's temperament, ask yourself the following questions:

- Is my baby always on the go, or laid back?
- Is my baby unpredictable, or does he or she follow a regular schedule?
- How does my baby react to new situations?
- Is my baby easily distracted, or able to focus?
- What's my baby's general mood?
- Is my baby hypersensitive to light, noise, touch, or textures?

A more sensitive child may not like your "playing airplane" with the spoon to get the food into his or her mouth. On the other hand, if your baby thrives on stimulation, feel free to whoop it up as long as the focus remains on eating.

One of the gang

Pull the baby's highchair right up to the table at family mealtimes. You'll notice that he or she will be increasingly interested in what everyone else is having for dinner.

In addition to being spoon-fed, your baby may like to take charge a bit by feeding himself or herself a teething biscuit and holding—though not really using—his or her own spoon while you do the actual feeding. Once your baby grows accustomed to eating, have him or her join the rest of the family at mealtimes. It may seem more efficient (and less messy) to feed the baby separately, but this is a missed opportunity. By nine months or so, your baby will enjoy being part of the family action.

Feeding themselves at nine to twelve months

Your child's relationship with food is about to get messier and more delicious. He or she is now old enough to leave those baby purées behind in favour of foods with real texture—and to start eating them without help from mom and dad.

Discovering tastes and textures

Now that they're joining the rest of the family at the table, older babies are ready—and often willing—to try more table foods. This will mean additional work for whoever is preparing the meals for the family, but often dishes can be adapted for the baby. For instance, your baby can have some of the zucchini you're making for dinner, as long as you cook his or her portion just a little longer—until it's soft—and cut it into small enough pieces for the baby to handle. Soups are another good choice. (See opposite for some ideas on how to cook a special soup for your baby.)

While your child's menu is getting more exciting, so is his or her means of eating. The older baby is able to use developing fine motor skills to pick up small pieces of food. During these months, your baby will be able to take hold of food between forefinger and thumb in a pincer grasp. Sometimes the baby will eat the food, sometimes not. The pincer grasp will start out a little clumsy, but with practice it will soon evolve into a masterful and efficient skill.

Offer your infant a choice of "safe foods" (see below for suggested finger foods) and let your child feed himself or herself. Do this as much as possible. Though it can be a little slow, it's consistent with how you want to approach feeding throughout childhood: You present the child with healthy food and the child decides what to eat, or even whether to eat at all. It's normal to worry that your infant isn't getting enough, but remember how small his or her body and stomach are. Portions must be small.

The small portions should include food that has been cut up into small pieces. The size of the pieces varies depending on the food's texture. A piece of chicken, for instance, needs to be smaller than a piece of watermelon, which even a pair of baby gums will quickly smash.

Some children are more sensitive to texture and may reject anything coarse, such as meat. Parents may worry if their child doesn't seem to like meat, but this is not a concern with such a young child because the baby's protein needs are still being met through breast milk or formula.

tips

Which finger foods are safe for my baby?

At around nine months, babies can start trying finger foods. But which foods are best? If you are unsure about a food, pop it in your mouth and ask yourself these questions:

Does it melt in the mouth? Some dry cereals will melt in the mouth as will crackers that are light and flaky.

Is it cooked enough so that it mushes easily? Well-cooked veggies and fruits will mush easily as will canned fruit and vegetables (choose those that are canned without added sugar or salt).

Is it naturally soft? Cottage cheese, shredded cheese, and small pieces of tofu are soft.

Can it be gummed? Pieces of ripe banana and well-cooked pasta can be gummed.

To introduce meats, start with well-cooked ground meats or shreds of thinly sliced deli meats, such as turkey. If your child doesn't like meat (or any other food), don't let that stop you from offering it at future meals. Present it, but don't force your baby to eat it. This allows the baby the opportunity to grow more accustomed to the food and eventually accept it.

Hold the sweets

At first bite, your baby probably will love the taste of cookies, cake, ice cream, and other sweets, but do not introduce them now. Your child needs to eat nutrient-rich foods instead of consuming empty calories found in desserts and high-fat snacks, such as potato chips. It's tempting to want to see the baby's reactions to some of these foods, but now is not the time. Grandparents and others may want to rush your baby into trying triple-chocolate cake or some other family favourite. Politely and firmly explain that the baby isn't ready for those foods. If grandma persists and says you had your first bite when you were an infant, blame this tough stance on your child's doctor. The doctor won't mind.

Finger foods to avoid

Finger feeding is fun and rewarding for the older infant, but it's important to avoid foods that can cause choking. Parents and caregivers also can help prevent choking by supervising the baby while he or she is eating. Foods that are choking hazards include:

- pieces of raw vegetable or hard fruits
- raisins, whole grapes, or cherry tomatoes (instead, serve grapes and cherry tomatoes cut in quarters)
- whole hot dogs and kiddie sausages (peel and cut these in very small pieces)
- white bread
- pieces of hard cheese

A middle-of-the-night feed

Just as you are enjoying your baby's new eating habits, you may be surprised that—out of the blue—he or she wants a bottle in the middle of the night. But something other than hunger may be at work if your child has started awakening during the night again. Infants nine to 12 months old are aware enough of their world to notice when parents are not around. They may express this realization quite loudly in the middle of the night and parents may assume that the crying means their baby is hungry.

Q: My nine-month-old isn't ready for most food I cook for my family. What's a good meal to serve her?

A: Sometimes you can adapt the family's meal to suit your baby's limited palate, but other times you'll need to cook something separate. Vegetable soup for baby is easy to prepare and a batch can be divided into small containers and kept in the freezer.

Start with store-bought low-sodium chicken or vegetable stock, or make your own stock. Use just enough to cook everything, and include only those vegetables your child has already tried. Carrots, zucchini, potatoes, and sweet potatoes are good choices for soup. Add canned peas or green beans, or scan the fridge for leftover veggies to toss in the pot. Cut all vegetables into small pieces.

For protein, add small pieces of chicken, tofu, or kidney beans. And don't forget the noodles. Choose a pasta shape that will be easy for the baby to pick up, such as elbows or small shells. Cook the soup until everything is soft. Serve the soup on a plate so your child can pick up the pieces and enjoy.

If your baby was previously fine without an overnight feeding, he or she might just need some reassurance. It's normal for an infant at this age to experience separation anxiety. If your baby wakes up, go to him or her, pat them on the back, calm them down, and maybe offer a comfort item, such as a special blanket. But take care not to turn it into playtime, and try your best to avoid offering a middle-of-the-night feeding because it can disrupt everyone's sleep and lead to a pattern of overeating.

Drinking on their own

By 12 months, a baby is ready for the switch from formula to cow's milk. If you've made it to the one-year mark with breastfeeding, congratulate yourself. You can continue breastfeeding for as long as you like, or you can stop now.

You probably have already introduced the cup to your baby, so let him or her keep working at using it. Little by little, cut back on the use of the bottle. This might be a tough transition for your child, so don't rush it. Offer praise when your child sips from a cup, because it's an important step toward eating like a big kid.

Activity for babies

The first year of a child's life is filled with the most amazing physical achievements—a series of predictable milestones. Like building blocks, each new skill provides the foundations for the next one.

Encouraging physical activity

Guidelines have been developed to encourage physical activity in babies. And those guidelines are very easy to follow. Babies need no formal programs, the experts say; they simply need the daily opportunity to explore their environment. These guidelines apply to all babies, wherever they are cared for— at home, at a relative's house, or at a childcare centre. What children should have are a safe environment, room to explore, and a chance to use their muscles.

A young infant needs opportunities to develop head and neck strength. Next, babies work on the strength in their trunks, which allows them to sit up at around six months. And nearing the end of the first year, babies want to seize every opportunity to move, whether it's by scooting, crawling, creeping, cruising, or walking.

The guidelines caution against letting babies spend too much time in confined spaces, such as car seats, strollers, swings, and cribs. These places and devices can discourage physical activity because babies are restrained from moving and exploring. Instead, let your baby spend time trying out newly acquired skills, from reaching for a rattle to sitting without support and then taking first steps.

New parents are often easy targets for advertisers selling the latest toy or gadget designed to educate and entertain their precious baby. But you can provide enriching experiences without spending much money. Expensive toys, baby massage classes, and videos that introduce classical music or art are not necessary for healthy physical and cognitive development.

"building blocks"

Baby **development chart**

Your knowledge of normal infant development can help you encourage your child to be active and practice new skills, as well as having a lot of fun. Strengthening muscles and mastering these basic skills are the first steps toward lifelong physical activity. Your child's doctor can help you understand your baby's development and which skills to look for next. There's no need to rush to the next stage. With support from their parents, babies will progress and develop successfully at their own pace.

AGE	WHAT BABIES CAN DO	RECOMMENDED ACTIVITIES
0–3 months	• focus and follow objects, especially faces and brightly coloured or shiny toys • spontaneously wave arms and kick legs • raise head while on tummy • swipe for dangling objects • hold rattle placed in hand • smile and coo	while supervising, place baby on tummy to strengthen neck and shoulders; try an infant gym with dangling objects; put a rattle in the baby's hand
3–6 months	• on tummy, prop self up and lift head • roll over • reach for and grasp objects • hold head steady while sitting • sit with support • laugh	continue tummy time; let baby sit supported on your lap; let baby reach for favourite toys and objects
6–9 months	• sit without support • sit and pivot • stand with support • start to use finger and forefinger to grasp objects • wave bye-bye • babble	keep a variety of toys within baby's reach in a safe play area; help baby pull to stand; play Peek-a-Boo
9–12 months	• get on hands and knees • crawl, scoot, or creep • pull to stand • cruise along furniture • stand alone • first steps—maybe • say "mama" and "dada"	help pull to stand; hold baby's hands and practice walking; let baby climb stairs with supervision; offer push-and-pull toys; sing action songs, such as "Itsy Bitsy Spider"

Babies want and need to spend time with the people who love them, who are the best teachers to help them with their developing skills. Looking at books together, singing songs, or going for a stroller ride under the autumn leaves are wonderful experiences at a very reasonable price.

Being active is important, but don't forget that all babies need down time, too. After an energetic day of moving around, banging blocks together, playing peek-a boo, and singing, take some time to turn down the lights and cuddle with your baby in your favourite rocking chair. The peaceful moments will be good for you both and will reinforce the baby's feelings of security and love.

Sensible safety precautions

Here are a few things to remember and steps to take before your baby becomes more mobile.

- Don't leave babies unattended on beds, couches, or tables. Normally, infants start rolling over at four to six months, but even newborns can fall after unexpectedly scooching, squirming, or rolling.
- Place safety gates in front of all staircases. Stairs are often the reason why babies and toddlers get injured. Be sure to keep gates closed at all times.

- Use the safety strap on swings, strollers, and high chairs. Without a T-strap, which goes between a baby's legs, the child can get stuck or slip out and fall from these devices. Older children may stand up and fall over.
- Keep curtains, cords, and tablecloths out of a baby's reach. Between six and nine months, babies are eager to pull to a stand and they will use anything they can get a hold of to do it. They can be injured by falling objects or get tangled in cords.
- Don't use a baby walker. Walkers on wheelers don't help babies learn to walk any sooner, and in fact they may delay walking because they don't encourage the baby to use the muscles involved in walking. On top of that, they're dangerous, and are often the cause of serious falls down stairways. Choose a stationary walker or exercise saucer instead.
- Don't use borrowed baby equipment or buy used equipment from a garage sale or consignment shop. These items aren't bargains because they are old and often don't have the instructions that inform parents how to use them properly. Even products that are just a few years old may not reflect the latest in safety design and buyers may not know if the item has been recalled.

tips

Choosing a childcare provider

Because children spend many hours in childcare, it's important to know that your provider understands the importance of being active—even for infants. When making a choice, look for a provider that:
- understands physical development (such as when a baby is ready to roll over, sit with support, or pull to a stand), so the staff can help your child develop new skills;
- understands cognitive development, so the staff knows which activities are right for your child's age and how to foster learning;
- limits the amount of time a baby spends in cribs, high chairs, swings, and other equipment that restricts movement;
- provides a safe environment so that your baby can explore freely;
- encourages lots of activity through interaction, singing, and playing;
- discourages the use of TV, videos, and DVDs as a means of keeping a baby entertained.

Kicking and smiling in the first three months

Though it may seem strange to think about "activity" for such a young baby, even at this early age, babies do move their bodies. They wave and kick in a jerky way, but these movements increase their flexibility and strengthen muscles.

Signs of progress

New parents often talk about how they simply stare at their baby, wondering at this little person. During the first two months, babies seem to do little more than sleep and eat, but here and there you'll begin to see glimpses of your child's unique self. Your child will start to recognize your face and smile at the sound of your voice.

As you care for your baby, you are laying the foundation for a strong, committed relationship, which is essential to your baby's development. Progress starts in small ways with this tiny infant, taking little steps toward important milestones that are reached during the first six months of life, such as holding his or her head steady, rolling over, grasping objects, and sitting up with support.

By two to three months, a baby is able to do more and is increasingly interested in the world. The child can swipe at objects, bring a hand to his or her mouth, and grasp a toy. Soon, your baby may realize he or she is the one causing the rattle to make noise—quite a discovery!

Tummy time

While awake, it's important for your baby to spend some time on his or her tummy, to help strengthen the neck and shoulders. Some parents are concerned about doing this, because they have been instructed to avoid placing their baby on his or her tummy to prevent Sudden Infant Death Syndrome (SIDS). It is true that babies should not be put down to sleep on their stomachs because of the increased risk of SIDS, but when the child is awake, alert, and supervised, "tummy time" is safe and beneficial.

Babies need constant supervision while they are on their tummies, in case they tire out and need a parent to pick them up or flip them over. Start by trying tummy time a few times a day, but keep these sessions brief, because your

baby may get frustrated in this position. As the baby gets better at this skill, he or she will enjoy it more and just might show off another new talent: smiling.

Have baby, will travel

Using a baby carrier or sling accomplishes two goals: it gets a parent out of the house while at the same time keeping the baby snug and happy. It also frees up a parent's arms to do light chores. These devices can be especially welcome to new moms who feel out of shape. With the baby in a carrier, a mom can take a walk and get a little exercise. Meanwhile, the baby gets to see the outside world. Be sure to choose a carrier or sling that is right for your baby's weight and age, and follow the instructions so you use it safely.

A happy baby
Learning new skills, such as holding his or her head steady, grasping toys—and your fingers—and sitting up, will make your baby smile with delight.

Exploring at three to six months

Your baby's movements, which once seemed random and jerky, are becoming more orderly and purposeful. Now is a great time to create a child-proof play space that will make it safe for your baby to explore his or her new world.

Improving coordination

During these months, your baby will learn to hold his or her head steady and sit with support. He or she will be able to open and close the hands that were once locked in tight fists. Tummy time remains important because your baby needs it to further improve head control and upper body strength. While on the floor, he or she will learn to prop themselves up—the first step toward exploring their new environment and rolling over.

A safe space for exploration

Exercise saucers and bouncer seats, as well as other baby equipment, keep babies in one place, but they don't provide the kind of activity needed. Exercise saucers are fun and let the baby bounce, spin, and play with different toys. But they shouldn't be used for more than 30 minutes a day, broken into two or more brief sessions. If your child starts crying and seems bored, he or she probably is.

Avoid the temptation to let your baby use a walker with wheels (for information about these, see page 86). A safe play space is a better choice (see below for how to create such a space.) In addition to being safe, the space should also be inviting and fun. To do that, place toys in reach, sit on the floor to play with your child, and make sure your baby has room to wiggle, squirm, and stretch.

Social butterflies

Babies seem to come alive socially during these months. They stare intently at faces and enjoy their first laughs. They enjoy being out and about, even if you are just going to the grocery store. Because they're more interactive, and physically able, it opens up new possibilities for activities. Babies draw you in with a smile or a coo and are able to have extended play sessions. Playing can simply mean holding out a toy and letting your baby reach for it—even better if the baby is in your lap, where he or she can practise sitting up at the same time.

tips

A child-proof play space

Creating a child-proof space doesn't mean spending a lot of money. It simply means finding a room or part of a room and making it safe for the baby to explore—with supervision.

- Install baby gates to block entrances or staircases.
- Cover outlets and tie up curtain cords.
- Put breakable items out of reach.
- Remove tables or other furniture that could tip over, and pad all the corners.

When the room is safe, let your baby move around, finding toys and other fun things to do.

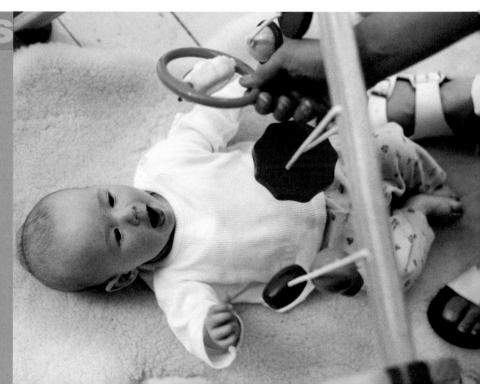

Sitting and standing at six to nine months

Because babies are increasingly active at this age, parents have the opportunity to encourage the accomplishments they're so eager for their child to achieve, which include sitting without support and starting to stand up.

The balancing act

Being able to change positions is one of a baby's greatest achievements during these months. They can roll in both directions, sit without support, sit and pivot (without falling over), get from their tummy to a sitting position, and, finally, pull up to a stand. They also may have devised novel ways of transporting themselves where they want to go: scooting, creeping, or rolling. A parent can help a child work on balance in the sitting position by strategically placing objects within reach so the baby can practise this skill—and feel a sense of accomplishment when the desired toy is grabbed.

Standing up

When your child can support his or her weight, it's time to practise standing with support. Let your child lay on your lap or the floor and let him or her hold your hand and pull up to a stand. Once the child is good at that, he or she also might like to stand and bounce, so turn on some music and let the baby feel the beat. He or she also may be able to stand with support from the crib rails or couch. Before you know it, your child will be doing this without any help.

Mind-body connection

Babies make huge cognitive strides during these months as they figure out the world around them. For instance, a baby learns how an object—or person—is still there even if partially covered. Place a blanket over a toy and voila! It's still there. That's why Peek-a-Boo is a great game for babies of this age. (See below for more games to play with your child.)

Your baby also starts to grasp cause and effect. Maybe you have found yourself trapped in this game: baby drops the toy, you give it back, and he or she drops it again. Or, your baby may delight in hitting a wooden spoon against a pot. That's another example of cause and effect because your baby realizes that banging the pot makes a noise. It's satisfying because it's a way of demonstrating "I am here!"

Let's play

At six months, a baby will hold a toy and explore it with his or her hands and mouth. Banging and throwing toys seems to be a universal response. By nine months, babies show more interest by carefully inspecting and manipulating toys as they try to figure things out.

Playing games with your baby is a way of reinforcing new concepts. It's a great time to introduce "This Little Piggy," "Pop Goes the Weasel," and other nursery rhymes. Other popular games that babies age six to nine months enjoy include Pat-a-Cake, Peek-a-Boo, and So Big!

On the move at nine to twelve months

During this last phase of their first year, babies seem to be going somewhere all the time—up the stairs, under the table, from one end of the room to the other, pulling themselves up and along with whatever they can get their hands on.

Getting into trouble

Most babies at this age can scoot, creep, or crawl. They will pull to a stand and "cruise" around using the furniture as support. Walking may be just around the corner for many of them. Parents can hold their baby's hands so the child can practise walking. Push and pull toys also can come in handy because they give a child something to hold onto, offering a bit of support. Many babies also love trying to climb the stairs—with a parent close by, of course. Trailing this busy person is a great workout for parents, too.

Babies can get into trouble very quickly, even in the short amount of time it takes for a parent to answer the phone or check on dinner. So remember to keep baby gates closed and, when possible, close doors to those rooms that might contain hazards, such as the bathroom, basement, or kitchen. Also ensure that all dangerous or poisonous products are kept up high, well out of their reach, because babies will be sure to open all the cabinets at their level.

Because so much is off-limits, your baby will enjoy it if one of the floor-level cabinets is fair territory. Fill it with safe toys or household objects, such as plastic containers or pots. This also gives the baby something to do while adults are in the kitchen, preparing meals or doing other kitchen chores.

While sometimes it seems your baby is just bent on making a mess, remember that he or she benefits from all this stimulating activity. Babies are learning critical skills and they're understandably determined to learn to move around and figure out how things work.

info

The baby who's not walking yet

While people look for babies to walk by age one, the truth is that most babies don't walk that early. As with other big achievements, such as sitting up, there's no one magic age that is associated with developing a skill. Rather, there's a range of months during which most children are expected to reach that milestone. The usual range for starting to walk is between nine and 16 months, but that doesn't mean some normal children won't walk a little later, or take a few steps sooner.

It's also important to know that walking early isn't a sign of superior intelligence. Later walkers usually can look forward to being just as bright and physically active as their peers who walked sooner.

A child may be a late walker because his parents walked later. In extreme cases, such as in some foreign orphanages, a child may have been confined in a crib and didn't get the opportunity to develop the strength and skills necessary for walking. But sometimes a child who isn't walking by 18 months may have a medical condition. If you have any concerns about your child's development, discuss them with your doctor.

If your child has been growing and developing normally until this point, there is no cause to be concerned that your one-year-old hasn't taken his or her first step. It's just one more achievement to look forward to as your child enters the second year of life.

What's on the agenda?

It's true what people say about babies being more interested in the box and wrapping paper than in whatever gift the packaging held. Stuff around the house may interest babies as much as—or more than—any toy.

Between nine and 12 months, kids like big cardboard boxes they can stack or crawl through and crinkly paper they can crunch. When it's time to open the toy box, reach for balls and blocks. Roll or hand a ball to your baby, and demonstrate how to stack blocks, letting your child knock down your tower.

Books of all types will be of interest to your child. Fabric books and board books make it easy for babies to turn the pages. Look for books that have flaps to lift, textures to touch, and sounds to hear. When you run out of books to look at, visit the library for a fresh supply. It's a whole new place for your baby to explore.

Parents need to be vigilant

Close supervision, always important, takes on new significance now because babies can really get from one place to another in a flash.

Q: My ten-month-old baby isn't crawling. What should I do?

A: Crawling is a favourite infant milestone, but not every child crawls. This is no cause for alarm if your child has made steady progress in his or her motor development by rolling over, sitting, pulling to stand, cruising, and so on. You may have noticed that prior to learning to walk, a child devises some unique ways of getting around, including rolling, scooting on his or her bottom, or creeping.

While it's not a critical motor skill, here are some ways to encourage crawling in the older baby:

- Allow for tummy time so your baby is in the right position to practise crawling.
- Help your baby get into the crawling position on hands and knees.
- Position a favourite toy out of reach and encourage your baby to move toward the desired object.
- Limit the time your baby spends in strollers and cribs so he or she has more opportunity to move.

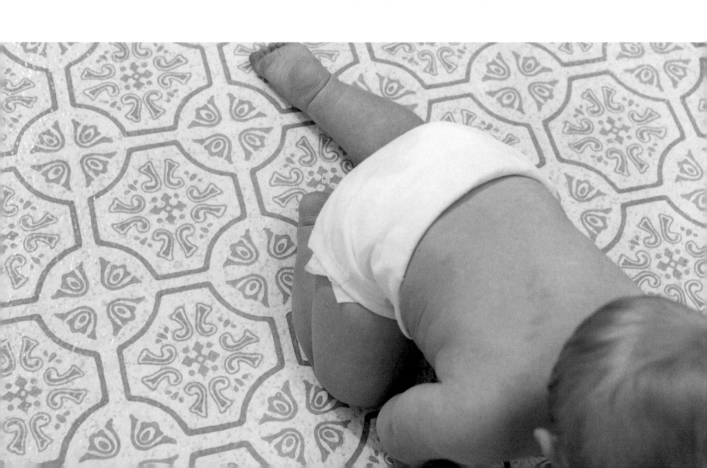

5 TODDLERS

Between the ages of one and three, children **walk away from babyhood** in search of independence. Parents should let them **have their independence**—in measured amounts—when it comes to eating and activity.

age 1-3

"kick it"

Toddlers on the move

Between the ages of one and three, children are both formidable and lovable. Toddlers push the limits—and their parents' buttons—as they try to figure out how to navigate the world.

Parents provide the structure

Toddlers want their independence and may express it loudly—it's during this period that the "terrible twos" take hold. But they also don't want to stray too far from mom or dad, who are the source of security and safety. Parents can provide the right environment for their child by setting boundaries when it comes to eating and activity.

Parents should provide the kinds of foods that an active toddler needs. But anyone who has a child of this age knows how independently minded they can be, so savvy parents will have to work with their toddler and exert control in a crafty way. For instance, try presenting two healthy snacks and let your child choose which one to eat. In this

way, your toddler will feel in control, but you will accomplish your goal of getting him or her to eat a nutritious snack—and without the usual battle.

Parents should also provide structure for physical activity. It's not difficult to get toddlers to be active—their high-energy style can wear a parent out—but toddlers need creative adults to help them channel that energy into activities that are both fun, productive, and safe. A parent can fill the role of activity coordinator by leading a game of "Simon Says," playing catch, or helping the child sing action songs like "Head and Shoulders, Knees and Toes." Toddlers also need their parents to be there when it's time to stop exploring and settle in for a good night's sleep.

Toddlers are picky eaters

A toddler may express his or her independence through eating—or not eating, as the case may be. Nearly all toddlers could be described as picky eaters. Children of this age are famous for their reactions to new foods. They are naturally suspicious and, if they agree to try a spoonful, they may reject the new taste or texture. A toddler may also choose to play with food rather than eat it, or may want to eat only macaroni and cheese for days. But because you choose the foods on your toddler's plate, you don't have to serve macaroni and cheese every day. Instead, you can influence your child's food preferences by presenting a variety of healthy foods to make up the menu.

Feeding guidelines

What does this mean when deciding what to offer your toddler? Refer to the chart below to get an idea of what—and how much—your child should be eating. The number of servings per day is based on Canada's Food Guide to Healthy Eating, produced by Health Canada. The serving sizes are often smaller than what is recommended for older children. However, toddlers need the full two servings—480mL—of milk, but this can be spread out over the course of a day. The chart recommends the number of servings per day of each group. Keep in mind that younger toddlers may not be eating this much—at least at first.

Growing from baby to child

Babies grow at a lightning pace—8cm or so every three months. The toddler, in contrast, grows at a much slower rate—only 8–13cm in an entire year. Growth slows markedly by 18–24 months. A toddler actually needs fewer calories per kg than an infant. This remains the case in the preschool years and beyond.

Toddlers are in the midst of a transformation from baby to young child. During the toddler years, they will lose that "baby" look as they get leaner, stronger, and more active. It's also a period of amazing physical accomplishments as toddlers progress from barely walking to being able to run with agility by the age of three.

How much should **your toddler eat?**

Compared to older kids, toddlers need fewer and smaller-sized servings from each of the basic food groups, with the exception of dairy foods. The chart below can be used as a guideline when feeding your toddler, but remember that each child is unique. Your doctor can make specific recommendations based on your child's individual needs. Serving size may vary, and your child may eat more or less on any given day.

FOOD GROUP	DAILY SERVINGS	CHILD SIZE SERVING (24–48 MONTHS)
Grain products	5	½–1 slice of bread; 4–8 crackers; ¼–½ cup (60–125mL) cooked rice or pasta; 15–30g ready-to-eat cereal
Milk products	2–3	1 cup (250mL) milk; ⅓–¾ cup (85–185mL) yogourt; 25–50g cheese
Meat and alternatives	2	25–50g meat, fish, or poultry; 1 egg
Vegetables and fruit	5	¼–½ cup (60–125mL) fresh, frozen, or canned vegetables or fruit; ¼–½ cup (60–125mL) juice

"I love bananas"

Nutrition for toddlers

Toddlers are beginning to discover what they like, and don't like, to eat—remember that it wasn't so long ago they were trying solid food for the first time. Parents are in charge of providing healthy choices.

What toddlers need

In general, toddlers need about 1,000–1,200 calories a day, which they get in little bites and nibbles of food. From 12–24 months they are in transition from an infant diet, which is high in fat: From the age of two, a toddler should be getting only 30–35 percent of daily calories from fat.

Here's a breakdown of some of the important components in a toddler's diet. (See pages 34–39 for more information about these components.)

Protein: About 1g per kilogram of body weight every day. A child weighing15kg therefore needs about 15g of protein daily.

Fibre: 6–8g a day (the child's age in years plus five).

Calcium: 500mg a day. This requirement is easily met if your child gets the recommended two servings of milk products every day.

Iron: 7mg a day.

Milk matters

An important part of a toddler's diet, milk provides calcium and vitamin D to help build strong bones. Children under age two should have whole milk to help provide the dietary fats they need for normal growth and brain development. After a toddler turns two, most kids can switch to lower-fat or nonfat milk, although you should discuss this decision with your child's doctor.

Some kids initially reject cow's milk because it doesn't taste like the familiar breast milk or formula. If your child is around 12 months and having this difficulty, mix whole milk with some formula or breast milk. Gradually adjust the mixture over time so it becomes 100 percent cow's milk.

Meeting iron requirements

After 12 months of age, toddlers are at risk of iron deficiency because they no longer drink iron-fortified formula and may not be eating iron-fortified infant cereal or enough other iron-containing foods to make up the difference. Drinking a lot of cow's milk (more than 800mL to 1L every day) can also put a child at risk of developing iron deficiency. Here's why:

- Cow's milk is low in iron.
- Toddlers who drink a lot of cow's milk may be less hungry and less likely to eat iron-rich foods.
- Milk decreases the absorption of iron and can also irritate the lining of the intestine, causing small amounts of bleeding and the gradual loss of iron in the stool.

Iron deficiency can affect a child's growth and may lead to learning and behavioural problems. And it can progress to anemia, which is a decreased number of red blood cells in a person's body. Iron is needed to make red blood cells, which carry oxygen throughout the body. Without enough iron and red blood cells, the body's tissues and organs get less oxygen and don't function as well.

To help prevent iron deficiency:

- Limit your child's milk intake to about 500–750mL a day.
- Increase iron-rich foods in your child's diet (see page 157 for a list of these foods).
- Continue serving iron-fortified cereal until your child is 18–24 months of age.

Talk to your child's doctor if your child drinks a lot of cow's milk or you are concerned that he or she is not eating a balanced diet. Many toddlers are checked for iron-deficiency anemia. A child who has anemia will need to take an iron supplement, but never give your child a vitamin or mineral supplement without first discussing it with the doctor.

One-day menu planner **for toddlers**

DAILY CALORIES

This plan will provide 1,105 calories.

You'll notice in this sample menu plan that the milk is given in 1/2 cup (125mL) servings, which is half of a full serving. Nutrition guidelines recommend two full servings each day, but toddlers may not be able to down that much in a sitting. The cereal snack is also half a serving because a full serving is too much for most toddlers.

breakfast
- 1/2 cup (125mL) milk
- 2 blueberry pancakes (see recipe on page 190)
- 1 tbsp syrup

FOOD GROUP	SERVINGS
grain products	2
milk products	1/2
meat and alternatives	0
vegetables/fruit	0

snack
- 1/2 cup (15g) oat "O" cereal
- 3/4 cup (185mL) orange juice

FOOD GROUP	SERVINGS
grain products	1/2
milk products	0
meat and alternatives	0
vegetables/fruit	1

lunch
- 1/2 cup (125mL) milk
- 1 canned pear half
- 30g sliced turkey
- 4 crackers
- 4 tbsp steamed zucchini

FOOD GROUP	SERVINGS
grain products	1
milk products	1/2
meat and alternatives	1
vegetables/fruit	2

snack
- 1/2 cup (15g) oat "O" cereal
- 1 banana

FOOD GROUP	SERVINGS
grain products	1/2
milk products	0
meat and alternatives	0
vegetables/fruit	1

dinner
- 1/2 cup (100g) steamed brown rice
- 30g diced chicken
- 1/2 cup (75g) steamed carrots and green beans
- 1/2 cup (125mL) milk

FOOD GROUP	SERVINGS
grain products	1
milk products	1/2
meat and alternatives	1
vegetables/fruit	2

snack
- 1/2 cup (125mL) milk
- 1 apple bar (see recipe on page 200; leave out walnuts)

FOOD GROUP	SERVINGS
grain products	1
milk products	1/2
meat and alternatives	0
vegetables/fruit	0

Food preferences at 12–24 months

Young toddlers become experts at eating as they come to accept new tastes and textures and feed themselves with increasing proficiency. For the parent, it is a golden opportunity to influence what a child chooses to eat for years to come.

Adjusting to a changing menu

Just when you had the routine mastered, your toddler's diet is changing. Bottles and baby food are on their way out. Milk and more table food are on the way in. But none of these changes occurs overnight, so parents can help toddlers ease into the new eating routine. Use the chart on page 95 and your own judgment to make sure your child is satisfied and getting adequate nutrition. Parents of toddlers have another important job: to help kids develop a taste for healthy food. Children are more likely to reject nutritious foods if they don't try them early in life. Kids given the easy option of cookies, ice cream, and doughnuts will often tend to choose these foods over healthier fare later on.

If kids don't like a food, they won't eat it—no rocket science there. But don't be discouraged if your toddler doesn't like a food the first time you offer it. Children are naturally slow to accept new tastes and textures, and you may have to present the food ten or more times before they'll finally give it a try.

If, for example, your toddler doesn't like green beans the first time around, don't stop serving them. Just keep reintroducing the beans without nagging or forcing your child to eat them. Simply make small portions of the food available so the child can give them another whirl. And be sure you're setting a good example by eating the food yourself! Serve nutritious foods that you like, so your child will see you enjoying what you're asking them to eat.

Letting your child not eat

While the goal may be to broaden a child's palate, a parent also needs to relinquish a certain amount of control to the child—even at this young age. A parent's role is to present

tips

Learning to eat like big kids

Toddlers are beginning to eat more independently—first with their fingers and then using utensils to feed themselves. This transition can be messy, because toddlers are notoriously sloppy eaters, but given the opportunity to experiment, they will improve their skills over time.

Finger foods

While fostering independent eating, parents should watch out for choking risk by serving finger foods that are easy to chew and cut into small pieces. (See page 82 for guidelines about safe finger foods.) In general, avoid foods such as raw carrots, hot dogs, peanuts, and popcorn.

Minimizing the mess

Here are some suggestions to help you limit the mess caused by your toddler's sloppy eating:
● Use appropriate size utensils.
● Place a plastic mat on the floor under the high chair.
● Use large plastic bibs, or bibs with pockets.
● Serve drinks in no-spill sippy cups.
● Keep washcloths on hand, so you can wipe your child's hands and face after the meal.
● If your child will be eating on the road, bring a wet washcloth or disposable wipes, a bib, and a change of clothes so you're prepared for anything!

healthy foods and let the child decide which ones to eat—or whether to eat at all. Be alert to what your toddler is saying through his or her actions. A child who is building a tower of crackers or dropping carrots on the floor may be telling you he or she is full.

Allowing a child to skip a meal is a difficult concept because many of us were raised to clean our plates and not waste food. But children should be allowed to respond to their own hunger cues—a vital skill to maintaining a healthy weight. That means eating when hungry, and sometimes not eating, even if it's time for Thanksgiving dinner.

Pushing food on a child who's not hungry may dull the internal cues that help a child know when he or she is full. But that doesn't mean that it's practical or advisable for the child to eat on demand all day long. That's why structured meals and snack times are important. Your child will come to expect that food will be available during certain times of the day. At those times, your child can decide whether to eat, as

Good things to eat
Use this golden opportunity to broaden a child's palate by exposing your toddler to a wide range of healthy foods, from fruits and vegetables to whole grains.

well as which foods to eat and how much of them to eat. If the child chooses not to eat anything at all, simply offer food again at the next meal or snack.

Practising feeding skills

At mealtime, let your child finger feed and practice using utensils, a skill typically learned at 15–18 months. Give your child many opportunities to do these things. Early on, make sure the child isn't too hungry, or the experience may lead to frustration. During this transition, jump in and help feed your child when necessary, but try to pay attention to the child's hunger cues and note signs that he or she is full. You can always offer more if your child still seems hungry, but you can't take the food back if you overfed your child.

tips

Toddler teeth need brushing

It's important to keep a toddler's teeth clean, to reduce plaque and the risk of cavities. While older toddlers may be able to brush on their own with supervision, younger ones will need some help from mom or dad.

- Brush your toddler's teeth twice a day, preferably after breakfast and before bed.
- Use a child-sized toothbrush with soft bristles.
- Avoid fluoride toothpaste until a child turns two, and after this age use only a pea-sized amount.
- Take care to brush all tooth surfaces to remove plaque and debris. Don't forget the back teeth and tongue. Remember—as your dentist has probably told you—most adults miss a lot of spots when they brush. So don't expect a toddler to hit them all without your help!
- To prevent cavities, limit sugary snacks and don't allow your child (of any age) to sip on juice or milk for extended periods.

When you're controlling the fork or spoon, resist the urge to slip in one more bite. And as your toddler gets the hang of eating, step back and let your child take over.

Little and often

Many toddlers need to eat often—as much as six times a day, including three meals and three snacks. Keep this in mind as you establish a pattern of meal and snacks. And remember that the schedule only establishes the times that you will present food to your toddler. Your child may not take every opportunity to eat.

Try to avoid offering snacks just before mealtimes or pacifying hungry kids with cups of milk or juice right before a meal. Eating and drinking just before meals can diminish appetite and decrease your child's willingness to try the new food you are offering at mealtimes.

When to stop bottle feeding

Around 12 months of age your child will be switching from breast milk or formula to cow's milk. By 12 months, most children have learned to drink from a cup, so it can be a natural transition from formula in a bottle to milk in a cup. If you are breastfeeding, only offer milk in a cup and avoid

the bottle habit altogether. Between 12 and 18 months is a good time to make the transition to a cup. At this age children should be drinking 500–750mL of milk per day. Drinking more milk than this can get in the way of eating a balanced diet and may also put the child at risk for iron deficiency. (For more information about iron deficiency, see page 97.)

Some young toddlers may be attached to the bottle as a source of comfort. Practically speaking, it's best to stop giving the bottle sooner rather than later because, over time, kids get increasingly resistant to giving it up and will have more to say in the matter.

Instead of cutting out bottles all at once, gradually eliminate them from the feeding schedule, starting with mealtime. Offer cow's milk from a cup after the child has begun the meal. Generally, the nighttime bottle is the last to go because it is part of the bedtime routine. If this is the case, let your child have a cup of milk with his or her evening snack and continue with the rest of your nighttime ritual (bath, bedtime story, teeth brushing, etc.). No matter how old the child is, no child should go to bed with a bottle because it can cause serious tooth decay. (See above for information about looking after your toddler's teeth.)

Eating by themselves at 24–36 months

The older toddler's desire for independence and control is intense. It's no wonder this age is called the "terrible twos." By anticipating problems and offering choices, you can teach your child which behaviours will yield positive results and which ones won't.

Conflict at mealtimes

When a two-year-old doesn't get what he or she wants, be prepared for a major tantrum. Although this behaviour is challenging, to say the least, it has a purpose. Toddlers are learning how to navigate the world, communicate in it, and figure out how to exert control over aspects of their lives. Although toddlers actually have control over very little, they are starting to master eating and using the toilet. A child can't—and shouldn't—be forced to do either one of these.

Because older toddlers often use eating to express their independence, food and mealtimes can cause conflict. You want your child to eat the vegetables on his or her plate; the child drops them onto the floor. You want him or her to eat the meal you prepared for the family; the child is clamouring for chicken nuggets, which is the only food he or she is willing to eat. A well-meaning parent's impulse may be to pick up the spoon and start feeding the child the healthy food on the plate. You also might start talking up those nutritious foods, telling the child how big and strong broccoli will make him or her. Or you might start bargaining: "Well, if you eat three more bites of chicken, I'll give you a cookie." The problem is, none of those tactics work in the long run.

Playing with their food
Toddlers are explorers in all realms, including the food on their plate or in their bowl. Finger feeding allows them to investigate the feel of the food before they eat it.

info

Don't use food as a reward

During the toddler years, avoid the temptation to reward a toddler with food, particularly with sweets and snacks. Toddlers respond to positive reinforcement and food rewards can be very powerful. But there's a big downside to using food as an incentive: It can start a pattern of unhealthy eating behaviour. Also, if the child is offered a cookie, not a piece of fruit, for good behaviour, the child may get the message that snacks and desserts are more valuable than other, more nutritious foods.

Instead of rewarding your child with food, take a deep breath and try to find another solution.

- If your child appears to be bored, try to get him or her interested in a toy or game.
- If your child wants some of your time, take a few moments and give him or her a little attention.
- If your child is hungry, provide a healthy snack.
- If your child needs a reward for a job well done, offer a big hug instead of a sugary treat.

As with all toddler behaviour, consistency is key, so both parents and all caregivers should adopt the same tactics. If this is not done, the toddler might get confused, or learn which parent to ask for a snack.

Parents taking over

You may think that not letting your child feed himself or herself is for the child's own good, but it takes away control that rightfully belongs to a child of this age. Kids need to decide whether to eat, what they will eat, and how much to eat—this is how they are going to learn to recognize their own internal cues that tell them when they are hungry and when they're full. Just as important, toddlers need to learn and practice the mechanics of feeding themselves.

Talking up certain foods

Who hasn't used the line about spinach making you strong? But this cajoling approach may build dislike for the healthy food, rather than increase acceptance. By the same token, forbidding less nutritious foods makes them more desirable. This doesn't mean you shouldn't teach your child about the benefits of healthy foods, but don't push too much by celebrating every bite of spinach or broccoli your toddler eats or disapproving when he or she refuses.

Making deals

Because older toddlers need to decide for themselves if they are hungry, it's not a good idea to bribe them into eating a certain amount of food. It creates an unnecessary power struggle at the table as the bargaining gets more intense. This tactic can lead to conflict when the child whines about reducing the number of bites or refuses to eat any more food. It is a battle you will not win. Worse yet, the child learns to use food as a bargaining chip.

For some children, dinner becomes a negotiation session from the very start, and parents have been using dessert as an incentive for decades. But this doesn't encourage healthy eating. Instead it creates the impression that "treats" are more valuable than mealtime food. Foods like candy and cookies are not essential to your child's diet and it is not a deprivation to avoid serving them during the toddler years.

If your child has tried sweets and demands them, it's time to stop buying them. As a parent, you control which foods are in the house and you decide which ones to serve to your child. If you do not regularly stock candy and less nutritious snack foods, your child won't see them, clamour for them, and feel angry when you do not oblige.

If your toddler asks for candy, simply say, "We don't have any candy." Then present the child with two healthy snack alternatives and let him or her choose one. Even if the child mourns the loss of the candy, he or she will still feel a sense of control by getting to make the decision about which of the healthy snacks to eat.

How to get a toddler to eat right

In addition to everything else toddlers are learning, they are also learning how to get what they want. Parents need to stand firm. Doing so will limit clashes and encourage healthy eating. Here are some additional guidelines.

- Stock the house with healthy foods: Toddlers aren't going to run out to the store for a bag of potato chips; they'll eat what's served to them and ask for what they know is in the cabinet.
- Serve right-sized portions: Parents often overestimate how much food a child should eat. Especially with foods that aren't yet favourites, a couple of tablespoons is a good portion to start with. Small portions are less overwhelming for a child, while bigger portions may encourage overeating.
- Offer variety no matter what: If a child is stuck on one food, a parent might feel forced to serve that food every day so the child eats something. But eventually the child may tire of that food—and then what? In addition, you're missing an opportunity to introduce new foods and increase the number of foods your child is willing to eat. It's a good idea to continue offering a variety of foods even if your child rejects them repeatedly. Your toddler may surprise you one day. Most "food jags," as they're sometimes called, don't last long if parents don't accommodate them. Children won't starve and they will learn to be more flexible rather than go hungry.

Q: My child will only eat food that is white. Should I force him to try other foods?

A: No, don't force him, but continue offering a variety of foods even if he often rejects them. Eating can be an emotional issue, so try to keep a cool head and be smart about the strategies you employ. Help him establish healthy preferences that will serve him well through the years. Know that most healthy kids eat enough food to grow and develop normally, but also trust your instincts if you're concerned your child isn't eating enough, or failing to eat enough healthy foods. Talk with your child's doctor about your concerns. Going over your child's growth chart is a good way to make sure he is staying on track. Most toddlers don't need a multivitamin, but your doctor may recommend it if your child is a particularly picky eater.

- Have family meals together. Children eat a more nutritious diet, with more fruits and vegetables, when they regularly have family meals.
- Create positive peer pressure: Toddlers are more likely to eat fruits and vegetables if they see their peers eating them, so look for opportunities where your child can eat healthy with friends, at home or at playgroups.

tips

Helping your toddler learn to eat at mealtimes

- Set your toddler's place at the family table—it's good for kids of this age to see their parents and siblings eating together and eating the right foods.
- Present a variety of foods, including some established favourites and some new foods.
- Serve small portions.
- Cut food into small pieces.
- Serve the drink after the child has started eating.
- Talk about something other than what the child is (or isn't) eating.

"Here we go"

Activity for toddlers

Toddlers have reason to be proud of their accomplishments, such as walking, running, and climbing. Over these years, they master basic skills as they gain muscle control, balance, and coordination.

Physical skills to learn

Each new skill mastered allows a toddler to progress to the next one, building on a foundation that one day will enable him or her to perform more complicated physical tasks, such as jumping rope, kicking a ball, or turning a cartwheel. For a toddler, those days of turning cartwheels can't come soon enough. Children in this age range want to do more than they may be physically capable of doing. This can be a powerful motivator that drives them to keep trying until they acquire a new skill, no matter what it takes.

That's not to say that toddlers can do it alone. They need their parents to support them as they make progress. Here are some ways parents can help their child.

- Know which physical skills your child is working on now, and which ones will come later. (See the developing skills chart, opposite.)
- Provide opportunities for the child to be physically active.
- Choose activities the whole family can enjoy.
- Keep the child safe during all forms of activity.
- Minimize sedentary activities such as watching TV.

The more opportunities a parent provides, the more active the child will be. Take advantage of your toddler's natural desire to keep moving. Even at this early age, a child is establishing patterns of activity that set the stage for the rest of childhood. If a toddler is inactive at three, there's a good chance that child will remain inactive later in life.

Developing **skills**

Playing and learning are completely enmeshed for toddlers, so acquiring the long list of skills below should be fun and games for them. Parents should give toddlers many opportunities to practice their developing skills—and provide a lot of supervision so they stay safe while they learn. In addition to these physical accomplishments, toddlers are developing in other ways. Provide opportunities for your child to explore, ask questions, use his or her imagination, and practice skills, such as stacking blocks or colouring.

EARLY TODDLER SKILLS (12–24 MONTHS)	OLDER TODDLER SKILLS (24–36 MONTHS)
• walks independently	• balances one to two seconds on one foot
• pulls toys while walking	• climbs well
• carries toys while walking	• throws ball overhand
• stoops and gets back up	• bends over easily without falling
• begins to run	• runs and jumps well
• kicks a ball	• kicks ball forward
• holds railing up/down stairs	• alternates feet up and down stairs
• walks backward	• pedals tricycle

Walking shoes

Going barefoot indoors is fine when toddlers are learning to walk. Outdoors, though, shoes are needed. The shoes won't help your child walk, but they will protect tender feet from injury. Choose comfortable sneakers or shoes that fit well, instead of those big, clomping, white baby shoes that just get in the way.

A toddler's shoes should:
- have easily bendable soles;
- be flexible enough to allow foot and ankle movement;
- fit well enough that they don't slip and cause tripping.

How much **activity is enough?**

Current guidelines recommend that toddlers get 30 minutes or more a day of physical activity, such as playing on a playground, going for a walk, or taking a parent-and-child tumbling class. In addition, toddlers should get at least one hour of free play, when they can explore and play with toys.

Though it can be a workout for their parents and caregivers, toddlers ought to be moving most of their waking day. Children in this age range shouldn't stay inactive for prolonged periods of time—no longer than one hour unless they're sleeping. To achieve this, avoid TV-watching or long stints in high chairs, in favour of free time down on the floor, so your toddler can move around.

	PHYSICAL ACTIVITY	FREE PLAY
Younger toddlers (12–24 months)	• listening to music and dancing together • holding your child's hands while he or she jumps • exploring the backyard or playground together • climbing stairs and using climbing equipment, with supervision	• using push and pull toys (popcorn popper, play broom, vacuum) • imitating animals or adults at work (mowing lawn, making dinner, using tools) • playing with shape sorters and other floor toys
Older toddlers (24–36 months)	• playing on a playground or in the backyard together • playing follow the leader, "Ring Around the Rosy," and other similar games • playing ball • taking a mommy-and-me movement class for toddlers • exercising together (see the suggested activities opposite)	• enjoying imaginative play (playing with toy cars, making play figures talk, caring for a doll) • building with blocks • drawing with crayons

Limit TV time

When caring for a toddler at home, there are so many hours to fill that a parent or caregiver may be tempted to turn to passive activities, such as watching TV. But limiting television is a good way to help keep your child physically active. TV is not recommended at all for children under age two. Those guidelines relax for older toddlers, but there's really no reason why your child must watch any TV. A toddler will get much more out of playing with a shape sorter, swinging on a swing, or hearing a book read by a caring adult. Even educational programs aren't as enriching as real-life activities, such as figuring out how a toy works, or playing games and singing songs together.

If you choose to allow some TV time for your older toddler, try to limit it to one to two hours of quality children's programming per day. If possible, choose noncommercial TV because commercial TV exposes children to food advertising, which often pushes low-nutrient snack foods and drinks. Another option is age-appropriate videos, especially those that invite the child to play along.

Provide a safe environment

Wherever a toddler is being active, the play area must be safe. At home, use gates and other safety equipment to make at least one room in the house safe enough for a toddler to explore. Away from home, look for childcare

Q: My toddler wants to watch videos all the time. What should I do?

A: Children like repetition, which can lead to repeated requests to watch the same video over and over again. A toddler may be very insistent and even throw a tantrum if the desired movie or show isn't played on demand. Remember that you, the parent, are in charge. You can say "No" in a matter of fact way, and direct your child to a different activity.

Very few parents can claim that they have not used a video or DVD to keep a toddler occupied for a while. But try not to use the TV as a babysitter or a replacement for your time and attention. Even if it means delaying dinner by 15 minutes, take a little time in the evening to reconnect with your child, especially if you've been away from him or her all day.

Toddlers are time-consuming little people because they need so much supervision, direction, and attention. But your efforts will help them learn to play independently and keep them from getting hooked on TV. Stick to your guns, and the next time your child wants to watch the video offer alternatives, such as colouring or doing puzzles together.

facilities and playgrounds that have newer, high-quality equipment that's not too big or challenging for your toddler. Also ask about whether children are separated by age—a practice that helps prevent injuries.

But no matter how "safe" the environment, there's no substitute for supervision. Many toddlers seem to subscribe to the "no fear" philosophy and may climb to the top of the monkey bars without reservation. Close supervision is important because, even as they show improving skills, toddlers lack sufficient balance, coordination, and judgment.

Activity away from home

If your toddler spends time with a caregiver or at a childcare centre, it's important to investigate how much activity the children get on a regular basis.

- Do they go outside most days?
- Is there a schedule of activities that they adhere to?
- Do they watch videos or TV on a regular basis?

Another option is a playgroup, which is a great way to get children together for some active time. A playgroup is also a welcome change of pace for stay-at-home parents, who benefit from the social time with other moms and dads.

The parents could plan some time for structured group activities, such as playing a game, and let the kids do their own thing for some of the time. Meeting at a playground or large, indoor space is ideal.

If you've ever seen a group of toddlers playing, they don't seem to be interacting as much as older children. Still, be assured they enjoy this time together. Eventually, they will start playing in a more cooperative way.

tips

Physical activities for parents and older toddlers

- Walk like a penguin, hop like a frog, or imitate other animals.
- Sit facing each other and hold hands. Rock back and forth, and sing "Row, Row, Row Your Boat."
- Bend at the waist and touch the ground. Walk your hands forward and inch along like a caterpillar.
- Sit on the ground and let your child step over your legs, or make a bridge with your body and let your child crawl under.

6 PRESCHOOL KIDS

Is your preschooler ready to **learn and grow**? You can help make this possible by **serving nutritious foods**, encouraging lots of physical activity, and helping your child get **ready for kindergarten**.

age 3-5

"lucky me"

Taking their place in the world

The preschool years are a time of transition, when children become less dependent on parents and increasingly reliant on themselves. But because they idolize adults, they are eager to please.

Emerging as individuals

Between the ages of three and five, children will start to move from a magical world to the real one, where the moon is made of moon rocks, instead of green cheese. As preschoolers become more rational thinkers, they can better follow rules and instructions. They also will begin to understand the concept of consequences—another change that prepares them for the road ahead.

During the preschool years, your child will emerge as an individual. No longer a toddler, he or she is less likely to throw a tantrum and should be more likely to cooperate— children of this age want to please their parents. And your preschooler will want to be involved in whatever is going on, whether it's playing a game with older siblings or helping a parent do the household chores or prepare dinner.

Inquisitive and opinionated

To be sure, preschoolers still get frustrated and they are still learning how to behave. But they can communicate more effectively. Preschoolers are keenly aware of the world and are, by nature, inquisitive. Their drive to discover is evident in the many questions they ask their parents.

- What is that bug?
- Why is ice cold?

- Why do I have to wear shoes?
- Where does the sun go at night?

Children learn by asking questions and parents should try to answer them. One great place to talk is around the family dinner table. Through conversation, children acquire language skills that help get them ready to learn at school.

In addition to talking, children like listening, especially to a story being read. Now that your child is older, try to involve him or her more in the reading. Here are some ideas:

- Ask your child to "read" you a story, paging through a book and telling you what's happening.
- Stop and ask questions like "Where is Goldilocks going?" or "What do you think will happen next?"
- Ask your child to act out parts of the story.
- Encourage your child to create a picture about the story you've read. Most preschoolers enjoy colouring, cutting (with child-safe scissors), pasting, and painting. Display your child's artwork and say how much you like it.

While preschoolers are people-pleasers, they also can be quite opinionated. They want to be heard. Whether it's a new food on their plate or their first swimming lesson, preschoolers are able to tell you—in no uncertain terms—if they liked it or not. But no matter how independent or well-spoken they are, preschoolers still need an adult to call most of the shots. By limiting TV and computer time, parents can

help lead their children toward becoming more physically active. Adults also guide their children toward better nutrition when they buy, prepare, and serve healthy foods and drinks.

Learning how to be fit and healthy

The give-and-take of communication creates opportunities for parents. Whether it's playing or eating, preschoolers want to do it themselves, but they are willing to learn from mom and dad. It's a great time to teach kids about healthy food choices and how to be active in new and exciting ways.

Preschoolers are old enough to begin understanding the concept of being full, known as satiety. Kids who stop eating when they feel full are less likely to become overweight. Most children naturally know if they are hungry or full and they can use these cues to properly control their food intake. Children who are encouraged to ignore these cues may learn to override this internal control mechanism.

A balanced diet gives children the nutrients necessary for optimal growth and development, and the energy for the exploration they want to do. Physical activity encourages children to develop muscle strength and endurance and to improve their motor skills. Through eating right and playing a lot, preschoolers can maintain a healthy weight and stay energized as they get ready for the next big step in their young lives: kindergarten.

tips

How does my garden grow?

Growing a garden can introduce children to nature and get them interested in healthy food. And, as you know if you've cared for a garden, it's good exercise. Here's how to cultivate your child's green thumb.

- Buy child-size garden tools, such as a shovel and watering can, for your child. Larger tools can be difficult to use and frustrating for a small child.
- Consider starting out with seeds instead of young plants—children enjoy watching them germinate and grow. Pick seeds that are easy to care for and produce quick results, so children can see the fruits of their labour soon. Green beans, cucumbers, and pumpkins are good choices, as are

sunflowers, zinnias, and marigolds. Carrots take a while to germinate, but are fun to pull out of the ground.

- Let your child play a key role by helping you decide what to plant in the garden and helping you plant the seeds or seedlings. You also might turn over a small section to the child, who can choose to plant something there or just dig in the dirt.
- Keep your little gardener safe by avoiding the use of pesticides and other chemicals.
- Have your child wear a hat and apply sunblock, especially between the hours or 10 a.m. and 4 p.m. Also use a child-safe bug-repellent, if necessary.

"I don't like it"

Nutrition for preschoolers

Many food preferences are already established by the preschool years, but parents still hold a lot of sway, and it's a good time to introduce new foods to your children.

What preschoolers need

Growth is slow and steady for preschoolers, whose daily needs increase by about 100 calories a year between the ages of two and five. Preschool children typically eat 1,200–1,600 calories a day, depending on their activity level. Here are some key nutrients and guidelines for how much your child should have each day (see pages 34–39 for more information about these nutrients).

Protein: About 1g per kg of body weight, so a 20-kg child should have about 20g of protein daily.

Fibre: 8–10g a day (add five to your child's age, in years, to calculate fibre requirements).

Calcium: requirements increase during these years—from 500mg to 800mg by the time a child is four. The calcium requirement can be a challenge if your child doesn't like milk. But calcium can be found in other milk products and in calcium-fortified foods.

Iron: 10mg a day.

The parents' role

At a parent's request, a preschooler may be willing to try new foods—especially if mom and dad are eating the same thing. In addition to watching what you eat, your child learns other lessons at the family table, including how to act at mealtime. You can expect more of a preschooler than a toddler, but don't expect perfection. Work on teaching your

Q: My four-year-old just will not try new foods. I'm at my wits' end. Should I give up?

A: Research shows it may take as many as ten tries before a child accepts a new food. So if your child doesn't seem to like a new food, don't give up. Never force or bribe a child to eat, and don't make a big issue out of it if your child chooses not to eat. By presenting the new food over and over again, you increase the chances your child will try it. Eventually, your child may decide to try the food and might even like it!

child proper use of utensils, where the napkin goes, sitting up straight at the table—and how to say "No thank you" instead of "Yuck!"

Guiding a child's eating habits is delicate work. You want to encourage your child to make good choices, but without hovering or pestering. You should take charge by presenting mostly healthy foods, but you don't want to teach your child that certain foods are "bad." You want your preschooler to eat enough nutritious food, but you don't want to start negotiating the number of bites of dinner that must be eaten to get dessert. These approaches don't work, and may even make it more likely that a child will eat too many calories.

Parents can take these steps to encourage a well-rounded diet:

- Continue offering a variety of foods, even ones the child has rejected in the past.
- Keep healthy foods in the house and limit the availability of high-energy, low-nutrient foods.
- Involve children in meal preparation—for example, let them tear lettuce for a salad or help set the table.
- Create a structure for daily meals and snacks, so the child doesn't graze all day long.
- Have regular family meals and make them pleasant times for the whole family to get together.
- Set a good example by eating a nutritious diet yourself.

tips

Eye appeal

To tempt your preschooler, here are some ideas for making healthy foods look good and fun to eat.

Food faces Make facial features by arranging fruits or vegetables on a plate, or on a slice of bread or a bagel half spread with peanut butter or cream cheese. Try blueberry hair, kiwi fruit eyes, a strawberry nose, and a banana smile.

Flower power Arrange apple slices to make flower petals. Use a few slices of kiwi for the centres.

Cute cut-outs Use cookie cutters to fashion sandwiches or slices of cheese into hearts, stars, and favourite animal shapes.

Pleasing pancakes Make silver dollar pancakes or spoon the batter into shaped moulds on the griddle.

Is your child really hungry?

Parents need to talk to children about what it means to be hungry and what it means to be full. Most of us are born with the ability to gauge our body's need for food, but over time we can learn to ignore these signals, which may contribute to weight gain. Not surprisingly, kids who don't recognize when they're full are more likely to be overweight.

Around the preschool years, many children start to use the word "hungry" to express other feelings, such as boredom, loneliness, sadness, and other emotions they don't understand or are unable to name. Using food to relieve sadness, for instance, will establish the connection between food and feelings other than hunger. Over time, that can be increasingly difficult to undo. And it won't address the underlying reason for the sadness, either.

If your child complains of hunger, take a minute to gently probe and make sure that's what's really going on. When your child says, "I'm hungry," ask "What have you been doing?" or "Would you like me to come play with you for a while?" If your child quickly forgets about a snack, you'll know he or she was in search of your attention or just looking for something to do.

Likewise, it's important to avoid inadvertently encouraging your child to overeat. The first step is to stop praising the clean plate.

- If your child regularly leaves a lot of uneaten food, it may help to put smaller portions on his or her plate.
- Let your preschooler know that it is okay to stop eating if he or she feels full. This encourages children to respond to their own hunger and satiety cues.
- Draw their notice to how you eat more slowly as you become full. Pass on seconds if you're no longer hungry. And avoid saying, "I'm stuffed, but this is so good that I can't stop eating it."

Remember that your child is watching what others do and listening to what they say. If parents and siblings all model healthy eating habits, a preschooler will have lots of good examples to follow.

One-day menu planner **for preschoolers**

DAILY CALORIES
This plan will provide 1,586 calories.

These sample menus reflect a preschooler's need to eat frequently throughout the day. Note that the planner includes two 250-mL servings of milk. If you find your child can't drink a full serving in one sitting, offer milk in smaller amounts during the day. In addition to the milk, there is an additional serving of dairy foods at the evening snack, to ensure that your child meets the daily calcium requirement.

breakfast
- 1 egg
- 1 slice toasted bread (wheat or whole grain)
- 1 tbsp jelly
- 3/4 cup (185mL) orange juice

FOOD GROUP	SERVINGS
grain products	1
milk products	0
meat and alternatives	1
vegetables/fruit	1

snack
- 1/2 cup (125mL) applesauce
- 30g low-fat granola with raisins

FOOD GROUP	SERVINGS
grain products	1
milk products	0
meat and alternatives	0
vegetables/fruit	1

lunch
- 50g sliced turkey
- 1 slice bread
- 1/2 cup (50g) sliced cucumber
- 1 oatmeal cookie
- 1 cup (250mL) low-fat milk

FOOD GROUP	SERVINGS
grain products	1
milk products	1
meat and alternatives	1
vegetables/fruit	1

snack
- 3–6 whole-grain crackers
- 2 tbsp peanut butter

FOOD GROUP	SERVINGS
grain products	1
milk products	0
meat and alternatives	1
vegetables/fruit	0

dinner
- 1 cup (250mL) pasta with 1/2 cup (125mL) meat sauce (see page 199)
- 1/2 cup (60g) green beans
- 1 cup (250mL) lower-fat milk

FOOD GROUP	SERVINGS
grain products	2
milk products	1
meat and alternatives	0
vegetables/fruit	2

snack
- 1 strawberry-banana smoothie (see recipe on page 201)

FOOD GROUP	SERVINGS
grain products	0
milk products	1
meat and alternatives	0
vegetables/fruit	1

Kids hear the fast-food message

An average child will see an estimated 360,000 television advertisements by high school graduation day. Many of those commercials are for less nutritious foods, snacks, and drinks, including those sold at fast food restaurants. In fact, researchers have noted a surge in fast food commercials during Saturday morning cartoons. Those restaurant ads reel in kids by promising an inexpensive little toy with each meal—yet another reason to limit your child's TV-watching.

- Allow your child to watch television for no more than two hours a day.
- Choose noncommercial TV or videos to limit exposure to commercials.
- Look for opportunities to teach your child about advertising and how it can make some products, including food and drinks, seem more exciting and better for you than they really are.

Letting kids have some control

Parents may feel uneasy about giving preschoolers control over how much they eat. But it's a limited kind of control. The parent is responsible for setting the schedule for meals and snacks and deciding which foods to serve. A child of four shouldn't be getting his or her own snacks, but can be given a choice and allowed to decide whether to eat or not.

There's nothing wrong with serving foods you know your child likes, but they shouldn't always be on the menu. Serve a variety of foods and don't cater to a child's limited palate. It may seem illogical, but it's better to present a range of foods, even if your child sometimes refuses to eat anything on the plate. It's normal to want your child to eat dinner, but it's also important to know that skipping one meal will not harm a healthy child. Let the child know food will be available at the next regular meal or snack time—and not before then.

If your child chooses not to eat a meal, try to avoid arguing about it or criticizing the child. Staying neutral and calm will help prevent the more vexing problems that can arise when parents and children battle over eating habits.

Preschoolers who "eat all day"

The average preschooler eats three meals a day plus two or three snacks. But given the opportunity, many preschoolers would choose to snack all day long. A child who "grazes" like this might never feel hungry. You want your child to know

when he or she is hungry—and full—because then the child will be better able to regulate how much food to eat. Here are some additional reasons to discourage grazing:

- A child who's hungry at mealtime may be more inclined to try new foods and eat the healthy foods presented.
- Children who graze are often snacking on higher calorie foods and drinks, which put them at risk of excessive weight gain.
- A child who snacks frequently, especially on sweets, is more likely to get cavities.

Preschoolers can be easily distracted, so make sure they sit at the table for meals and snacks. Also, turn off the TV. And notice if there might be a reason—other than feeling full— why your child is always ready to leave the table quickly. Maybe your child is in a hurry to get back to playing or always leaves the table when an older sibling is done eating.

Set times for eating are also beneficial because children like having a daily routine. Then they know what to expect. For example, if they start to feel hungry at preschool, they'll remember that they always get a snack right after story time. Or, if they don't feel hungry when it's time for an afternoon snack at home, they'll know that dinner is just around the corner. On a very active day, though, it's perfectly normal for a child to be extra hungry and need more than the usual amount to eat. On those days, be flexible if your child wants an extra snack or eats more at mealtime.

When preschoolers are thirsty

Soft drinks are commonly served to children in Canada. These carbonated drinks have no nutritional value, are often high in sugar, and often contain caffeine, which can have negative effects on kids (see below). One North American study found that one in eight preschool children drank 270mL or more of pop a day, which is 110–150 empty calories. That's ten percent of a preschooler's daily calorie needs.

It's easy to drink too much pop, and children are more likely to drink increasing amounts as they get older. In older kids and adolescents, drinking pop has been linked to overweight and other problems, including tooth decay. The best strategy is not to serve soft drinks at all.

Preschoolers should not drink any pop because it can get in the way of good nutrition. For instance, a four-year-old needs 800mg of calcium, which is the amount in about three glasses of milk. A child is unlikely to drink that much milk if pop is available at home.

The best drinks for preschoolers—and indeed for children of all ages—are milk and water. Whenever possible, try to discourage the habit of drinking pop and other sugary, energy-dense drinks to quench your child's thirst, when water or milk will do just as well.

If your child doesn't like plain milk, try adding a touch of flavouring, such as chocolate or strawberry. The little bit of flavour may make a big difference and it won't add a significant amount of sugar. But avoid premixed chocolate or strawberry drinks, which often contain considerably more energy, sugar, and fat than milk you flavour yourself.

Decaf kids

Most parents wouldn't dream of giving a preschooler a cup of coffee, but they may routinely serve cola and other soft drinks that contain caffeine. For children, the effects of caffeine are similar to those seen in adults. Too much caffeine can cause:

- jitteriness and nervousness
- upset stomach
- headaches
- difficulty concentrating
- difficulty sleeping.

And because preschoolers are not very big, it doesn't take a lot of caffeine to produce the effects. Caffeine also acts as a diuretic—something that makes a person urinate more. For young children, especially on hot days, this can contribute to dehydration. (See page 67 for more about dehydration.)

Drink calories **count**

All drinks are not created equal. Milk has just as many calories as pop, but it's rich in nutrients where pop provides only empty calories. Orange juice has about as many grams of sugars as a powdered drink mix beverage, but the fruit juice is the better choice because it is naturally rich in vitamin C and provides fibre. Choose milk and water most often for your preschooler and limit juice to no more than ¾ cup (185mL) a day.

DRINK	SIZE	CALORIES	SUGARS
Water	250mL	0	0g
1% milk	250mL	100	11g
Orange juice	250mL	110	22g
Juice drink (10 percent fruit juice)	250mL	150	38g
Powdered drink mix (with sugar added)	250mL	90	24g
Soft drinks	250mL	100	27g

Pack a picnic

A picnic can be a fun adventure for kids of this age. Consider heading to a nearby park, college campus, or somewhere with a water view. If you can't or don't want to go far, the backyard will do just fine.

- Work together to prepare a list of picnic foods. Be sure to take along at least one fruit and one vegetable per person.
- Let kids help prepare the lunch or pack the cooler. Pack paper plates with characters on them, special cups, or even some silly coloured straws.
- Don't leave home without lots of napkins, hats, sunblock, bug spray, and a big, soft blanket to spread out beneath your feast.

To avoid giving your child too much caffeine, be sure to read food and drinks labels. In addition to colas and some other soft drinks, caffeine is found in chocolate, coffee ice cream, and iced tea drinks.

Canadian guidelines recommend that preschool children consume no more than 45mg of caffeine a day. This is equivalent to the average amount of caffeine found in a 355-mL can of cola or four 45-g milk chocolate bars.

Helping in the kitchen

Involving your child in food preparation is a great way to keep mealtimes upbeat and positive. Your preschooler's natural curiosity extends to food and cooking, and you can assign him or her small tasks to help you, such as pouring ingredients into the mixing bowl or adding the various toppings to a pizza.

Unfortunately, though, their curiosity can get preschoolers into trouble in the kitchen, so be sure to keep a close watch on your child when you cook together. Preschoolers need to be taught not to touch whirring electric beaters, hot pans, and stovetops.

Here are some simple steps you should take to keep your child safe in the kitchen.

- Give frequent reminders about what's okay to touch and which items can hurt them
- Talk about which kitchen tasks are for grown-ups and which are for kids.
- Establish kitchen rules, such as not touching stove knobs or picking up knives.

Even as a child gets older, he or she may need reminding about how to work safely in the kitchen. (For more information on this topic, see page 49.)

Having your child help you in the kitchen is a wonderful opportunity for fun and learning. Following a recipe together is a chance for your preschooler to apply math skills as he or she counts out scoops of flour or spoonfuls of nuts and is introduced to fractions. Your child also will enjoy the process of packing a picnic basket (see above for some tips).

It's also a great time in childhood for toys related to food and cooking. Kitchen sets, play pots and pans, and pretend food items are good choices. Point out the healthy foods in your child's mini kitchen and have your child "prepare" a meal for you. If your preschooler likes to draw, have him or her create a menu card for that night's dinner. You might even have your child take your order and then serve you as if you were in a restaurant. Bon appetit!

"watch me"

Activity for preschoolers

Like toddlers, preschoolers have a lot of energy, but they are able to use it in a more organized fashion. Instead of just running around in the backyard, a preschooler will ride his trike or chase a butterfly.

Preschoolers need to play

Kids of this age are movers and shakers, quite literally. Talk about an airplane, and a preschooler just might thrust out his or her arms and start jetting around the living room. Put on some music, and your child will be happy to dance along.

Preschoolers are also discovering what it means to play with a friend instead of just alongside one, as toddlers do. If your preschooler has spent most of his or her time with family, or the only group experience has been a "mommy and me" class, it's time for your child to branch out and meet new friends. Having this opportunity to be around other children will help your preschooler learn important social skills, such as sharing and taking turns. No doubt there

will be disputes, but preschoolers are at an age when they can learn to cooperate and interact while they play. They might play a simple board game, work together on a castle in the sandbox, or play house.

How much activity is enough?

Preschoolers should have at least an hour of structured play time every day. In addition, they should get at least one hour—and up to several hours—of free play. They are likely to get structured play at childcare or their preschool program. They might play "Duck, Duck, Goose" and "London Bridge," or simply practice catching or kicking a ball. They also love a trip to the playground. Just be sure that the equipment is safe and that you keep a close watch on them. (See more safety tips on page 121.) Lots of fun things can be organized indoors, such as setting up a child-friendly obstacle course (see below for this and other activity ideas). Designate a play area and clear the space of any breakables. Or go outdoors into the backyard and plant a section of the garden together (see page 111).

Unstructured or free play is when the child is left more to his or her own devices—within a safe environment, of course. During these times, a child should be able to choose from a variety of activities, such as exploring, playing with toys, painting and drawing, doing a puzzle, or dress-up.

During pretend play, preschoolers often like to take on a gender-specific role because they are beginning to identify with members of the same sex. A girl might pretend to be her mother by "working" in the garden, while a boy might mimic his dad by pretending to cut the lawn. It's clear your preschooler is keeping an eye on how you spend your time, so set a good example by exercising regularly. Your child will pick up on this as something parents do, so naturally he or she will want to do it as well.

Helping your child learn new skills

Preschool-age children are developing important motor skills as they grow. Some of the new skills your preschooler may be showing off include hopping, jumping forward (broad jump), catching a ball, doing a somersault, skipping, and balancing on one foot for five seconds or longer. Parents can help their children practice these skills through playing and exercising together. Here are some ideas.

- Play follow the leader. Take turns being the leader and mix it up with jumping, hopping, and walking backward.
- Kick a ball back and forth with your child, or set up a "goal" for your child to aim for.
- Play bounce catch.
- Practice hitting a ball off a T-ball stand.
- Use paper airplanes to practice throwing.
- Balance a beanbag while walking. Make this more challenging by setting up a simple slalom course.
- Practice balance by pretending to be statues.
- Play freeze dance.
- Play wheelbarrow with your child by holding his or her legs while your child walks forward on his or her hands.

tips

How to keep kids active indoors

When kids are stuck inside, it's easy to get into the TV habit. Instead, suggest ways to be active indoors. Here are ideas for keeping kids busy.

Treasure hunt Hide little "treasures" throughout the house and give clues where they may be found.

Obstacle course Set up chairs, boxes, and toys for the children to go over, under, through, and around.

Soft toys Use soft foam balls to play indoor basketball, bowling, soccer, or catch. You also can play volleyball using a balloon, or play catch with lots of balloons.

Forts and tents Set up a small tent or build a fort out of sheets and cardboard boxes or chairs.

tips

Keep 'em moving

You know your child has energy to spare, yet when you go out for a family walk, your preschooler almost instantly complains: "I'm tired!" Most likely, the child isn't worn out—just bored. A brisk walk, while invigorating to an adult, may be dull to a young child. When you're going out the door, tell your child you're going on an adventure, treasure hunt, or parade. Then make it fun by using these tactics to live up your family stroll.

- Set goals, such as walking to a nearby park, stream, or friend's house.
- Walk backward, skip, or jump part of the way.
- Race your child to the next tree or mailbox.
- Point out interesting bugs, plants, rocks, or clouds.
- Play "I spy" along the way.
- Sing songs or recite nursery rhymes while you walk to your destination.

The very active preschooler

Some parents worry that their active preschooler may be hyperactive or have attention deficit hyperactivity disorder (for information about ADHD, see page 179). In fact, these disorders usually aren't diagnosed in preschool children because it's normal for them to be active and have short attention spans. As children get older, more is expected of them, and it is then that it may become clear that a child is less focused, has poorer judgment, and is much more active than his classmates.

To gauge whether overactivity might be a problem for your child, consider these questions:

- Is your child's activity level unusual for kids of the same age?
- Is your child highly active in all settings (home, preschool, etc.) or just in some settings, such as in church?
- Is your child highly active all or most of the time? Or, is it mostly on days when he or she can't get outside to run and play?

If your child is very active, try to avoid situations where he or she is forced to sit still for long periods of time. Also, look for safe ways for the child to be active, even if you can't get outdoors (for some ideas about how to keep kids active indoors, see page 119). Many preschoolers will become

more calm and focused by the time they reach the early school years. But if you're still concerned about your child, make an appointment with the doctor to talk about it.

Getting ready for school

Being active together can be great fun because preschoolers like to learn as they go. A walk outside can become a nature hike as kids notice the ladybug crawling across the sidewalk, the leaf floating in a puddle, and the bird perched on the fencepost. The same walk can become a scavenger hunt if you give your child a list of things to find: a red door, a cat, a flag, and something square. Your walk together can even become a mathematical experience if you emphasize numbers and counting: How many windows are on the garage door? Do you see any number threes?

Without realizing it, these kinds of activities prepare children to start school. They begin to understand more about the world and how it works. And they can learn basic concepts, such as counting, letters, and colours. Other organized activities, such as swimming or dance classes, also can help prepare children for the world of school. Through such classes a child can be part of a group and learn to follow instructions, as well as getting a little practice separating from mom and dad for a short while—all important skills to learn for school readiness.

Old enough for team sports?

Many parents are eager to enroll their preschool child in organized sports. Although some leagues may be open to children as young as four, organized and team sports are not recommended until a child is a little older. Preschoolers can't understand complex rules and often lack the attention span, skills, and coordination needed to play sports.

Instead of learning to play a sport, preschoolers should continue to work on fundamental skills, such as hopping on one foot, catching a ball, doing a somersault, and maybe riding a bicycle. If you want to teach your child to play baseball, start by teaching him or her basic skills, such as throwing, catching, and hitting off a T-ball stand. Then, if you play a game of whiffleball, don't expect your child to understand all of the rules or follow them. Don't worry if your child doesn't tag first base—it's enough that he or she is running in the right direction!

Safety concerns

No matter what type of physical activity your child gets, safety remains a concern because preschoolers are still developing coordination, balance, and judgment. As a parent, you must strike a balance between letting your child try new things, while doing what is necessary to keep him or her safe and to prevent injuries.

- A child on a trike or bike should always wear a helmet.
- If you haven't done so already, it's time to talk about street safety, because even the most cautious preschooler may dart into the street after a ball.

- A preschooler in the swimming pool needs constant adult supervision, even if he or she has learned to swim. It's a tricky age because kids want more independence, and should have some, but they cannot be left unsupervised.

Preschoolers still need their parents to set limits. For instance, a preschooler won't know when it's time to take a break on a hot, summer day. Likewise, a preschooler may not know when he or she has had enough TV or computer time. Preschoolers shouldn't be inactive for more than an hour at a time unless they're sleeping, so it's easy to understand why a lot of TV isn't advisable. It can start a pattern of inactivity that could lead to weight problems or lack of physical fitness for your child.

Should a preschooler use a computer?

Like watching TV, using a computer is a sedentary activity that should be limited. If your child plays on the computer, make sure the combined TV and computer time doesn't exceed two hours a day. If you decide to allow your child to use the computer, carefully choose the software and the websites your child can visit. Place the computer in a part of the house where you can easily monitor your child and be aware of how long the computer is in use.

Even though many websites and computer games are marketed to preschoolers, using the computer is not as valuable as other pastimes, such as playing, going outside, talking to a parent, or drawing a picture. As one pediatrician put it, "A computer can't teach values, relationships, self-assurance, or the ability to set goals and to dream."

Playground safety

The playground can be a great place for young children to explore and get some exercise. To keep your child safe, follow these tips:

- Select playgrounds that appear to be in good condition and have soft surfaces for landing (sand, a deep layer of wood chips, or rubber mats).
- Teach your child simple safety rules, such as holding on when using a swing and going feet-first, not head-first, down a sliding board.

- Supervise your child at all times. Be nearby to help out as your child climbs and uses other equipment that could cause injuries. Don't let preschoolers climb higher than about 1.5m. Be sure your child doesn't wander outside the play area.
- Direct your child to equipment that is appropriate for his or her age.
- Watch out for open "S" hooks or protruding screws that might snag your child's skin or clothing.

7 SCHOOL-AGE **KIDS**

School-age children are **growing in independence** and are learning to take care of themselves. During these years parents instill **good nutrition and fitness habits** by setting limits and being role models.

age 6–12

"I hate veggies but I love gum"

A time of dramatic change

Between the ages of six and 12, children grow from first graders still clutching their parent's hand to near-adolescents trying to create their own identities, often in the image of their peers.

Becoming independent

Physical growth continues its steady pace for school-age kids, but will pick up dramatically with the onset of puberty, which is usually between eight and 12 for girls and ten to 14 for boys. Good nutrition and adequate physical activity are essential during these years. As children begin to gain more control over what they eat and how active they are, there will be new challenges for parents.

Keep them eating healthy

Although children at this age are making more of their own choices, parents still need to take the lead when it comes to eating so they can steer kids in the right direction. This means providing a variety of nutritious foods for them to choose from, because much of what children eat at this age is still, to a large extent, determined by what is served and stocked at home.

At school, the movies, birthday parties, and other special events, kids may well be influenced by what their friends are eating. It's fine for kids to enjoy less nutritious foods from time to time, but the trick is to keep the occasional from becoming the norm. An otherwise healthy diet can help offset the effects of occasional lapses; however, this approach doesn't work the other way around. Eating healthy foods once in a while cannot compensate for a diet that lacks balance and proper nutrition.

A positive attitude toward fitness

School-age children need regular physical activity, not just an occasional afternoon of bike riding. Parents often look to organized sports to fill this need during the school-age years. These early experiences can cultivate a child's love for a sport like soccer—or they can create feelings of frustration and inadequacy that lead to a more sedentary lifestyle. It's okay if your child doesn't like team sports or show interest in them. There are plenty of other ways to be active without being a member of a team or club.

Individual activities, such as swimming or walking, may lead to an exercise habit that lasts a lifetime. Playing hopscotch or tag can provide as much—or more—sustained, vigorous physical activity as a soccer game. Even if your children are involved in organized sports, make sure they still have time for the fun and frolic of free play. You might even join them once in a while. It's a chance to teach your kids to love physical activity, in whatever form suits them, and they will see it as a pleasure, not a chore.

Reassurance helps

Being active improves coordination and strength, helping kids develop confidence and a positive attitude about their bodies—feelings that lead to good self-esteem. This is of particular importance for school-age kids, who begin to pay close attention to their bodies and worry about whether they are normal. If they think they are less coordinated, less athletic, or a different size from their peers, this can make them feel out of place. As they get closer to puberty, kids will scrutinize their bodies even more. Some boys may worry that they are smaller and less muscular than their friends. A girl, on the other hand, may fret about her weight or when her period is going to start.

A visit to your doctor can provide reassurance for you and your child. A child who is overweight may welcome a chance to talk with the doctor, especially if the child is worried about his or her weight. Dealing with this now also may spare kids from being teased and feeling left out, which can be intense for children of school-age, especially as they approach adolescence.

If you look around your child's schoolyard, you'll see children of various body types and athletic ability. It's important to remember that regardless of their physical characteristics and athletic talents, all children need frequent reminders that they are loved.

Fit for a life change
School-age kids need to eat a nutritious and balanced diet and get plenty of regular physical activity to be in the best shape for the great change they face—the onset of puberty.

"I love my new lunchbox"

Nutrition for school-age kids

When kids start going to school it's an opportune time to give them more control—within parental boundaries—over which foods they eat. Lunch and after-school snacks are the places to start.

Making good decisions

Letting kids decide what to eat may mean giving them a more active role in food preparation and, as they get older, teaching them to be informed consumers who read food labels and make healthy decisions based on that information (for more about this, see page 48). Help your child make the right decisions now so they can avoid nutrition problems.

- A child who eats too little—or doesn't get enough healthy foods—is at risk of a nutritional deficiency. Calcium is a concern, especially for kids aged nine and older.
- A child who overeats could end up with a weight problem, joining the 15 percent of six- to 12-year-olds already struggling with too much weight.

Nowhere is decision-making more challenging for kids than in the school cafeteria. Prepared school lunches may offer balance and portion control when eaten in their intended form, but students often have other options that allow them to overeat or eat too much of one food. Double helpings, à la carte items, snack foods, candy, and pop are often readily available at or near schools and are difficult for many young people to resist.

Packing a child's lunch, or helping a child pack a healthy lunch enables parents to stay in the driver's seat when it comes to lunchtime and after-school nutrition. After-school snack attacks can add to the problem, particularly when kids come home before their parents do (see page 134).

Daily nutrition needs

Here are the dietary requirements for school-age kids. You'll notice that as they get older they will eat more and take in more calories, so the total amount of each component increases. A child who's very active, tall for his or her age, or participating in competitive sports may need more calories than the recommended amount. Use these figures as a guide as opposed to tracking them gram by gram. (See the sample daily menu planners on pages 130 and 133 for ideas on how to put the requirements for your child's age group into practice.) Remember that nutrition is an average.

DIETARY COMPONENT	KIDS 6–8	KIDS 9–12
Carbohydrate	200–250g	300g
Protein	22–30g	30–45g
Fat	48–60g	00–75g
Fibre	10–15g	14–17g
Total daily energy	1,600–2,000 calories	2,000–2,500 calories

info

Cereal is g-r-r-reat

School-age children will usually get all the vitamins and minerals they need by eating a varied diet. A good way to be sure your child meets his or her daily requirements is by serving them fortified breakfast cereals. Of course, cereal is great for breakfast, but it's also good for quick snacks, especially if the cereal contains little added sugar. And the milk poured on top adds calcium and vitamins A and D, which kids need.

School lunch

It's tempting to let your kids buy lunch at school each day, but what they pick and choose from the menu may not be as nutritious as you think. They might even have the option of a fast-food meal. A packed lunch is often a better choice.

Eating well at school

While Canadian schools may make efforts to ensure that the lunches they provide for their students meet healthy standards, most kids have the option of mixing choices—and the choices they make are very likely to be heavy on fat and light on vegetables and whole grains. A glance at your child's cafeteria menu may tell the tale: you are probably going to find such items as chicken nuggets, cheeseburgers, and hot dogs.

Some schools have taken steps to offer salads and other more nutritious fare, such as grilled chicken sandwiches or lean beef entrees. But even if the prepared meal is a healthy one, it is very easy for kids choosing their lunch to bypass the healthy option in favour of pizza, nachos, candy, and ice cream—foods better suited to the ballpark than the school cafeteria. Some school districts have even partnered with fast-food chains so that a child can choose fast food for lunch every day of the week.

Older kids also may have access to vending machines whose proceeds support school groups. Legislation in some places has aimed to remove these machines or require that they be stocked with healthier snacks. Be aware of fund-raisers that sell food, such as candy and baked goods, to students. And talk with your child about what lunchtime is like.

- What do they usually eat?
- Do they ever get "double lunch?"
- Do teachers on lunch duty push them to eat everything on their trays?
- Is the time relaxed or is it rushed, especially for kids who choose to buy a prepared meal?
- Is the cafeteria pleasant or is it noisy and chaotic?
- Do kids swap foods?
- Do kids critique each other's food?

If you want to improve the school cafeteria experience, your best bet is to talk with other parents and to lobby the school administration for changes that promote healthy eating at

tips

Be on the safe side

It's important to take a few food safety precautions when packing your child's lunches.

- Use a thermos for hot foods.
- Use a cold pack to keep cold foods cold. One study found fewer than a third of parents included a cold pack when packing yogourt, deli-meat sandwiches, and other foods that need refrigeration.
- As an alternative to cold packs, you might experiment with freezing some foods and drinks overnight, and letting them thaw in the lunchbox.
- Wash out lunchboxes every day or use brown paper lunch sacks that can be discarded.
- Whoever packs the lunch should wash their hands before packing it. Then toss in some moist towelettes to remind kids to wash their hands before eating—and to clean themselves up afterward.

Lunches at home, at school, and on the go

A lunch eaten at home, or brought from home, is often the best choice because parents can control the contents by keeping healthy foods on hand or including them in the lunchbox. Here's how a homemade lunch stacks up against a school cafeteria lunch and a typical fast-food meal, in terms of approximate calories and fat content, and food group servings provided.

homemade lunch

- turkey on whole-wheat with lettuce, tomato, and mustard
- 1 banana
- slice of low-fat brownie snack cake
- 1 cup (250ml) skim milk

FOOD GROUP	SERVINGS
grain products	2
milk products	1
meat and alternatives	1
vegetables and fruit	1 1/2

This meal provides 648 calories, of which 21 percent comes from fat.

school lunch

- beef and vegetable stew
- dinner roll
- apple
- brownie
- 1 cup (250ml) skim milk

FOOD GROUP	SERVINGS
grain products	1
milk products	1
meat and alternatives	1
vegetables and fruit	2

This meal provides 757 calories, of which 35 percent comes from fat.

fast-food lunch

- cheeseburger
- fries
- chocolate shake

FOOD GROUP	SERVINGS
grain products	2
milk products	1
meat and alternatives	1
vegetables and fruit	1

This meal provides 958 calories, of which 33 percent comes from fat.

school. Be sure to discuss these issues with your child. While you can't stop kids from swapping foods, you can explain why it's important to have a variety of foods at lunch and help clear obstacles that prevent them from eating well at school.

Bringing lunch from home

It's worthwhile encouraging kids to eat a packed lunch. Older kids can pack their own, or—if they don't like doing it—you can make it for them, with two rules:
- They must work with you on choosing items to pack.
- They must agree to eat the packed lunch.

Get younger kids excited about the idea by buying them a special lunchbox. Though they may not be particularly interested in the nutritional advantages of a packed lunch, you may pique their interest by letting them select and pack foods they like to eat. Make a list of healthy foods that are lunchtime fare—such as cheese sticks, yogourt, fruit, raisins, nuts—and let your child pick which ones to pack. Leftovers from last night's dinner also can be a good choice. When kids like what's in their lunchboxes, they'll eat more, giving

them the energy they need to learn and play. If your child has an after-school sports practice, their lunchbox is the perfect place to pack an extra snack and drink.

Healthy packables

Prepackaged lunches for kids usually include deli meat, a juice drink, and a sweet treat, making them high in fat and calories. It's easy to create your own versions at home with healthier ingredients. Use these components and pack them in plastic containers, resealable plastic bags, or colourful plastic wrap.
- cold-cut roll ups (turkey, ham, or roast beef with lower-fat cheese in a flour tortilla)
- pizza (mozzarella and pizza sauce on an English muffin)
- cracker sandwiches (whole-grain crackers filled with peanut butter and jelly or cream cheese)
- peanut butter and celery sticks
- veggie sticks with low-fat dip or dressing
- fruit juice box
- optional dessert, such as flavoured gelatin, fresh fruit, low-fat pudding, oatmeal raisin cookie, or Graham crackers.

Helping six- to eight-year-olds eat healthy

During the pre-puberty years, seize the opportunity to affect your child's eating habits and attitude toward food, as this will have lifelong benefits. Let your child get involved in shopping and meal preparation, and start teaching him or her about good nutrition.

Leading by example

Kids need the same variety in their diet as preschoolers do, but at ages six to eight they are more able to understand why nutritious food is important to their health and general well-being. You are just the person to guide them in this because, at this age, kids still want to please their parents and often follow their lead. If young school-age kids begin to understand nutrition—even at a very basic level—they will be able to apply that knowledge to the choices they make on their own, such as when they are in the school cafeteria. To encourage good decisions, create a healthy eating chart at home so your child can track his or her own progress toward the goal of eating five servings of vegetables and fruit every day. You can help your child meet this goal by stocking fruits and vegetables at home. Also, help your child eat a healthy diet by serving a variety of foods that meet his or her nutritional needs. Talk—in terms your child will understand—about why making the right food choices is important.

DAILY CALORIES
This plan will provide 1,875 calories.

One-day menu planner **for kids six to eight**

No single menu can account for a child's individual tastes and preferences, so don't feel limited by the foods presented below. Use this menu planner to help you get a feel for the amounts and types of food that a young school-age child should be eating. You also can use this format for a food log to analyze your child's diet for a week or so, but don't feel pressure to analyze each day in this detailed way. Instead, keep your eye on the big picture.

breakfast
- 1 cup (30g) low-sugar cereal
- 1 cup (250mL) 1% or 2% milk
- 1/2 banana
- 3/4 cup (185mL) orange juice

FOOD GROUP	SERVINGS
grain products	1
milk products	1
meat and alternatives	0
vegetables/fruit	2

snack
- 1 45-g box raisins
- 30g twisted pretzels

FOOD GROUP	SERVINGS
grain products	1
milk products	0
meat and alternatives	0
vegetables/fruit	1

lunch
- 2 slices whole-wheat bread
- 2 tbsp peanut butter
- 1 tbsp grape jam or jelly
- 10 baby carrots
- 1 cup (250mL) low-fat milk

FOOD GROUP	SERVINGS
grain products	2
milk products	1
meat and alternatives	1
vegetables/fruit	1

snack
- 1/2 cup (70g) sliced cucumber
- 1 small whole-wheat pita bread
- 55g hummus for dipping

FOOD GROUP	SERVINGS
grain products	1
milk products	0
meat and alternatives	1
vegetables/fruit	1

dinner
- 55–85g roast chicken
- 1/2 cup (100g) steamed brown rice
- 1/2 cup (75g) steamed broccoli
- 1 chocolate sandwich cookie
- 1 cup (250mL) low-fat milk

FOOD GROUP	SERVINGS
grain products	2
milk products	1
meat and alternatives	1
vegetables/fruit	1

tips

Make your own pizzas

Pizza is popular with kids of all ages (adults too), and it's easy to make. Kids will particularly enjoy eating pizza they've made themselves. Here are some ideas for crusts and toppings.

- **Crusts** (choose whole-wheat if possible): prepared thin-crust pizza dough, large or personal size pizza crusts, English muffins, bagel halves, and pita bread.
- **Sauces:** pizza sauce (homemade, canned, or bottled), olive oil, pesto sauce, salsa, and barbecue sauce.
- **Cheeses:** mozzarella, Monterey Jack, Cheddar, Swiss, Parmesan, and romano.

- **Toppings** (precook all meats, seafood, and some vegetables, depending on desired crunchiness): artichoke hearts, green and red bell peppers, broccoli, carrots, cauliflower, olives, eggplant, onions, mushrooms, red potato, scallions, spinach, fresh or sun-dried tomatoes, zucchini, pineapple, shredded chicken, lean ham, turkey sausage, shrimp and other seafood, and lean ground beef.
- **Seasonings:** salt, pepper, fresh garlic or garlic powder, fresh ginger, oregano, thyme, basil, rosemary, and crushed red pepper flakes.

Doing it for themselves

Another way to teach children about making good choices about food is to involve them in the process of preparing it, both for themselves and for the family. Cereal may be one of the first "meals" your young child is able to prepare independently, but it can be the first of many.

When it's time for a family dinner, invite your child to help you choose recipes, select foods at the market, and cook the meal. Your child might even be able to do some of this on his or her own, especially if you choose something easy to start with, such as pizzas (see above). A pizza party is a great introduction to what cooking is all about. Add to the fun by inviting a few of your child's friends over.

Create a pizza assembly line in your kitchen. Have the components—crusts, sauces, cheeses, toppings, and seasonings—prepared in advance, and set them out on the counter so kids can select their own. The novelty of being able to choose from a variety of ingredients may encourage your child to try foods he or she otherwise wouldn't. As you work, talk about how varied selections can pack the pizza with nutritional punch: for example, a whole-wheat crust will provide complex carbohydrates; broccoli offers vitamins and fibre; and cheese is rich in calcium. Explain the cooking process—what oven temperature for how long—and let the children decide if the pizza should be tender and gooey or

crisp and crunchy. When the pizzas are ready, sit down together, applaud the kids for a job well done, and enjoy their efforts. Take time for a little conversation, too.

Snacking before mealtimes

Strategic, healthy snacking is better than letting your children get too hungry, especially if they must wait several hours before getting their evening meal. The hours after school are often spent doing homework, or attending sports practices or other lessons. Kids need a nutritious snack to keep them from getting fatigued and grumpy when they need to be focused and alert.

Another advantage of snacking before a late dinner is that your kids won't come to the table so hungry that they overeat. Rather than a snack, if you're serving soup or a salad you might allow your kids to eat these early, before the main meal is on the table.

It's good to have your child ask permission before diving into snacks, but start letting them fix their own whenever possible. Opt for healthy snacks, such as fresh fruit, cheese and crackers, or peanut butter and celery (turn to page 134 for a list of more healthy snack ideas). With a little coaching, they can learn to wash fruits and vegetables, put peanut butter on celery or crackers, and pop open a yogourt without too much trouble (and only a few splatters).

Keeping nine- to twelve-year-olds eating healthy

Boys and girls at this age are nicknamed "tweens" because they're between stages—not quite kids anymore but not yet teens. For most kids, the first signs of puberty will occur during these years, bringing increased appetite and nutritional needs.

Growing up

The growth spurt that marks the passage through puberty starts, on average, at 10½ for girls and 12½ for boys. As growth picks up, energy needs grow too. This is especially true for boys. Kids at this time generally require an additional 200–300 calories per day. If kids are very active, they'll need even more calories. Athletic children may require as much as 2,500 calories a day or more during these years.

Getting enough calcium

Boys and girls age six to eight need 800mg of calcium per day. But around nine, due to the onset of puberty, their needs for this mineral increase dramatically, and 1,300mg of calcium is recommended every day to ensure the development of healthy bones. Milk is a great source of calcium, but some kids this age dislike milk and may refuse to drink it, or they may be unable to drink milk because of lactose intolerance (for more about this, see page 175).

Here are some calcium-rich alternatives to milk:

- 1 cup (250mL) yogourt (315mg calcium)
- 55g cheese (300mg calcium)
- ½ cup (65g) frozen yogourt (120mg calcium)
- 1 cup (250mL) calcium-fortified juice (300mg calcium)
- ½ cup (95g) cooked white beans (120mg calcium)
- 1 cup (155g) steamed broccoli (70mg calcium)

Raising savvy consumers

If your children are interested, show them how to read food labels (see page 48). And send the message that eating the right foods will help a child feel good and grow properly. That message is especially important as kids move from elementary school to middle school and start making more of their own choices about what to eat. Peer groups wield more influence and no one likes to be seen as different during these years. As a result, it may be difficult for a child to make healthy choices, in the cafeteria for example.

What parents say...
about food at home

"I try to cook well-rounded meals and we rarely eat fast food (I can't stand it so the kids never got too used to it). I don't keep pop or junk food in the house either, but of course they sometimes have it when we go out or they are out with friends. Nothing is 'off limits.' I just try to teach them to eat some things in moderation. It is also important for us to sit down together for family dinner. So even with a crazy schedule, we manage to eat together most nights, even though it is usually at 8:30 p.m.

"Both of my daughters are aware of how important it is to be physically fit but not to go overboard with dieting and such. They know that the models they see are airbrushed pictures and that the really thin images and girls on TV are not necessarily healthy. Fitness has always been part of my daughters' lives."

One-day menu planner **for kids nine to twelve**

DAILY CALORIES
This plan will provide
2,110 calories.

More than any other age group, this is a time when you may notice a dramatic difference in the amount of food your child eats, even when compared to other children of the same age. The biggest factor will be the onset of puberty, when the older school-age child's appetite will take a sudden upswing. Use the following one-day menu planner as a guideline and adjust it when your child's energy needs increase.

breakfast
- 3/4 cup (185mL) apple juice
- 2 whole-grain waffles
- 2 tbsp syrup

FOOD GROUP	SERVINGS
grain products	2
milk products	0
meat and alternatives	0
vegetables/fruit	1

snack
- 1 string cheese

FOOD GROUP	SERVINGS
grain products	0
milk products	1
meat and alternatives	0
vegetables/fruit	0

lunch
- 2 slices whole-wheat bread
- 85g lean turkey, ham, or beef
- 1 tbsp mustard
- 10 baby carrots or celery sticks
- 1 apple or other fruit
- 1 cup (250mL) low-fat milk

FOOD GROUP	SERVINGS
grain products	2
milk products	1
meat and alternatives	1
vegetables/fruit	2

snack
- 1/2 cup (115g) cottage cheese
- 1 cup (125g) fresh raspberries or other berries

FOOD GROUP	SERVINGS
grain products	0
milk products	1
meat and alternatives	0
vegetables/fruit	2

dinner
- 1 1/2 cups (200g) spaghetti
- 1 cup (250mL) tomato and meat sauce
- tossed salad with 2 tbsp low-fat dressing
- 2 oatmeal-raisin cookies
- 1 cup (250mL) low-fat milk

FOOD GROUP	SERVINGS
grain products	3
milk products	1
meat and alternatives	1
vegetables/fruit	2

Peers are not the only ones with the power to influence what your child eats. Advertisers of food and drinks have recognized the buying power of kids. Just watch a little Saturday morning TV. Many commercials tell kids they will be cooler, stronger, and more fun if they eat or drink the advertised products. Unfortunately, these sugary drinks, high-fat snacks, and high-energy foods offer little nutritional value.

Help your child be a savvy consumer by questioning the claims commercials make. Also encourage kids to start comparing labels on heavily advertised foods with healthier ones. They may still want those foods, but you have given them a new, more sophisticated way of looking at advertising.

Busy schedules
During the later school-age years, kids are apt to have more extracurricular demands. Soccer games or music lessons can interfere with your plans for a healthy dinner, but don't give

up on eating as a family. Keep beating the drum about shared meals, healthy snacks, and a varied, nutritious diet. Both kids and parents need them even more during these busy years. Stock the house with easy snacks that you can toss in your child's backpack. Try granola bars, cereal bars, fresh or dried fruit, and trail mix (there's a recipe for this on page 200).

Quality time together
Making dinner together accomplishes the dual goals of spending quality time with your child and everyone eating a well-balanced meal. Consider planning an ethnic food night at home. It may be more fun if you let your child invite a friend over that night. Spend time together looking for recipes, then make a trip to an ethnic market to get the ingredients you need. If the meal is a hit, consider venturing out to try the same cuisine at a restaurant. And get your child involved in choosing other ethnic themes for future meals.

How to keep snacking under control

As school-age kids get older, they grow more independent and capable of taking care of themselves. But left to their own devices, they may not always make healthy decisions, especially when it comes to snacks after they get home from school.

The snack attack

After a long day, kids need fuel to get them through to dinner. After-school snacks can be part of a nutritious diet. The trick is providing the right food in the right amount. A perfect snack will ease after-school hunger pangs, but not so much that the child loses interest in eating dinner.

If making their own choices, kids—and in particular the latchkey child who lets himself or herself into an empty house after school—may opt for chips and pop in the hours before dinnertime. Solve this problem by limiting the kinds of snacks available. Make it easy for your child by keeping fresh fruit and cut-up vegetables in plain sight. Don't keep high-fat or salty snacks in the house—or store them in an out-of-the-way spot. You also might try preparing an after-school snack the night before, so your child can grab it out of the refrigerator when he or she arrives at home.

If your child seems "starved" after school, look into what he or she is eating—or not eating—for lunch. Your child might be spending lunch money on something other than food, tossing out an undesirable packed lunch, or just not getting enough to eat at mealtime.

Coming home to an empty house also can lead some kids to snack too much. The child might be bored or not have the judgment necessary to go without adult supervision. Even kids as old as 11 or 12 may not be ready to be left alone. Look for alternatives, such as after-school clubs or spending time at a neighbour's house. The less time the child spends alone, the less time there will be to snack.

Kids like to snack
Parents need to keep an eye on what kids are eating. No food should be forbidden—not even ice cream—but it's not a good snack for every day.

tips

Healthy snacks

Kids can easily brand nutritious snacks as yucky, if they try a food you call "healthy" and don't like it. To avoid this, serve a variety of nutritious snacks and be responsive when your child really likes one of them—or really doesn't. Keep the snack menu fresh by serving new items occasionally.

If your child tires of one type of snack, let him or her help choose new ones. Some great snacks for after-school munchies are:

- breakfast cereals
- lower fat granola bars
- rice cakes and corn cakes
- English muffins, bagels, and pita breads
- homemade fruit and bran muffins
- air-popped popcorn
- low-fat tortilla chips
- peanut butter—great spread on apple slices or whole-grain crackers
- raw fresh vegetables (broccoli, carrots, cauliflower, celery, cucumber, green beans, snow peas, and zucchini) with dressing, sour cream, or hummus for dipping
- raw fresh fruit (apples, apricots, bananas, berries, grapes, melon, grapefruit, nectarines, peaches, pears, oranges, and pineapple) with cream cheese or yogurt for dipping
- fruit salad
- dried fruit (apples, apricots, bananas, and raisins)
- hard-boiled eggs
- low-fat string cheese
- low-fat fruit or flavoured yogourt

"I swim like a fish"

Fitness for school-age kids

It's okay if your child doesn't like team sports or show much interest in them. He or she simply may prefer free play to organized games, or like individual sports such as swimming and bicycling.

The benefits of physical activity

With school-age kids spending more time on sedentary pursuits like watching TV and playing computer games, the challenge for parents is to help their children find physical activities they enjoy and feel successful doing.

For some children, their preferred activity may be in a traditional area, such as gymnastics or being on the baseball team. Other kids may be fast runners—or they may find they have a great talent for hopping on one foot. Many school-age children enjoy scouting, camping, and other outdoor pursuits, which get them outside and teach them valuable skills. The real challenge comes with those kids who dislike all forms of exercise.

Whatever they like to do, school-age kids should be active every day. That means at least 30 to 60 minutes of physical activity, including ten- to 15-minute bursts of more vigorous activity. This can be time spent in a gym class or at recess, practicing an organized team or individual sport, or playing outside with friends. School-age children also should participate in an additional 60 minutes or more each day of age-appropriate activities, which can include anything they like to do, such as putting on a play, looking for bugs, or building a snow fort.

Expose your kids to a variety of activities, games, and sports so they can get the recommended 90 minutes or more of activity every day. School-age kids don't care about activity recommendations, but they won't mind being physically active if they're having fun. Make yourself part of the action and help keep them moving by:

- organizing family outings;
- letting kids take classes to learn different sports;
- considering a noncompetitive sports league;
- leaving time for free play;
- setting aside some time to be active with your child.

For the child who would rather be reading, listening to music, or playing video or computer games, you might try an incentive chart that offers small rewards, such as stickers, for every day he or she gets some exercise. (See pages 60 and 138 for more information about how to create an activity log to motivate kids.)

In the early school-age years, while children are learning basic skills and simple rules, there may be only a few athletic standouts. As kids get older, differences in ability become more apparent. Commitment and interest level often go along with ability, but it's possible for any child to be intensely committed to a sport. It's also possible for a very talented athlete to lack interest. Help your child choose the activity that is right for them (see below).

Choosing an activity **that suits your child**

Different sports emphasize some skills over others. The chart below shows a variety of sports and activities alongside the physical and mental abilities needed. You can use this information to find an activity that suits your child's strengths and the areas in which he or she wants to improve. If your child doesn't have much endurance and wants to try the swim team, what better way to improve stamina than competitive swimming?

SPORT	STRENGTH	FLEXIBILITY	COORDINATION	CONCENTRATION	BODY CONTROL	QUICKNESS	STAMINA
TEAM							
baseball	✔✔	✔	✔✔✔	✔✔✔	✔	✔✔	✔
football	✔✔✔	✔	✔✔	✔✔	✔	✔✔	✔✔✔
basketball	✔✔	✔	✔✔✔	✔✔✔	✔✔✔	✔✔✔	✔✔✔
soccer	✔	✔	✔✔✔	✔✔✔	✔✔	✔✔✔	✔✔✔
hockey	✔✔✔	✔	✔✔✔	✔✔✔	✔✔✔	✔	✔✔✔
INDIVIDUAL							
swimming	✔✔	✔	✔	✔	✔	✔	✔✔✔
ice skating	✔	✔✔✔	✔✔✔	✔✔✔	✔✔✔	✔	✔✔
inline skating	✔	✔✔	✔✔✔	✔✔	✔✔✔	✔	✔✔
dancing	✔	✔✔✔	✔✔✔	✔✔✔	✔✔✔	✔	✔✔
gymnastics	✔✔	✔✔✔	✔✔✔	✔✔✔	✔✔✔	✔	✔
bicycling	✔✔	✔	✔✔	✔✔	✔	✔	✔✔✔
running	✔	✔✔	✔	✔✔	✔	✔✔✔	✔✔✔
golf	✔	✔	✔✔✔	✔✔✔	✔✔✔	✔	✔
tennis	✔	✔	✔✔✔	✔✔✔	✔✔✔	✔✔✔	✔✔
fencing	✔	✔✔	✔	✔✔✔	✔✔✔	✔✔	✔
martial arts	✔	✔✔✔	✔	✔✔✔	✔✔✔	✔	✔

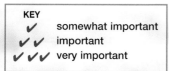

KEY
✔ somewhat important
✔✔ important
✔✔✔ very important

Helping six- to eight-year-olds be fit

Parents love to watch their infants and toddlers grow and develop—we know what to expect and can measure the rapid progress. But it's easy to forget that older children pass through developmental stages, too.

Encouraging exercise

Between the ages of six and eight, kids are learning and mastering fundamental physical skills, such as jumping, throwing, kicking, and catching. It will take a few more years before most children can combine these skills, to throw on the run, for instance, the way many 11-year-olds can. They aren't ready for the pressure of competition and they can't grasp complex strategy.

Now is the time to teach your kids basic skills, simple rules, and a sense of accomplishment. Your aim is to create a foundation that will help your child develop a lifelong love of exercise and physical activity.

Free play

When you were a kid, you probably did quite a bit of free play, though no one called it that. Free play isn't something a child takes lessons in or needs special equipment for—it's what kids do naturally when given the opportunity to decide how to spend their time outdoors. Free play includes hopscotch, jump rope, dancing, tag, scavenger hunts, and bike riding, to name just a few.

Encouraging free play may seem challenging at first, but left to their own devices and creativity, it's amazing what kids will come up with. And nothing encourages free play like turning off the TV and computer. You can also help by reminding your child that it's time to go outside and by having a selection of games, toys, and sporting equipment always on hand (see opposite for some suggestions). In warm weather, sprinklers and hoses inspire a lot of darting and dashing. If your backyard loses its charm, you can simply branch out to nearby playgrounds and athletic fields. On snowy days, bundle up and head outside to make a snowman or have a friendly snowball fight.

Free play may involve more vigorous activity than a gym class or a team sport, where a child may spend 20 minutes being active and the rest of the time on the bench, changing

What parents say...
about motivating kids

"I have two kids, a girl eight and a boy ten, and we were looking for a fun way to get them up and moving. So we decided to make a weekly activity log, to keep track of how active they are each day. We all created the chart together. We put the days of the week across the top of the chart and then listed our kids' favourite activities down the left side (both free activities and more organized sports). Our daughter's choices were swimming, hopscotch, and dancing. Our son opted for riding his bike, playing soccer, and skateboarding. Every day our son or daughter did one of the activities we put on a star or a sticker. The chart idea was so successful at motivating them we decided to carry on for a month. And we set a goal for each of them to achieve during the month. The reward for reaching their goal was to let them choose a family outing, such as a trip to the movies."

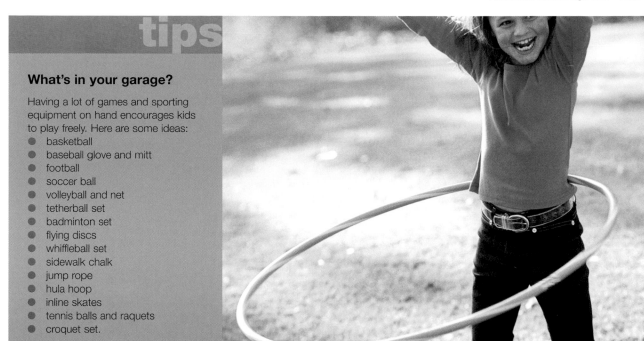

What's in your garage?

Having a lot of games and sporting equipment on hand encourages kids to play freely. Here are some ideas:

- basketball
- baseball glove and mitt
- football
- soccer ball
- volleyball and net
- tetherball set
- badminton set
- flying discs
- whiffleball set
- sidewalk chalk
- jump rope
- hula hoop
- inline skates
- tennis balls and raquets
- croquet set.

into a uniform, or lining up. Studies also show a decline in the frequency of P. E. classes as well as the amount of physical activity during an average class. It's a good idea to learn more about the physical education program at your child's school. Here are some steps to take:

- Inquire about how gym classes are run in your child's school and how active they are.
- Let the school know that physical activity for your child is important to you.
- Ask whether the P. E. teachers are certified in physical education and whether non-P. E. certified teachers are allowed to coach.
- Help your child be prepared for gym day with the right clothes and shoes, so this chance to be active during the school day isn't missed.
- Find out if the physical education program also organizes before and afterschool games, such as kickball.

For more information about P. E. classes, see page 141.

Organized sports

Many young school-age children enjoy organized activities, which can be anything from gymnastics (tumbling) and ballet to volleyball. They offer kids lots of opportunities to be active, learn new skills, and feel good about themselves.

Team sports

Playing on a team can teach children about sportsmanship and teamwork while building self-esteem. But there are many ways team sports can go wrong for a young child. It's not enough for coaches to explain the rules of the game or how to do a particular skill. A child must be emotionally or physically able to do it. At this age, there are skills some children won't be able to master. That can lead to a sense of failure and frustration, especially if parents or coaches have unrealistic expectations or are harsh in their judgment of the child's performance.

If you think that participation in a team sport is right for your child, look for classes or leagues and coaches that share your philosophy. At this age, the emphasis should be on having fun while learning basic skills and being physically active. Remember that success doesn't mean scoring the winning goal. It means that the kid who used to run the wrong way on the soccer field now runs the right way and takes a shot at kicking it in the net. Or, even better, the kid passes it to his teammate who's closer to the goal.

Noncompetitive sports leagues are the best choice for the early school-age child. Although some naturally gifted child athletes may take to competitive sports, for most children it's better to avoid teams that put a lot of emphasis

tips

Sneaky exercise

By assigning active household chores or suggesting outings where exercise just happens, you can sneak physical activity into your kids' schedules. Try these:
● cleaning their room
● folding laundry
● sweeping or vacuuming
● washing the car
● dusting
● watering the garden
● raking up leaves
● shoveling snow off the driveway
● birding
● shopping
● walking a dog.

on winning. Here are some questions to ask when choosing a sports program for your child:
● Do all players get equal playing time?
● Does the coach rotate players so everyone gets a chance to play the more desired positions?
● Are players ever benched for poor performance?
● Do award ceremonies honour only winning teams and star players or are players also recognized for participating and showing good sportsmanship?

Watch for signs your child simply doesn't enjoy practising or playing in the games. Talk to your child about it, and if necessary, meet with the coach to talk about what's bothering your child.

Team sports have so many potential benefits that many parents are anxious to get their child signed up, dressed in a uniform, and on the field ready to play. But early failure at any sport may turn children off, causing them to give up on all sports completely because they think they're just not good enough.

Individual sports

Team sports are fine for kids who enjoy them, but how many adults regularly play football? Yet long after high school, many adults continue to enjoy swimming, tennis, running, and bicycling—the individual sports and activities they learned in childhood. Like team sports, these promote fitness and give kids confidence and control over their bodies. But with individual sports, it's easier for kids to set their own pace and improve skills independently.

Of course, the level of intensity will vary from kid to kid. A child pursuing excellence in gymnastics or figure skating may require many hours of practice. In fact, these sports depend so much upon repetition that some kids do specialize in them, even at a young age. However, a child can get a lot out of gymnastics or figure skating without ever pursuing an Olympic medal.

Which sport?

To help prevent kids from feeling frustrated and quitting, parents can help their child choose the right sport or sports to try. Start by taking into account the child's interests, and then consider his or her physical and mental abilities, as well as body type. A bigger child might be suited for football because size is an advantage. A smaller child might succeed at baseball or might consider an individual sport.

Also, consider your child's temperament. A mild-mannered boy may not be comfortable playing football, but may like the challenge of karate. Likewise, an active girl may not have the patience and control required for ballet, but be better suited to a more fast-paced activity, like soccer.

myth : **Physical education at school provides enough exercise.**

fact: More than half of parents surveyed ranked their child's physical education classes as important as math, science, and English. But gym classes often aren't enough to keep a child fit. Few students get physical education every school day, and one study of third graders found that only five minutes of a typical gym class were spent doing vigorous physical activity. Time for physical activity is shrinking in some schools due to budget cutbacks and pressure to increase time spent on academics.

At your child's school, ask about how recess and physical education classes are structured. Are there any organized activities during recess? Are children encouraged to go outside or can they stay in? With P. E. classes, how much time is spent changing clothes in the locker room, on instruction, or lining up? Encourage schools to keep gym class and recess periods active, and encourage your children to participate. If you're dissatisfied with the state of physical education at your child's school, work with other parents and with teachers and school officials to implement change.

You can guide your children, but remember that the choice of sport should be left largely up to them. As with food, parents can help by presenting the child with a menu of good choices. (See the chart on page 137 for guidelines on how to match your child's abilities with a sport.)

Even if your child is not the tallest kid on the block but wants to play basketball, definitely let him or her give it a whirl. Remember, the goal isn't to produce a scholarship-winning athlete, it's to raise a child who likes being active and is happy to run outside on a sunny day.

Family fitness

Don't just put the onus on your kids to be active—make fitness a family affair. If you want your children to keep moving, set the right example by showing them that you enjoy being active as well, especially when it comes to family time. Maybe it's time to take a golf lesson together, or make a trip to the tennis court to volley back and forth, or spend a rainy Saturday at the bowling alley. A little friendly family competition can be fun, but don't take it too hard if your ten-year-old beats you!

Summer camp

For kids, summer is a major change of pace. In one respect, this is good, especially if the school year has been a demanding one. But if summer is too lazy, children may get bored and might not get enough physical activity. One answer is summer camp. Some families have a tradition of sending kids to sleep-away camps, but there are also plenty of day camp options. Some are expensive, so you might also want to consider day camps run by the city or county, the local YMCA, or Boys and Girls Club. Whichever camp you choose, your child will enjoy being active. When September rolls around, you may find your child is sad to bid farewell to new friends and can't wait to go back to camp next year.

Keeping nine- to twelve-year-olds physically fit

Being physically active can be exciting for the older school-age child as he or she becomes more coordinated. Whether your child is a natural-born athlete, a casual athlete, or a nonathlete, there are lots of possible sports and activities to try.

Parents can make a difference

All kids can refine and improve their skills and feel successful during these later school-age years. Now that they've got the fundamentals of their chosen sport or activity down pat, they can work on individual skills, such as perfecting their free throw, improving their back dive, or finessing a goal, sending the ball into the corner of the net. Parents can help at this time by reminding kids that success at sports also includes having fun—and learning how to handle setbacks.

Questions to ask

For kids who play team sports, parents need to check that their child's sports program is still filling all of the child's needs. There are five important questions for a parent to ask.

- How competitive is this sports league? For nine- and ten-year-olds especially, the right answer is: "We play mainly for fun."
- Is there a policy that every child gets to play at least part of the game? No kids should feel left out.
- How often does the team practice? Three nights of practice plus a game each week will be too much for most school-age children.
- How are injuries handled? The coach and assistants should be trained in first-aid and have taken a life-saving course. Referees (umpires) also should be trained in basic safety procedures.
- How can I help? Ask if you can help coach or take on other tasks, such as scorekeeping, working in the concession stand, and making phone calls.

Switching activities

It may have been a few years since you and your child chose a sport or activity from the many available options. The novelty of the uniform may have worn off and it's possible that the activity or sport is no longer the right one for your child. He or she may want to follow their friends into a new activity or just try something new, which is perfectly natural at this age.

tips

Brainstorming for activities?

Traditional sports aren't the only way to be active. Here are some alternatives your child might enjoy (see also associations for various sports and activities listed on page 203):
- **Archery** (shooting at a target with a bow and arrow)
- **Fencing** (two opponents each use a flexible, narrow, blunt-end sword to attack and defend)
- **Judo** (an art of self-defence that overcomes an opponent by skill rather than sheer strength)
- **Croquet** (players knock wooden balls through hoops on the ground using long-handled mallets)
- **Bocce** (an Italian game, similar to bowling, played with wooden balls on a long, narrow court)
- **Horseshoes** (players toss horseshoes to try to encircle a heavy stake)
- **Golf** (players use long-handled clubs to hit a small ball into a series of holes on a large course)
- **Curling** (teams slide heavy stones along an ice court)

If your child isn't enjoying an activity—or is feeling frustrated by failure—it may be time to switch to something else. That doesn't mean the time spent playing basketball or doing gymnastics or tumbling was wasted. You should expose your child to a variety of activities and that was just one step along the way. As children grow and change, their activities should reflect what they enjoy and feel competent doing. If they feel sports are a burden, they may choose to be sedentary, putting them at risk of becoming overweight.

Most kids are casual athletes

Some children will want to pursue excellence in a sport, while others may be perfectly happy—and fit—just being casual participants. Most kids fall into this latter category, but in a culture that is obsessed with winning, it's easy to overlook these kids as athletes. Yet they stand to gain no matter how well they perform. That's why it's important to encourage kids to remain active even though they aren't the top performers.

Participation in sports drops sharply between the ages of ten and 18. But why would a child who likes sports lose interest? The answer may be increasing pressure or time requirements (see more about children quitting sports on page 144). If your child is turning away from sports and physical activity, look for ways to make adjustments. Here are some examples:

- A child who loves gymnastics, but doesn't like competitions or the idea of long practices, could be switched to a noncompetitive class.
- If a kid who loves playing basketball is discouraged because he's not scoring as many points as his teammates, look for clinics he could attend and encourage him to keep practicing.
- If a child simply wants to try something new, like inline skating for example, make sure he or she has the right equipment (see page 65 for information about sports gear), the right instruction, if needed, and a safe place to practice. If the first time out is disappointing—and it probably will be—encourage him or her to keep trying.

Each child's fitness personality is different
The athlete will want to be on the basketball team, while the casual athlete may just enjoy shooting hoops in the playground or on the driveway. The nonathlete, on the other hand, is likely to need a parent's help and encouragement to get physically active.

The nonathlete

Some children are not natural athletes and they don't like participating in sports at all. They may shy away from activity because they're overweight and self-conscious about it, or it may be that they aren't as coordinated as their peers. Other kids might have a physical condition or health problem that slows them down.

By this age, children are aware of these differences, and some kids may have even been teased about them. This may push a child to drop out of a sport or physical activity—something that can hurt his or her confidence. The danger for a child like this is not leaving one activity that didn't work out; it's abandoning all physical activity altogether, and becoming a couch-potato kid.

If your child is not interested in physical activity or has quit a sport, try these strategies:

● Look for something new and different to pique your child's interest (see page 165 for some ideas).
● Limit the amount of time used for sedentary pastimes, such as watching television and playing video and computer games. Remember that reading is sedentary, too, so suggest your child takes regular breaks from the books to move around a bit.

Be helpful and sensitive

Almost all kids will be able to find something that they do well enough and feel good about, but the nonathlete may need a parent's help to find that special activity. Start with what you already know they like. If the competition of swim team proved too much, let the child continue enjoying the sport during free swim at the local pool, gym, or YMCA. Find out which activities interest them and what their friends are doing. Comb through course catalogues from your local YMCA or community recreation department, presenting your child with a menu of possibilities. If possible, sweeten the deal by arranging for the child to take the class with a friend. (For more activity ideas, see the list on page 142.)

Cultivate other interests

Every moment of your child's spare time doesn't have to be filled with aerobic exercise. The nonathlete will benefit from having other kinds of scheduled activities that engage his or her interests.

Think about the child's weekly schedule. Can an after-school club fill some unproductive time? For evenings and weekends, you might want to investigate course offerings at local museums, theatres, and cultural groups. In summer,

info

The child who wants to quit a sport

Quitting—and the thought of being a quitter—can stir emotions for parent and child. If a kid is unhappy in an organized sport or activity, the first thing to do is to talk it over. Remember that it can be okay to quit a sport as long as the child gets enough physical activity otherwise.

In dealing with this dilemma, parents should ask themselves these questions:
● Is my child well suited to this sport?
● Was my child as interested in this sport as I was?
● Does my child have enough unscheduled free time?
Common reasons for quitting include no longer enjoying the sport, feeling too much pressure, or not having enough time for the sport, plus school and other activities. Quitting may be reasonable if the child feels overscheduled.

After talking with your child, you may find there are steps you can take to improve the situation. You might talk with the coach about problems such as too little playing time. You also might help your child work on improving skills. If he or she wants to keep doing this sport, you might cut another activity out of the schedule to allow some free time during the week. If your child still isn't having fun, it might be time to quit this sport and move on to something new.

Also keep in mind that quitting a sport can be a sign of depression if your child seems sad much of the time and has lost interest in sports and other activities that they usually enjoy. There may be logical reasons why a child no longer enjoys a sport, but if you suspect depression, talk with your child's doctor.

Walking to school

If your child walks to school, ensure the journey is trouble-free. Here are some suggestions for making it safe.

- Teach your kids about pedestrian and bike safety.
- Identify the safest route to school.
- Encourage your child to walk or bike with other kids.
- Ask neighbours to keep an eye on kids walking to and from school.
- Make sure your school provides crossing guards at busy intersections.
- Use the "Walking School Bus" concept, where a designated adult "picks up and drops off" children at their homes (on foot), following a set route.

keep your child busy at a camp in your area that will cultivate his or her interests (see page 141 for more about summer camp). Organize family outings and vacations that reflect your child's hobbies. If he likes model trains, go to a local show. If she likes baseball, consider a trip to the Baseball Hall of Fame.

At home, continue to encourage "free play" as much as possible by having a variety of sports equipment and games on hand (see page 139 for a list of what to keep in your garage). If your child must be indoors, ping pong, foosball, and air hockey aren't going to burn off hundreds of calories, but they're a lot more active than dozing and snacking in front of the television.

The athlete

Some children are happily settled in a sport or activity by the older school-age years. They may have established bonds with coaches, good friendships with teammates, and a solid commitment to their chosen sport. In this situation, a parent can continue to support the child's efforts while watching for any changes. It's important to check that the child:

- is continuing to manage schoolwork;
- is getting enough rest;
- is still enjoying the sport.

Be there if your child wants help practicing at home, but think twice before you force it. Practicing with a parent can help some kids, but other children may be at risk of burnout if their parents push them too hard. Support your child's league or school by volunteering to clean up the fields, work in the concession stand, or participate in fund-raisers. Support your child by attending games and cheering them on unless they tell you they feel more relaxed when you aren't there. (Don't take it personally if they say this—many kids feel that way.) Either way, avoid making negative remarks about any player or either team, and definitely don't descend into squabbles over whose kid gets more playing time. Leave the coaching to the coach. And don't critique your child's performance.

Some parents can go overboard and put pressure on kids to specialize in one sport at this age, but this is not recommended. Instead, let your child try out new things and enjoy a variety of physical activities. Remember—you're trying to develop your child's lifetime love of exercise. Nothing but soccer may lead to burnout. It's also important that the child gets some down time to play other kinds of games and explore other avenues of interest, including those that have nothing to do with sports or exercise. (For more information about the needs of the child athlete, see page 182.)

"What's happening to my body?"

Puberty in school-age children

Most kids will begin to show the first signs of puberty during these years, at varying times. Early changes can cause embarrassment and fear, which may affect eating and exercise.

Creative parenting required

Growth and development will vary among kids, so your ten-year-old may be a lot bigger than his friends. Being bigger and taller can be an advantage in sports such as basketball or football, but a disadvantage in gymnastics or dance, which prize small bodies. That advantage also can fade away as other kids catch up—and maybe overtake—the early bloomer.

The first changes in puberty, like breast development and pubic hair growth, can make kids feel embarrassed about their bodies. They may be reluctant to participate in sports to avoid the locker room. A girl who is developing breasts may be self-conscious and need a bra to make her feel more at ease. Other kids may need the option of changing privately instead of in the open locker room. Keep the lines of communication open, but don't expect kids at this age to articulate all their needs. Help them through subtle intervention. Talk to their teachers and coaches, too.

While all kids go through puberty, their development occurs at such differing rates that it's easy for a child to feel odd because he's the first—or last—to begin developing. Parents need to explain these changes before they happen. Be sure children know that the changes are normal and that it would not be normal for them to get older without the changes taking place. While you're talking about their growing bodies, remind them that good nutrition and physical activity will help them grow up healthy and strong.

Some early signs of puberty

Entering puberty signals the beginning of a host of mental, emotional, and physical changes for a child, but it doesn't happen overnight. In addition to getting taller, here are some of the first changes that occur when a child starts to develop. Boys:

- enlargement of testicles and penis
- hair starts to grow in pubic area
- adult body odour
- skin becomes oilier and acne may begin.

Girls:

- breasts start to bud and grow
- hair starts to grow in pubic area
- adult body odour
- skin becomes oilier and acne may begin.

Gaining weight

It's normal to put on some body fat prior to puberty, and it's important to reassure children who think they're overweight but are not. However, the child who gains too much now is at risk of being an overweight adolescent. If you think your child might be gaining too much, visit the child's doctor to discuss the issue.

Body Mass Index (BMI) is a helpful tool for monitoring your child's weight. Because it is standardized for height, weight, and age, BMI generally should stay within the normal range while a child is growing. If BMI changes more rapidly than expected—from the 75th percentile to the 85th, for instance—it may be time to take action. Exactly which actions to take will vary from child to child.

Seek a doctor's input before putting your child on a diet, which is often inappropriate and unnecessary, and which can be harmful to a growing child. (See pages 18–19 for an explanation of BMI, and information about addressing a child's weight problem.)

Watch out for eating disorders

It's normal for children to gain 4–5kg or more a year during puberty, but some girls may look at the rising number on the scale and worry they are overweight. They may grow out of their clothes and no longer have the fashionably lean figure seen on magazine covers. A preoccupation with weight and appearance can lead to an eating disorder, such as anorexia nervosa (starving oneself) and bulimia (binge eating followed by self-induced vomiting).

Eating disorders are most common among teenagers, but younger girls who start puberty earlier, especially if they're a little overweight, are at risk as well. The early bloomers are bigger and more mature than their friends, which may make them feel fat. Girls who are uncomfortable with the idea of growing up may fear puberty and view the changes as things they don't want.

Watch for signs that your child is concerned about size and weight, and is taking steps such as dieting or exercising to excess. Note any changes, such as ruling out certain foods, skipping meals, refusing to eat with the family, or growing preoccupied with food labels. If you're concerned, discuss it with your child's doctor. You may be able to prevent an eating disorder if behaviours are recognized early and addressed. (For more about eating disorders, see page 163.)

Q: **My daughter is very overweight and wants to attend a weight-management camp. Should I send her?**

A: It's great that your daughter is motivated to make a change in her life. It could be a positive experience for her to attend a camp where she can meet other kids facing the same problem. If your daughter is overweight, she should have already seen her doctor to talk about the best steps to take in attaining a healthier weight. Ask your child's doctor how this kind of camp might fit into her overall weight-management program.

Carefully check out any camps that you're considering. The program should focus on encouraging healthy eating (not dieting), and on increasing activity levels. Kids may learn about proper nutrition, and about making better food choices, but they should also be focused on having a good time and enjoying the camping experience.

Avoid any camps that take a "boot camp" approach to weight loss, where strict discipline about eating and exercise are the rule. Remember that no camp can completely solve a child's weight problem. When she returns home, your daughter will need your help in living a healthier, more active lifestyle.

8 ADOLESCENTS

As they **progress toward adulthood**, teens can learn how to take good **care of themselves**. A teenager's home environment remains an important source of **structure and support** when it comes to **eating and exercise**.

age 13–18

"I like my brother" (sometimes)

Becoming mature

It's true that the teen years from 13 to 18 are ripe for conflict as it's a time of great change. But these years are also filled with pride and pleasure as you watch your children move toward adulthood.

Teenage challenges

Almost from the moment you bring a new baby home from the hospital, you'll start to hear those warnings about the teenage years:

"She's so adorable. Just wait until the boys start calling."

"Before you know it, he'll be asking for the car keys!"

Once your baby has grown up and is a teenager, you'll understand these comments all too well.

As a normal part of their passage into adulthood, teenagers will align themselves more with their friends and, at the same time, will seem to turn away from their parents. This is a normal stage that allows teenagers to create their own identities. This identity may start out as a carbon copy of their friends, but by the time the teenage years are over, most parents are—more often than not—pleased with the unique, finished product.

Rapid growth and big changes

Good nutrition and adequate physical activity are important as children enter adolescence, a period of rapid growth second only to the first year of life. By the start of the teen years, many girls already have experienced a major growth spurt and have started menstruating (see page 146 for more information about puberty). Most boys, who reach the peak of their growth spurt a year or two later than girls, are in the midst of big changes during these years. While teens' bodies are changing, the way they think about their bodies and themselves is changing, too. As they move through the teenage years, they'll begin feeling less self-conscious and more comfortable with how they look. Teenagers are better able to make this transition if they eat well and remain physically active.

Your teen's job is to become an independent person who can make good decisions and take care of himself or herself. You are the guide along the way. If your own approach to eating and exercise is healthy, it will increase the likelihood that your child will adopt and maintain the same smart habits.

Mom and dad are still role models

Though teenagers say and act otherwise, parents continue to wield strong influence as role models during the adolescent years. One survey found that 65 percent of 15-year-olds said they still wanted their parents' advice and guidance. Parental influence is particularly important when it comes to fitness and nutrition, because today an increasing number of teens are overweight.

Younger teens have a better chance of overcoming weight problems, but overweight teens are more likely to become overweight adults, and also suffer the associated health problems (see below and also pages 20–23 for more information about the medical consequences of being overweight). Even if your teenager resists some of your efforts, don't give up on good practices, such as stocking and serving healthy snacks, preparing family meals, and promoting regular exercise habits.

Make every effort to include your teenager in family activities and mealtimes, and always remember that they're still watching what you do. Your actions and the choices you make may leave a more lasting impression than a lot of long-winded advice or lectures.

It's a fine balance to determine when to give advice and when to let your teenager call the shots. The teen years are a time of transition, when a parent needs to relinquish some control—but gradually and within clearly defined limits. All the while, a parent needs to remain a constant and consistent presence in the child's life, because even as teenagers test their independence, they still need mom and dad.

info

Teens at risk for type 2 diabetes

A person with diabetes has elevated blood glucose levels due to a problem with insulin, a hormone produced in the pancreas. Insulin helps glucose (a simple sugar that comes from the food we eat) move out of the bloodstream and into the cells, which use it as fuel. In type 1 diabetes, the body no longer makes insulin. (For more about type 1 diabetes, see page 176.) In type 2 diabetes, insulin is still produced, but is less effective in handling blood sugar. Overweight often plays a role in the development of this condition, known as insulin resistance. Overweight, insulin resistance, and diabetes all increase the risk of teens developing heart disease, stroke, and kidney problems later in life.

Overweight teenagers
Once considered an adult disease, type 2 diabetes has increased dramatically among children. Now, about one in five children

diagnosed with diabetes have type 2. The dramatic increase is linked to an equally startling trend—the percentage of overweight children in Canada doubled between 1981 and 1996, and continues to rise. (For more about type 2 diabetes, see page 21.)

Screening for diabetes
As many as 80 percent of children who have type 2 diabetes are overweight at the time of diagnosis, which often occurs around puberty. Overweight children should be screened for diabetes, especially if there is a family history of type 2 diabetes, the child has high blood pressure (a risk factor for heart disease), or the child has a skin condition called acanthosis nigricans. This condition—dark, velvety skin in the folds and creases of the body— is often associated with insulin resistance. Screening is important because a child with type 2 diabetes may not have any obvious symptoms.

"delicious"

Nutrition for teenagers

Adolescence is a period of rapid growth that must be fueled by additional calories. But not just any calories will do. Teens need foods that will build strong bones and healthy bodies for a lifetime.

The hard sell won't work

You know about good nutrition and what your child needs, but you can't force it on a teenager. However, while your teen may resist your efforts to promote healthy eating, remember that you're still in control of which foods you serve and make available at home.

Keep promoting good habits by eating well yourself and by serving family meals. Children who have regular meals with their family eat healthier and even make more nutritious choices when they're away from home. Try to make arrangements so your teenager can be there at mealtimes. Providing structure like this can help your teen stay grounded while so much else in his or her life is in flux.

Freedom of choice

While you're providing that overarching structure, it's also a time to be flexible and to give your teenager some freedom to make choices about food. Here are some good ways to involve your child:

● Your teen's likes and dislikes may have changed over the years, so invite him or her to go shopping with you or make a list of foods for the dinner menu.

● Have your teen help you prepare dinner once a week or take responsibility for certain tasks, such as making salad, on a regular basis. Your teen will learn about making healthy food choices, and at the same time he or she will acquire some basic cooking skills and gain an

Daily nutrition needs

On average, teenage girls need fewer calories than teenage boys. An active teen (of either sex) will eat more, while a sedentary teen will need less. As teenagers mature, their nutritional requirements become more similar to the recommended daily allowances for adults.

DIETARY COMPONENT	TEENAGE GIRLS	TEENAGE BOYS
Carbohydrate	300g	400g
Protein	45–55g	45–65g
Fat	60–75g	75–95g
Fibre	18–23g	18–23g
Total daily energy	**2,200 calories**	**2,500–3,000 calories**

appreciation for what it takes to make a home-cooked meal. As a bonus, you'll get a little extra time together to catch up with each other.

- Occasionally, let your teen take the lead by selecting the menu for a family dinner or even preparing the meal—with you as the assistant.
- Suggest that your teen invite over a few friends to enjoy a special meal together. They can plan the menu and prepare it themselves. How about a pasta party? Here's a menu that's easy and fun: garden salad, garlic bread, fresh tomato sauce with basil (see recipe on page 198) spooned over fun-shaped pasta, and Italian ice or gelato with fresh berries.

Why teens need breakfast

While teenagers are in charge of choosing what to eat, they still should eat three meals a day. Yet many teens don't do this, and may start the day on an empty stomach. Without a good nutritious breakfast, teenagers:

- are less able to learn;
- actually eat more calories during the rest of the day;
- are twice as likely to have diets low in iron;
- may have a higher body mass index (BMI).

On the other hand, teens who eat breakfast regularly:

- tend to eat a healthier diet overall;
- do better in school and are more attentive;
- are more likely to participate in physical activities.

Ideally, your child would have time in the morning to sit down for a complete breakfast before dashing off to school. But many teens start school at a painfully early hour of the day. So, when there's no time for breakfast, do the next best thing by offering a variety of ready-to-eat breakfast foods.

Cereal is a quick meal and can even be eaten dry. Buy single-serving cereal boxes or make your own single servings, using bags or containers. Choose higher-fibre cereals or hot cereals that aren't loaded with sugar. Try pre-packaging your own mix of nuts, dried fruits, and pretzels or crackers that your teen can grab on the run. Fresh fruit and yogourt are also good choices. Any breakfast is better than no breakfast, but you should limit fat, so don't let your child get into the toaster pastries or doughnuts habit. (See below for more fast breakfasts.)

The vending machine looms

If kids eat a healthy, sustaining breakfast, they are less likely to resort to eating at a school snack bar or at a vending machine—at least in the morning hours. These easily accessible snacks and drinks are available in schools across the country. In fact, 98 percent of high schools have a snack bar or vending machines. They appeal to teens for obvious reasons: They're convenient and inexpensive. But the foods typically offered don't provide much in the way of nutrition. The most commonly available products are higher-fat salty snacks, candy, higher-fat bakery items, and sweet drinks, such as pop and sports drinks. Fewer than a quarter of high school vending machines or snack bars offer 1 percent or skim milk, low-fat or nonfat yogourt, or fruit and vegetables.

Schools like selling these foods and drinks because it translates into dollars. Some proceeds may go to support school groups. But some schools also sell contracts to corporations who then have the rights to sell soft drinks at the school (which gives the school revenue). In recent years, lawmakers and nutrition advocates have been critical of these arrangements and of the overabundance of unhealthy foods in schools. While some changes are underway, it's likely your child still has easy access to these low-nutrient foods.

The solution is not an easy one because you can't follow your teenager around and police what he or she eats. But just as you've been doing right along, you can be sure that your child gets healthy, satisfying food at home. You can also encourage your children to pack their own snacks to get them through the busy school day.

tips

Quick breakfast ideas

If your teen doesn't care for typical breakfast fare, be creative by offering a favourite sandwich, a fresh fruit smoothie (see page 201 for some delicious smoothie recipes), or even leftovers. Here are some quick breakfast fixes to tempt your teen.

- **Fruit and cream cheese sandwich** Layer cream cheese and fresh fruit, such as sliced strawberries, on bread or a bagel.
- **Fruit and nut oatmeal** Add dried fruit or nuts to instant oatmeal.
- **Banana dog** Spread peanut butter in a whole-grain bun, plop in a banana, and sprinkle with raisins.
- **Breakfast taco** Sprinkle shredded Monterey Jack cheese over a corn tortilla, fold in half, and microwave for about 20 seconds; serve topped with a spoonful of tomato salsa.
- **Waffle sandwich** Spread peanut butter and jelly on a toasted whole-grain waffle.
- **Country cottage cheese** Mix apple butter with cottage cheese.

info

Why teens should eat family meals

What counts as a family meal? It's any time you and your family eat together—whether it's takeout food or a home-cooked meal with all the trimmings. Family meals are a comforting ritual for both parents and teens. Teens know they will be fed and that their parents will be on hand. Parents enjoy seeing their kids on this predictable schedule, giving everyone a chance to catch up.

Teens who take part in regular family meals are:

- more likely to eat fruits, vegetables, and grains;
- less likely to snack on unhealthy foods;

- less likely to smoke, drink alcohol, or use marijuana or other drugs.

Strive for nutritious food and a time when everyone can be there. This may mean eating dinner a little later if your teen is at, say, sports practice.

Some teens may turn up their noses at the idea of a family meal—which isn't surprising considering that they're trying to establish independence at this age. It may be a challenge to get your teenager interested—or home in time. If so, try letting your teen invite a friend to dinner, or prepare your child's favourite dishes. Above all, keep mealtimes calm and congenial—no lectures or arguing.

Temptations other than food

When parents teach children to eat well, hopefully they will pick up the broader message that their bodies need good care. This point is important because the teen years are a time when it's common for kids to try smoking, drinking, and other risky behaviours. Some parents will throw up their hands, believing there's nothing they can do about it. But this simply isn't true. With smoking and other dangerous habits, it's best to educate your child early on, so the risks are clearly understood.

No smoking or drinking

Your teen probably already knows that smoking can lead to serious illnesses, like lung cancer and heart disease. Your teen also probably knows that alcoholics often end up getting ill because of their heavy use of alcohol over the years. The trouble is that these health risks seem far off and not all that threatening to teenagers, many of whom feel invincible. You may remember this feeling from your teens.

Beating the drum about long-term effects may be less effective than highlighting immediate effects. For drinking, there's the risk of arrest for possessing it, using fake ID to obtain it, or driving while under the influence of it. A teen who smokes may have difficulty recovering from colds or other respiratory infections, decreased cardiovascular fitness for sports, and—perhaps worst of all—bad breath.

Be proactive by teaching your teen that part of a healthy lifestyle means avoiding tobacco products and alcohol. Share facts about substance use, but don't overdo the scare tactics. Most important of all, encourage open communication with your teen. Your child may not feel comfortable talking to you about everything, but if you are loving and welcoming, you may be surprised at how much your teen may share.

Q: **My daughter and her friends say they smoke to stay thin. How can I get her to stop?**

A: Your best approach is to get your daughter to understand that using cigarettes as a method of weight control now could be the start of a lifelong addiction. Encourage her to stop as soon as possible. If she does need to watch her weight, help her do it through healthier means, such as eating well and regular exercise. The best way to quit smoking is to gradually cut down the number of daily cigarettes. Quitting might be easier if she has a "buddy." Maybe your daughter can encourage her friends to join her and they can kick the butts together. And if by chance you are a smoker, it's very important that you set a good example and kick the habit at the same time.

Helping 13- to 15-year-olds eat well

The early teenage years may be hungry ones for your child, especially during the periods of fast growth associated with puberty. To build strong and healthy bodies, growing teens need nutritious food, especially food that is rich in calcium and iron.

The effects of puberty

Before puberty, girls and boys have similar nutritional needs, but adolescence changes that for several reasons. The average girl hits her peak growth spurt at about 12, while the average boy doesn't reach that point until about 14.

Most girls in their early teens have had their first menstrual period, after which growth slows over the next year or two as they approach adult height. As girls are slowing down, the average boy is revving up. During puberty, boys will need more calories than girls as they grow taller and more muscular, thanks to male hormones. Because each child will start puberty at a different time, energy requirements will vary widely among boys and girls of the same age. As teens get older, their nutritional needs start to resemble those of adults.

Differences for boys and girls

Just as daily energy requirements differ for boys and girls during these years, so does the need for certain nutrients. Both boys and girls need iron, but menstruating girls—especially those who are very active—will need more, to prevent iron deficiency and anemia. Boys and girls need calcium, but it is especially important for girls because they have a higher risk of developing osteoporosis later in life.

One-day menu planner **for kids 13–15**

DAILY CALORIES
This plan will provide 2,256 calories.

Milk products perform double duty in this menu. Milk, cheese, and yogourt are good sources of protein, with the added benefit of providing calcium. One thing dairy foods do not provide is iron, so look for alternative sources of iron, including iron-fortified cereals, dried beans, and nuts.

breakfast
- 2 cups (70g) raisin bran flakes or other iron-fortified cereal
- 1 cup (250mL) milk
- 3/4 cup (185mL) orange juice

FOOD GROUP	SERVINGS
grain products	2
milk products	1
meat and alternatives	0
vegetables and fruit	1

lunch
- 1 slice pizza
- 1 cup (60g) salad
- 2 tbsp low-fat dressing
- 1 cup (250mL) milk
- 1 low-fat granola bar

FOOD GROUP	SERVINGS
grain products	2
milk products	2
meat and alternatives	0
vegetables and fruit	1

snack
- 1/2 cup (85g) fresh fruit
- 1 cup (250mL) low-fat yogourt, plain or flavoured
- 1/2 cup (35g) almonds

FOOD GROUP	SERVINGS
grain products	0
milk products	1
meat and alternatives	1
vegetables and fruit	1

dinner
- 1 cup (200g) steamed brown rice
- 1/2 cup (125mL) broiled chicken
- 1 cup (75g) steamed broccoli
- 1/2 cup (75g) fresh pineapple

FOOD GROUP	SERVINGS
grain products	2
milk products	0
meat and alternatives	2
vegetables and fruit	3

snack
- 80g tortilla chips
- 1/2 cup (125mL) black bean salsa

FOOD GROUP	SERVINGS
grain products	1
milk products	0
meat and alternatives	0
vegetables and fruit	1

tips

Boosting iron intake

Here's how to ensure your teen is getting enough iron in his or her diet.

- Use foods high in iron (meat, poultry, fish, enriched grains, beans, tofu) in family meals, and be sure you have iron-rich or iron-fortified foods for snacking.
- To improve the body's absorption of iron, serve iron-rich foods alongside foods containing vitamin C, such as tomatoes, oranges, fruit juice, or strawberries.
- Avoid serving coffee or tea at mealtime. Both contain tannins that reduce iron absorption. Milk can also interfere with iron absorption; if getting enough iron is a problem, avoid drinking milk when eating iron-rich foods.

Building healthy bones

During childhood and adolescence, the body uses calcium to build strong bones—a process that is all but complete by the end of the teen years. Through the natural process of aging, bones then become less dense. For some older adults, bone loss is so great that bones weaken and break more easily, a condition known as osteoporosis.

When children get enough calcium and physical activity during the teen years, they can start out their adult lives with the strongest bones possible. But more than 85 percent of girls and 60 percent of boys fail to get the recommended 1,300mg of calcium per day. That's not surprising when you consider that teens now drink more pop than milk, which is one of the best sources of calcium. Teens who smoke, or who drink cola, caffeinated beverages, or alcohol may get even less calcium because those substances interfere with the way the body absorbs and uses calcium.

Teen girls may shy away from dairy foods, a rich source of calcium, because they believe milk and cheese are fattening. But a 250-mL glass of skim milk has only 80 calories and no fat, and it supplies one-quarter of the daily calcium requirement. In fact, people who eat diets rich in calcium weigh less and have less body fat. In one study,

adolescent girls who had an extra 300mg of calcium each day, which is equivalent to one glass of milk, weighed up to 900g less than girls who didn't get the extra calcium.

If, despite your best efforts, your teenage daughter adamantly refuses to eat milk products, then she should eat calcium-fortified foods and may need a calcium supplement. You also might want to talk with your child's doctor or a nutritionist. (For more information on calcium, see page 38. Find a list of calcium-rich alternatives to milk on page 132.)

Preventing iron deficiency

Both boys and girls need iron for a lot of body functions. When supplies of iron are low and iron stores become depleted, the body can't make enough of the red blood cells that transport oxygen to all the cells in the body. This is called iron-deficiency anemia. Teen girls need more dietary iron than boys because of blood lost during menstruation.

- Teen boys should get at least 12mg of iron a day.
- Teen girls need at least 15mg of iron a day.
- Athletes need more because iron is lost through sweat, and the gastrointestinal tract in some sports. Iron deficiency can develop so gradually that you and your child may not notice symptoms such as fatigue and weakness.

info

Different types of vegetarians

Many people who call themselves vegetarians are actually semivegetarians. They may have eliminated red meat, but still may eat poultry or fish. Even for those who have opted for a meat-free diet, there are different vegetarian regimens:
- **Lacto-ovo-vegetarian:** eats milk and egg products.
- **Lacto-vegetarian:** eats milk products; no eggs.
- **Ovo-vegetarian:** eats eggs; no milk products.
- **Vegan:** eats only food from plant sources; no eggs, milk products, or honey.

Be wary if your teen has self-imposed a very restrictive diet, because being a vegetarian should not be used as an excuse to drastically reduce calories or cut out all fat. A teen with an eating disorder may adopt a very restrictive diet and call it "vegetarianism" because it's considered socially acceptable and healthy. (For more information on eating disorders, see page 163.)

Going vegetarian

Teens often voice their independence through the foods they choose to eat. One strong statement is the decision to stop eating meat. This is common among teens, who may decide to embrace vegetarianism in support of animal rights, for health reasons, or because friends are doing it.

Avoiding meat may sound like a bad idea, but a well-planned vegetarian diet can be a very healthy way to eat, even for teens. Vegetarians often eat more of the foods that most teens don't get enough of—vegetables and fruit. And a diet rich in fruits and vegetables will be high in fibre and low in fat, factors known to improve cardiovascular health by reducing blood cholesterol and maintaining a healthy weight. To support your child, the whole family might try to eat vegetarian at least one night a week.

Meeting nutrient requirements

The less restrictive the vegetarian diet, the easier it will be for your child to get appropriate protein and enough of important nutrients. A vegetarian diet that includes milk products and eggs (lacto-ovo) is the best choice for growing

teens. A more strict vegetarian diet may fail to meet a teen's need for certain nutrients, such as iron, protein, zinc, calcium, and vitamins D and B_{12}. Calcium is a particular concern for any vegetarian who has eliminated milk products. It's important for teens to understand which nutrients might be missing in their vegetarian diet, so they can replace them. Failure to do so can lead to nutritional deficiencies.

Depending on the type of vegetarian diet chosen (see above), a teen can miss out on important nutrients. Here's a list of those they might be lacking and good food sources:
- protein: milk products, eggs, tofu, dried beans, and nuts
- vitamin B_{12}: milk products, eggs, yeast products, and fortified soy beverages
- vitamin D: milk products, fortified orange juice, and vitamin-fortified products
- calcium: milk products, dark green leafy vegetables, broccoli, chick peas, and calcium-fortified products, including orange juice, and soy and rice drinks
- iron*: dried beans, whole grains, brown rice, leafy green vegetables, and iron-fortified cereals and bread
- zinc: wheat germ, nuts, and legumes.

(*These foods contain iron, but are not as iron-rich as meat.)

The principles of planning a vegetarian diet are the same as planning any healthy diet—provide a variety of foods and include foods from all the food groups. A balanced diet will provide the right combinations to meet nutritional needs.

Variety and balance
Fresh fruit is an important part of a healthy diet, but restrictive diets that allow only raw foods or are limited to fruits or juices, should be avoided.

Keeping 16- to 18-year-olds eating healthily

For most older teenagers, dramatic growth has ended and they are settling into their new bodies. While taking on new responsibilities, it's easy to overlook an important one: taking care of themselves with a healthy diet and lots of physical activity.

Guidelines for parents and teens

Older teens might now be driving cars and working part-time jobs. They also may be learning to wash clothes and manage money. Among all these new responsibilities is one that is very important but often forgotten: how to eat well—even when mom and dad aren't around. Seven out of ten teens are making their own dinners, but are they preparing healthy meals that meet their nutritional needs? This question takes on added importance if your older teen is getting ready to leave the nest. Will the temptations of campus life prove too strong to resist?

A varied and balanced diet

You know what your teen needs, but how do you translate this information into guidelines your teen can easily follow? He or she won't want to count up grams of this and

percentages of that. A simple approach is to share with your teen the general principles of a balanced diet and the importance of eating a variety of foods.

The good news is that, by the late teen years, most kids are taking an interest in their own health. A parent can help by providing reliable sources of nutrition and health information, and encouraging a visit to the doctor to discuss any possible concerns. (See page 202 for a list of useful websites for nutrition and fitness information.)

Parental influence

Older teens need to understand nutrition and how to eat well because they spend more time outside the home. With their own money, and keys to the car, many teens have the funds and the freedom to eat as they choose. For some, this choice may be a huge soft drink and a bag of chips for lunch. However, you still can have influence by following these guidelines:

- Make family meals a priority.
- Be a role model by eating well yourself.
- Keep the house stocked with healthy foods.
- Teach teenagers how to make healthy meals and snacks on their own.
- Be aware of your teen's schedule.
- Without nagging, ask if they've eaten during the day and what they have had.

Beyond this, it has to be left up to the teenager. Though it can be difficult for a parent to accept, it is now largely the teen's responsibility to decide what and what not to eat. Hopefully the years of practising good habits have made an impact so your child will be ready when really put to the test: living away from home for the first time. (See opposite for tips on helping your child adjust to college.)

What's in the fridge, mom?
Older teens often fix snacks and meals for themselves, so be sure there are always plenty of nutritious and tempting foods available.

DAILY CALORIES
This plan will provide 2,717 calories.

One-day menu planner **for kids 16–18**

This menu is well suited for teen boys, who generally need more calories than teen girls. Cut back on serving sizes or lighten up the snacks for girls, to adjust down calories, but try to keep the balance and the right number of servings of all the food groups. For very active teens, especially boys, add a morning snack and look for other sources of meat and alternatives, rather than just piling on more pasta, rice, potatoes, and bread.

breakfast
- ½ deli-sized bagel
- 2 eggs, scrambled
- ½ cup (75g) strawberries
- 1 cup (250mL) 1% or 2% milk

FOOD GROUP	SERVINGS
grain products	2
milk products	1
meat and alternatives	2
vegetables and fruit	1

lunch
- 85g turkey on wheat bread with 1 tsp mayonnaise
- 1 cup (115g) raw veggies with 2 tbsp low-fat ranch dressing
- 30g pretzel thins
- 1 apple
- ¾ cup (185mL) fruit juice

FOOD GROUP	SERVINGS
grain products	3
milk products	0
meat and alternatives	1
vegetables and fruit	3

snack
- 2 whole-grain waffles with 1 tbsp peanut butter
- 1 cup (100g) grapes
- 1 cup (250mL) 1% or 2% milk

FOOD GROUP	SERVINGS
grain products	2
milk products	1
meat and alternatives	1
vegetables and fruit	2

dinner
- 1½ cups (200g) pasta with fresh tomato sauce (see recipe page 198)
- 115g chicken breast
- 2 cups (120g) salad
- 2 tbsp low-fat dressing
- 1 cup (250mL) 1% or 2% milk

FOOD GROUP	SERVINGS
grain products	3
milk products	1
meat and alternatives	2
vegetables and fruit	4

snack
- 1 piece (140g) apple crisp
- ½ cup (65g) low-fat frozen dessert

FOOD GROUP	SERVINGS
grain products	0
milk products	0
meat and alternatives	0
vegetables and fruit	1

info

Going to college

Even if your child was motivated to eat well and exercise at home, campus life can change all that. Unlimited cafeteria food, busy schedules, fast food convenience, and parties can add extra weight. The college years are prime time for older teens to gain weight and adopt unhealthy habits such as smoking.

Parents can't prevent teens from indulging in newfound freedoms, but they can offer some advice to their college-bound children. Explain that a lot of people gain weight when they go to college, but that it's possible to maintain healthy habits, even amid all the pressures and temptations. Here are some tips you can give your teen.

- Be smart about cafeteria eating by assessing all the options before choosing. Put together a balanced meal from the available choices.
- Be aware of portion sizes—it's easy to have seconds at a cafeteria.
- Don't study and eat at the same time.
- Stock the dorm room with healthy snacks, such as carrots, apples, microwave popcorn, and pretzels.
- Take advantage of campus exercise facilities—fitness equipment, swimming pools, and tracks.
- Take the stairs, ride a bike, inline skate to class, walk or jog around campus—whatever way they choose, encourage them to be active while at college.

tips

Fast food orders

If your teen is interested, offer these suggestions for eating lighter meals at fast food restaurants.

- Don't order "supersize" items.
- Order water, skim milk, or diet soda rather than regular soda.
- Hold the mayonnaise and choose lower-fat condiments.
- Avoid extras, such as bacon, sour cream, and more cheese.
- Check out the nutritional information for the items you're considering, so you can make an informed choice.
- Get a grilled chicken sandwich or a veggie burger instead of a burger or fried sandwich.
- Try side dishes other than fries, such as salad, fruit, baked beans, corn on the cob, or noncream soups.

Teens love fast food and snacks

Teenagers eat outside the home much more than they did 30 years ago and fast food is often the choice. Fast food restaurants may be hard for your teen to avoid because they often serve as hangouts. Some teens eat fast food because they need something quick for dinner as they rush between school and work. Others may like it because it's tasty and cheap. But it's not low in calories or fat. A large burger meal with fries and a soft drink may contain more than 90 percent of the total daily recommended amount of fat and more than 70 percent of the day's energy requirement.

Teens who have fast food three or more times a week consume more calories and fat than peers who eat fast food less often. Eating fast food frequently also makes teens likely to drink less milk and eat fewer fruits, vegetables, and whole grains. Though you won't be able to ban fast food, you may be able to help your teenager cut back.

Healthier alternatives

If you ask your teen to cut back on fast food, be sure to provide alternatives. If your child needs to eat on the run, suggest other restaurants that offer quick service and more

nutritious food. Stopping at a deli for a turkey sandwich is usually a good alternative to a supersized cheeseburger. Even a slice of pizza and a salad beats the typical burger meal, especially if your child skips the soft drink or chooses water, low-fat milk, or a diet pop. If a fast food restaurant is the only option, suggest ways to "lighten" their choices (see above). Another alternative is to pack a lunch or dinner to go. Keep healthy foods on hand at home, especially the ones your teens like, so he or she can put together a satisfying brown-bag meal.

Your child may be less likely to go looking for fast food if family meals are part of the routine. Family meals tend to be more nutritious, but the positive effects of sitting down together for dinner go beyond healthy eating. (For more about family meals, see page 155.)

The teenage girl who diets

More than half of teenage girls say they are dieting to lose weight or to avoid gaining weight. For a teenager who is overweight, this can be a positive step, as long as it's done with a doctor's supervision and in a healthy manner. However, teens may try fad diets and appetite suppressants, and may exercise excessively. In a recent North American survey, nearly 20 percent of girls said they had gone 24 hours or more without eating in an effort to lose weight. These methods usually don't work over the long term and they can be harmful, especially to a growing teen.

Girls who don't have weight problems may be dieting in pursuit of unrealistic weight goals. If your daughter is concerned about her weight, offer to set up a doctor's appointment. The doctor will check her height and weight and can calculate her BMI, to find out if there really is a problem. (For information about BMI, see page 18.) If your daughter is overweight, the doctor can suggest steps to take, which could include a visit with a dietitian. If her weight is fine, the doctor can reassure her that she doesn't need to diet to lose weight, and can reinforce the importance of healthy eating and regular exercise.

So many teenage girls choose to diet that it's worth opening a discussion about it with your daughter, even if you haven't noticed anything unusual. Talk about whether she has tried to lose weight and try to get a sense of how she feels about her body. What she says may surprise you. One survey found that 36 percent of girls thought they were overweight. Even if your daughter is comfortable with her weight, you may hear about her friend who isn't.

Going to extremes

About five to ten percent of teenage girls exhibit some of the behaviours associated with anorexia nervosa (starving) or bulimia nervosa (bingeing and purging). A smaller percentage meet the stricter criteria for diagnosis of these eating disorders. Both disorders can be very harmful to a girl's health and can even be life-threatening.

A girl who has anorexia refuses to maintain an acceptable weight, has an intense fear of gaining weight or becoming fat, and has a distorted body image. She may refuse to eat with the family or join in other social activities. Bulimia is marked by recurrent episodes of binge eating followed by an attempt to make up for the overeating by purging, which may include vomiting and using laxatives.

Restricting calories during puberty can affect growth and delay the onset of menstruation. Significant weight loss after menstrual cycles have become established can result in irregular or absent periods. Get medical attention if you suspect your daughter may have symptoms of anorexia or bulimia (see below for a list of early signs). Treatment should involve a team of professionals to address the complex medical, nutritional, and psychological needs of a teen with an eating disorder. Many teens with anorexia or bulimia may be dealing with depression or anxiety.

Signs of eating disorders

If your teen has an eating disorder, the best approach is to get help early. With anorexia nervosa, watch for a teen who:
- loses significant weight over a short period of time;
- seems to eat very little, cuts food into small pieces, or plays with food;
- wears loose-fitting clothes to hide weight loss;
- exercises compulsively;
- stops having menstrual periods.

Bulimia can be more difficult to spot, because the teen will not lose a dramatic amount of weight. With this disorder, watch for a teen who:
- shows a pattern of weight bouncing up and down (4–5kg up, 4–5kg down);
- spends a lot of time in the bathroom, especially after mealtimes;
- eats a lot without gaining significant weight;
- exercises excessively to make up for overeating;
- has irregular or absent menstrual periods;
- has damaged tooth enamel from self-induced vomiting.

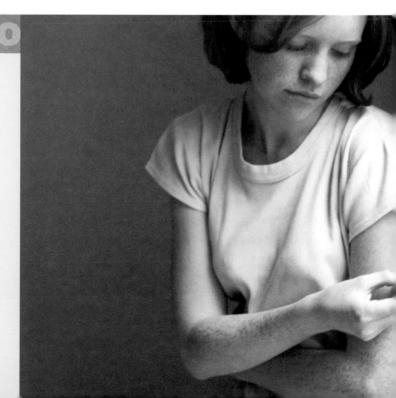

"I love hanging around"

Fitness for teenagers

It's a challenge to encourage physical activity in a technology-loving teen, who has a cell phone in one hand and a computer mouse in the other. But being active is very important during these years.

Wired teens

Hey parNts—RU sure yor teen gitz Enuf exercise? It's tough to answer this, when teens are spending 17 hours a week online—many of them text messaging friends in what looks like a foreign language. And while kids are using the Internet, they are simultaneously eating, watching TV, and talking on the phone. If they get tired of that, they might take a break and play a computer game.

None of these pastimes requires much physical activity, yet teens need to move their bodies just as they did when they were younger. In addition to the health benefits of exercise, they need time to be "unwired," so they don't get in the inactive rut that many adults fall into. For younger kids,

exercise often happens naturally at recess, by playing a team sport, or by riding their bikes around the neighbourhood. But by the teen years, physical activity must be planned and often has to be sandwiched between various responsibilities and commitments.

How much exercise is enough?

The activity recommendations shift for teenagers, recognizing that they are moving toward adulthood and are no longer playing tag in the backyard. Teens are encouraged to be active every day and to get at least three 20-minute sessions a week of more vigorous exercise. A teen can meet this recommendation by playing basketball, running, swimming, or doing aerobics—or doing any other activity that gets the heart beating faster, quickens the breathing, and causes the body to sweat.

To be active every day, teens can do traditional exercises as well as everyday activities that get their bodies moving. During the week, a teen might go to swim practice, take a long bike ride, and choose to walk to a friend's house, instead of going by car. Even activities that no one thinks of as exercise—such as taking the stairs, mowing the lawn, or mopping the floor—can contribute to a more active lifestyle. In short, encourage your child to make a commitment to being active whenever possible.

Experts recommend that adults be physically active for 30 to 60 minutes a day, so teens can keep that in mind as a goal. But it's even better if they can exceed it. Talk about these targets and let your teen decide how to achieve them. Keep your expectations reasonable, understanding that your child may have responsibilities, such as studying, that can't be eliminated from the schedule. But also encourage your child to take breaks during periods of inactivity—and to use free time in active ways.

Cool stuff to do

From the sedate to the wild, there's bound to be a sport or activity to suit every teenager's taste. Maybe your child doesn't like traditional sports—or is getting bored with the same old exercise program. If so, try suggesting some of these cool alternatives to your teen:

- paint ball
- laser tag
- dance (salsa, hip-hop, country, ballroom)
- water sports (swimming, diving, sailing, wakeboarding, waterskiing, canoeing, kayaking, rafting)
- fencing
- horseback riding
- rock climbing (indoor and outdoor)
- snowboarding
- skateboarding
- inline skating
- outdoor sports (hiking, mountain biking)
- fitness classes (Pilates, kickboxing, yoga)
- footbag
- flying disk.

What is geocaching?

If your teen is up for a high-tech treasure hunt, consider geocaching. This adventure sport, which is only a few years old, relies on global positioning system equipment to find "caches," which geocachers have placed in more than 100 countries. Getting to these caches can involve quite a hike, so you and your teen will get a lot of exercise along the way. Adult supervision is recommended, so teens don't get lost.

You never know what you'll find in a cache (CDs, a disposable camera, and small toys, for example), but they all include a log book, so you can leave a record of your success. To practice proper cache etiquette, the finder may take something from the cache and should leave something for the next hunter. (For more information about how it's done, see page 202 for the website address.)

Motivating 13- to 15-year-olds to be active

By the time they reach high school, only 35 percent of teenagers get regular, vigorous exercise. To encourage your teen to be active, talk about the benefits of getting regular exercise and the best way to make it happen.

Getting your teen off the couch

What you say: "It's such a beautiful day, why don't you go get some exercise?" What your teenager thinks: "You're always telling me what to do." Whether your child complies with your suggestion or stays put on the couch, this approach will fall short because it doesn't acknowledge what a teen wants: to be seen as an individual who can make independent choices.

One way to give your child some much-desired control is to let him or her decide how to be physically active. Before you ask your child for a list of exercise ideas, consider what will be practical, feasible, and affordable for your family. For example, if horseback riding is out, let your teen know up front, so you don't have an argument later. The possibilities for physical activity are vast enough that every kid should be able to find something that sounds interesting and fun. (For a list of possible activities, see page 165.)

Don't be surprised if your child is most interested in the activities that friends are doing. Peers carry a lot of weight right now, so seize the opportunity to hook a child on physical activity this way. Keep the group mentality in mind because it's likely to be an effective incentive. One good

Television hypnosis
Teenagers are spending more and more time in front of the "boob tube" and computer. They often snack during these sedentary activities.

A sample fitness contract

Some teens may be receptive to this kind of agreement, where the expectations and responsibilities of both child and parent are clearly outlined.

Teen portion

I agree to exercise three times a week for at least 30 minutes. I also agree to limit the amount of time I spend doing things that aren't active. They include:

- watching TV, a video, or DVD
- using the computer for fun
- playing video games

I will engage in these activities for a maximum of one hour on school days and a maximum of four hours over the weekend: no more than nine hours total per week. I can "bank" unused time for use later at a mutually agreeable time.

Signed,

_____
(Teen)

Parent portion

In return, I will support my teen's efforts to exercise three times a week. When needed, I will provide transportation to the swimming pool, park, or other recreational facility for my child and up to two friends. For agreed-upon activities, I'll provide the necessary equipment (clothes, shoes, protective gear). To manage TV time, I'll provide a TV schedule to help my child decide how to "spend" TV time. I'll also agree to pay for the rental of approved videos or DVDs.

Signed,

_____
(Mom or Dad)

---

idea is to suggest that your teen organize a group of friends to take a class or try a supervised adventurous activity, such as white water rafting, paint ball, or laser tag.

Young teenagers love a chance to show their age and take on the responsibilities that go along with being older and wiser. Look for opportunities that will help boost your child's confidence and self-esteem. Consider letting your teenager work as a junior camp counselor, mother's helper, or assistant coach of a younger sibling's sports team. As a bonus, part-time jobs like these are active, which means that your teen may get some exercise without even realizing it.

In addition to promoting regular exercise, parents need to limit the amount of time teenagers spend watching TV or playing video or computer games.

A parent-child fitness contract

If you and your teen squabble about exercise, it can help to negotiate a contract. A contract sends two key messages: that you are serious about physical activity and that you see your child's input as critical. Be clear that the contract isn't intended as a punishment, but that it will allow both parties to clearly state their expectations and their responsibilities.

A contract should include the stated goal, as well as the responsibilities of both the teen and parent. Here's a step-by-step approach:

- Parent and child separately create a list of goals.
- Work together to negotiate mutually acceptable goals and expectations.
- Create a contract based on the agreed-upon goals. Try to be as specific as possible and take small steps toward progress. (See above for a sample contract.)
- Post the contract in a prominent spot, such as on the refrigerator door.

You also might want to include your own commitment to exercise as part of the contract—it will be far more effective as an incentive if you are setting an example. If you don't, your teen will be more than happy to point out the contradictions in your behaviour.

As with any contract, the parent and teen should be flexible and willing to renegotiate as circumstances change. Remember, the goal isn't the contract itself. It's the positive changes in your teen's habits. At some point, you might even agree that the contract is no longer needed because your child has adopted a healthier lifestyle.

Helping 16- to 18-year-olds keep fit

As teenagers get older, their responsibilities increase and their free time decreases. And, like their parents, they may have little time to exercise. Parents have to take a back seat now, and let their teens work at fitting activity into their schedules.

Busy lifestyles

Many teens are juggling part-time jobs, relationships, academics, and extracurricular activities. Meanwhile, they're thinking about the future, and some may be filling out college applications. Their busy schedules rival that of their parents. The time crunch may lead some teens to drop out of organized sports, if they haven't already. For sedentary teens, the increasing responsibilities may become a reason not to be active.

If you have been preaching about the importance of fitness all along, you may be pleased to discover your kids seem to have gotten the message. In fact, older teens may be more receptive to what you have to say about fitness and exercise—without any nagging from you, some may even take the initiative to go for a run, have a swim, or join an exercise class. Though teens may not be swayed by warnings about their future cardiovascular health, they may be inspired by the immediate benefits of exercise, such as increased energy, a feeling of well-being, reduced stress, and a firmer, fitter body.

As your teen works to fit exercise into a busy schedule, parents can still help in these ways:

- Continue to have an active lifestyle yourself.
- Plan active outings as a family.
- Fit exercise into your own schedule.
- Encourage your teen to pursue lifetime sports, such as swimming, tennis, or cycling.
- As with younger kids, discourage watching TV or playing computer games.

A parent also can help by buying equipment or a gym membership, offering to be an exercise partner, or suggesting exercise videos or classes. Transportation can be an obstacle, so offer to drive your teen or give permission for him or her to borrow the car.

A part-time job can also help a sedentary teen be more active: Many jobs involve physical work, and even those that don't will reduce the amount of time that is spent passively at home. Be aware, though, that a working teen may turn to fast food when hunger strikes, so be sure to help them fit healthy meals into their schedule.

New partners
As they near adulthood, older teens still have an appetite for fun, but also are taking on more responsibilities, including romantic relationships.

If your teen has a job

Your child's job is your business, even though he or she is getting older. Help your child decide which jobs are worth applying for, and in developing a list of questions to ask prospective employers. Consider the various reasons your child wants a job: money, work experience, or something to do. No matter what the motivation is, the job should not interfere with school. It's also important that working teens have time to relax and to meet basic needs, like sleeping.

Once your teen has landed a job, monitor how it changes his or her eating habits. A teen working long shifts might not get much of a chance to eat regular meals. The result is that the teen might skip meals entirely, or pig out after work, eating far more than he or she would normally have at mealtimes. At the other extreme, a teenager working in a restaurant may have access to free food, which can be a problem if weight is a concern.

Getting a part-time job
Working can be an enriching experience for teenagers as long as they still have enough time to study and to participate in school activities.

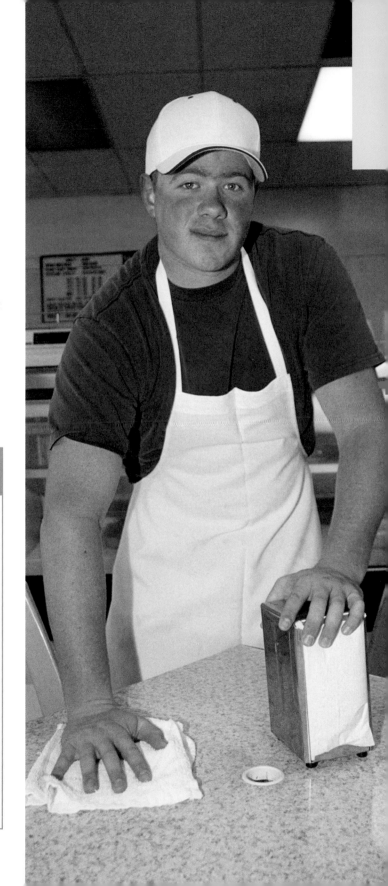

Q: **Should I limit the number of hours my 16-year-old son works?**

A: A teen shouldn't have a job that interferes with schoolwork. It's also important for your child to have other interests and participate in extracurricular activities. If your son's job is making this impossible, have him cut back his hours or suggest he quit working until summer. If you and your son decide he can continue working, keep these federal rules in mind. They are intended for 14- and 15-year-olds, but they are reasonable guidelines for all teens who are still in school.

During the school year, a teen should not:
- work before 7 a.m. or after 7 p.m.;
- work more than three hours a day on a school day, eight hours a day on weekends or holidays;
- work more than 18 hours a week.

When school is not in session, a teen should not:
- work before 7 a.m. or after 9 p.m.;
- work more than eight hours a day;
- work more than 40 hours a week.

9
SPECIAL **CONCERNS**

Some kids may face **nutritional and fitness challenges**. Whether they are gifted athletes or kids facing special **physical or medical needs**, parents have to look out for their **child's health** and well-being.

"I'm learning to swim"

Special challenges

Having a health condition can affect the way a child eats or gets physical activity. But parents can help their kids be part of the action—from eating cake at a party to joining the baseball team.

Before they play

If your child has a health problem and wants to get active, the first step is to schedule a physical exam. This should be done before any child begins a new activity or sport. It's a good idea even if it's not required, because these exams can identify potential problems and help minimize the risk of injury. Schedule the appointment with your family doctor or pediatrician, who should know your child's medical history.

Make sure children—especially older ones—know that the physical is intended to help them participate safely, not exclude them. The vast majority of kids, even those with existing medical conditions, will be approved for their sport or activity. For children with known health problems, your doctor may have to adjust medications or make suggestions about how to accommodate your child's participation in sports and other activities. (See opposite for information about some professionals who can be of help.)

The vital role of parents

Some medical problems, such as food allergies, and the less serious food intolerances, affect a child's diet because the problem food must be avoided. Asthma, on the other hand, may affect the way a child gets exercise, with certain sports being better choices than others. And some conditions, such as diabetes, require special attention to both nutrition needs and physical activity.

Whatever the circumstances, all children benefit from eating well and being active, and parents play a key role in helping their kids do both. It may mean choosing the right sport for a child who has attention problems, or being sure a child who has diabetes gets a snack during the soccer game.

When a child feels different

A child with a medical problem may feel self-conscious and worry about not being like everyone else. Even if the only outward sign is that your child must visit the nurse for medication, other kids will notice and wonder why. Reassure your child that everyone is different in some way. Here are some ways to help your child feel better about a condition that requires special attention.

● Educate your child. A child who's educated about a health condition is better equipped to handle situations that arise, including questions from peers about why they're taking medicine or eating a special diet. Role playing may help reinforce what your child has learned.

● Make a "cheat sheet." Type up a list if your child finds it difficult to remember special instructions, such as foods they must avoid or when to take medication. You may want to laminate the sheet so it won't be ripped.

● Inform teachers. Your child's teacher can keep an eye on your child and watch for teasing or harassment from other students.

● Be supportive. Children with special needs will feel different, so it's important for parents to let them know they are loved for who they are.

It's important for all children to be active, so don't let your child's special needs be an excuse for being sedentary. Keep in mind that there are many ways to be active and you can tailor the type of activity to your child's interests and abilities. Young children benefit from adult-led activities, and with the help of your doctor you can decide the best approach. Time for free play, where your child is left to his or her own devices, is a great way to let your child set his or her own pace. Refer to the age-specific chapters for some ideas, though appropriate activities may vary depending on your child's situation.

As children get older, parents also might want to search out sports programs and camps designed just for their child. Fortunately, there is a long list of organizations and professionals who can help you find the right program to meet your child's individual needs. (See page 202 for useful names and addresses.)

info

Professionals who can help

There is a variety of health professionals who can help you and your child's doctor address the child's particular nutritional and physical needs. They include:

Registered dietitians: can offer reliable information on a healthy diet, menu plans, portion control, and special dietary considerations.

Occupational therapists: help improve skills needed to do everyday things, including learning and playing; can provide adaptive equipment so kids with special needs can be active.

Orthopedic surgeons: treat sports injuries, especially serious ones that require surgery; also play an important role in the care of children who have physical disabilities.

Physical therapists: help improve flexibility, joint mobility, and muscle strength; can work with children who are recovering from sports injuries or with children who have physical conditions that limit them.

Sports medicine doctors: specialize in the care of athletes during all phases of training and competition; in addition to treating injuries, can help athletes optimize performance.

Allergists/immunologists: test for and treat allergies, including food allergies and sensitivities.

"Some foods don't like me"

The child with food allergies

Food allergies, and the less serious food sensitivities and intolerances, are increasingly common problems among kids. But they rarely have an impact on a child's overall nutrition.

Allergic to food

When a child has a food allergy, the body treats a food as a foreign substance, triggering an allergic reaction that can affect the skin, respiratory system, cardiovascular system, and gastrointestinal tract. Symptoms range in severity from a mild case of hives to a life-threatening anaphylactic reaction (see opposite). Foods that most commonly cause allergies are:

- peanuts and other nuts
- seafood
- milk, particularly cow's milk
- eggs
- soy
- wheat.

The chances of having a food allergy are increased if a child is exposed to these allergenic foods too early in life, or if a parent or sibling has a food allergy. (See page 79 for more about this.) In North America, as many as six percent of children under age three have food allergies. Peanut allergies have become a particular problem because peanuts are so commonly found in many commercially prepared foods.

With any food allergy, the best strategy is to avoid the problem food. Improved food labeling laws and the variety of alternatives on the market make it possible to do this, while still getting the nutrients required. For example, if your child has an allergy to cow's milk, there are alternative sources of calcium, such as calcium-fortified orange juice.

Q: **How can my child deal with food allergies or intolerances at school?**

A: About 20 percent of children with food allergies or intolerances will have a reaction in school. Although most of these reactions are not serious—a rash, for example—some children will have difficulty breathing and, in some cases, the reactions may be life-threatening. If you need cooperation from other students in your child's class, you may want to send a note home to the children's parents explaining the severity of your child's condition and how you'd like them to help. For instance, ask them to choose allergen-free snacks when they send in a treat for the whole class.

Talk to your child's doctor or allergist about developing an emergency treatment plan that can be shared with the school. School personnel should be educated in carrying out this plan, and have necessary medications on hand.

Sensitivities or intolerances

Food sensitivities, also called food intolerances, can be confused with food allergies, but in general they are less serious and can be managed more easily. It does not mean your child is allergic to a particular food, but he or she can still experience uncomfortable symptoms. Lactose intolerance, for example, means that a child has trouble digesting lactose, a type of sugar found in dairy foods. The child with lactose intolerance may complain about gas, bloating, or diarrhea after drinking milk.

What parents can do

If your child must avoid certain foods because of allergies or sensitivities, discuss your child's nutrition with a doctor or registered dietitian. If you are concerned that your child is missing out on important nutrients, ask about giving your child a vitamin or mineral supplement. When they are old enough, teach children with allergies or food sensitivities to make good decisions for themselves. For instance, these kids shouldn't share or trade food with a friend. You also can teach your child to read food labels and ingredient lists, and ask questions about what's in a dish.

Talk with the doctor about what to do if your child has a serious allergic reaction. The doctor may recommend keeping antihistamine medication on hand and carrying an emergency epinephrine injection kit. Your doctor will help you learn when it's appropriate to give these medications, and at what age you can teach your child to take emergency measures. As an added precaution, have your child wear a medical alert bracelet at all times.

What is anaphylaxis?

A severe allergic reaction to a food or other allergens can result in anaphylaxis, or anaphylactic shock. This is a sudden, life-threatening reaction that can cause one or more of the following symptoms:

- tingling around the mouth
- tightness in the throat
- feeling of fear
- hives and flushing
- wheezing or other breathing difficulty
- nausea and vomiting
- low blood pressure and rapid heartbeat.

If the allergic reaction progresses, the child could lose consciousness. If you suspect that your child is suffering anaphylactic shock, call emergency medical services immediately.

When your child has a food allergy that can trigger anaphylaxis, prevention is the key. Be sure to read all food labels and to teach your child to be vigilant about avoiding the problem food. You'll also want to be sure that teachers, babysitters, relatives, and anyone else who cares for your child knows about the food allergy and what to do if a reaction occurs.

"time out for a snack!"

The child with diabetes

A person with type 1 diabetes no longer produces insulin, which is needed to turn food into energy. There are special considerations for kids with type 1 diabetes when it comes to eating and exercise.

Managing diabetes

Without the hormone insulin, the body can't use glucose from the bloodstream as it should. Glucose, a simple sugar that comes from the food we eat, is used to fuel our bodies. Fortunately, children with type 1 diabetes can meet their insulin needs through injections or a wearable pump system. This insulin replacement can help keep a diabetic child's body functioning properly.

Children with diabetes need to be more aware of what they eat, how much they eat, and when they eat. They also need to monitor their blood sugar levels regularly. A child with diabetes should work with a diabetes management team to learn how to balance diet, exercise, and insulin

intake. There's no single management plan that is ideal for everyone. The plan needs to be personalized, based the individual needs of the child and of the child's family.

Nutrition needs

Just like all kids, children with diabetes need a balanced diet that includes all the food groups (see page 40). However, special attention should be given to the amounts and types of carbohydrate in foods, because carbohydrate is primarily responsible for the rise in blood sugar that occurs after eating. Control of blood sugar depends upon the successful balancing of food (especially carbohydrate) intake with insulin dosage and physical activity. Children with diabetes and their parents may face a number of challenges in achieving this balance, particularly as the child spends more time outside the home.

Parents should make sure that adults who will be supervising their child, including teachers, coaches, and other parents, understand the importance of following the child's meal and snack schedule. They also should know how to deal with hypoglycemia (see below).

Many adults believe that sugary foods are completely forbidden for people with diabetes. In fact, most nutrition management plans for children with diabetes permit limited intake of these foods. Allowing a piece of cake or some ice cream at a birthday party can help prevent a child with diabetes from feeling deprived or different from peers, an important consideration in helping a child cope with the disease. Newer ways to get insulin, such as compact wearable insulin pump delivery systems, give a person more freedom and flexibility.

Exercise issues

While some precautions are necessary, children with type 1 diabetes can exercise safely and should be encouraged to participate in physical activities appropriate for their age. In fact, maintaining physical fitness is a key factor in the management of diabetes. Regular exercise improves the body's response to insulin and can help a person have better control of the condition. Also, regular exercise helps all children maintain a healthy weight, which reduces the risk of heart disease in adulthood. This is especially important for children with diabetes since diabetes in itself is a risk factor for heart disease.

One aspect of your child's diabetes management plan should cover how to make adjustments for activity that help prevent hypoglycemia. Talk with your child's diabetes team about adjusting insulin doses and adding extra carbohydrate snacks during times of increased activity. Good choices for snacks include fruit juice, granola bars, crackers, and fruit.

Be sure you tell the school nurse, teachers, and coaches about your child's condition and what should be done in case of emergency. Also have your child wear a diabetes identification bracelet or necklace.

Type 2 diabetes

The management of type 1 diabetes differs from type 2 diabetes, where being overweight and sedentary often play a role. Previously called adult-onset diabetes, type 2 is becoming increasingly common in children. (For more about type 2 diabetes, see page 21.)

info

What is hypoglycemia?

Low blood sugar, or hypoglycemia, is more likely to occur when a person with diabetes misses a meal, eats less, or exercises more than usual. It can also occur when too high a dose of insulin is taken. Common symptoms are:
- hunger
- jitteriness
- weakness
- dizziness
- sweating
- headache
- blurred vision.

If hypoglycemia is not treated, the person could become confused or even lose consciousness.

The treatment for hypoglycemia is to raise blood sugar levels. One quick way to do this is by eating carbohydrate-rich foods and other sources of sugar. That's why it's important for kids who have diabetes to carry an emergency snack. In more severe cases, a child may be given an injection of a medication that causes a rapid rise in blood sugar.

"Fresh air"

Helping all kids be active

There are numerous conditions that can affect a child's ability to exercise and play sports. Two of the most common are asthma and Attention Deficit Hyperactivity Disorder (ADHD).

The child with asthma

When someone has asthma, certain triggers, such as allergies or respiratory infections, cause airways in the lungs to narrow, making it more difficult to breathe. Symptoms are wheezing, coughing, chest tightness, and shortness of breath.

You might think that a child with a breathing problem shouldn't exercise, but for many kids with asthma, regular exercise is beneficial because it improves lung capacity and overall fitness. If kids with asthma don't exercise, being out of shape can make them more prone to breathing problems. Inactivity also increases the risk that a child will be overweight, which can make asthma symptoms worse.

If your child has asthma you should first talk with your child's doctor about exercise so that all the proper precautions can be taken to make physical activity safe and enjoyable.

Getting medication right

As part of an asthma management plan, most kids use inhaled medicine to relieve symptoms during an asthma attack. Your child may be on other medications as well. In any case, before your child takes up a new sport or activity you'll want to talk with the doctor about whether these medications or dosages need to be adjusted. Never adjust the medications yourself without consulting the doctor first.

You'll also want to inform coaches about your child's asthma, so they are aware and know what do to in the event of an attack. Your child also should know how to handle an attack. Tell the child to stop, rest, and use an inhaler, if needed. See your doctor if symptoms are severe, last longer than usual, or don't respond to the inhaled medicine.

While exercise generally benefits children with asthma, it can trigger asthma symptoms in some. This is more likely to occur in cold, dry air, so wearing a scarf or muffler may help to reduce the chance of an attack. Using an inhaler before any physical activity may also help.

Appropriate sports

Many professional athletes have overcome asthma to excel in a variety of sports. For a few children, some sports may not be feasible, so they should choose one that they can participate in despite their asthma. Sports that require sustained activity, such as distance running, soccer, and basketball, may be too much of a challenge for some children with asthma. Better alternatives include volleyball, baseball, gymnastics, and short-distance track and field events, because they require shorter bursts of energy. For kids with asthma, swimming is often an excellent choice because the warm, moist air at indoor pools makes it easier to breathe.

The child with ADHD

Many kids with Attention Deficit Hyperactivity Disorder (ADHD) are easily distracted and impulsive, and have trouble interacting with their peers, so their parents may think they would not do well in sports. But under the right conditions, sports participation can help a child with ADHD gain more control over his body and improve social skills.

Children with ADHD may face obstacles in sports participation, similar to those they face in the classroom or at home. They may be careless and take unnecessary risks with themselves or their teammates, or they may be less attentive and be injured by a ball or other player. But finding the right sport—with the right amount of supervision—can boost self-esteem, help them make friends, and help them learn control as they channel energy in a positive direction.

Choosing the right activity
Individual sports, such as martial arts, swimming, dancing, and tennis, are a good choice for kids with ADHD because they often get more attention from coaches and can improve body awareness.

What parents should do

Safety is a key concern for children with ADHD. They may need more supervision, especially when using sporting equipment—from baseball bats to balance beams. You might feel a bit uncomfortable drawing attention to your child's ADHD, but it's a good idea to talk with coaches about your child's needs. With the right coach, your child can benefit from team sports and the camaraderie of being on the team.

You should attend practices and competitions. Work with your child on waiting his or her turn, following directions, and practicing good sportsmanship. Just learning these basics are significant achievements that will spill over into other areas, making the child feel more confident and liked by friends.

While not every child with ADHD needs medication, it can help some kids be more focused. If your child takes medicine, ask your doctor if the dosage should be adjusted. A child who is less distracted can learn better, both in the classroom and on the playing field.

The child with special needs

Activity benefits children with disabilities. It improves their general health, and they can gain flexibility, strength, and confidence, all of which can improve their present and future quality of life.

Overcoming barriers

Children with special needs can enjoy the power and pleasure of physical activity. Consider the wheelchair athlete who's adept enough to make a basket or the Special Olympian who runs across the finish line all smiles. Although there are many physical, medical, and developmental problems that can create barriers to activity, nearly all kids can and should find ways of being active. Some disabilities that can affect a child's ability to exercise are: brain or spinal cord injuries; cerebral palsy and other birth defects; developmental disabilities; hearing and visual impairments; heart problems; hypotonia (decreased muscle tone); muscular dystrophy; and seizure disorders.

Exercise helps a child with muscular dystrophy maintain muscle strength for as long as possible. Staying active is also important for a child in a wheelchair, who may gain weight easily. Being overweight can compound the child's health problems and make day-to-day care more difficult. For a child with juvenile rheumatoid arthritis, physical activity has been found to decrease pain and improve mobility of joints. In addition to health benefits, children with special needs get an emotional boost as they feel a sense of accomplishment and—maybe for the first time—the thrill of victory.

Professional advice

Parents of children with health problems or disabilities may be reluctant to let their child play sports or exercise for fear that they will be injured or it will worsen their condition. But in most cases, doctors will permit children with health problems to participate in activities after having an evaluation, getting appropriate treatment, and taking safety precautions. Even then, though a child may be cleared for physical activity, some sports may be off limits. For instance, a child with an uncontrolled seizure disorder must avoid sports such as swimming or those where having a seizure would put the child—or someone else—at risk of injury.

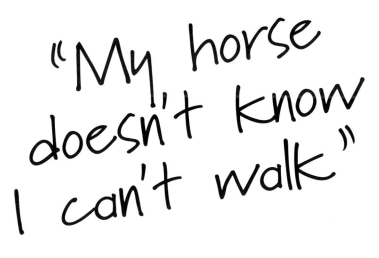

"My horse doesn't know I can't walk"

Q: **My child is disabled. Is summer camp a good idea?**

A: A camp experience can be rewarding for all children. For a child with special needs it's a chance to be with children who face the same challenges they do. They'll also get to enjoy the camp experience by being outside, participating in group activities, and getting a chance to be more independent. Camp also encourages physical activity, which may increase the child's confidence and desire to be active when they return home.

To find a good camp, seek opinions from professionals who know your child. Parents of other children with disabilities and advocacy organizations are great resources. Whether you choose day camp or overnight camp, ask about medical staff and facilities to be sure they are able to handle your child's special needs. Also, make sure the camp is accredited by a reputable organization, which provides some assurance that the camp adheres to standards for safety, staff training, first aid, health care, and transportation. (See page 202 for more information.)

Many children and their families work with physical and occupational therapists to improve flexibility, strength, and mobility. Therapists also can help parents select appropriate activities and make modifications, such as getting an adaptive tricycle with a hand crank and foot straps.

In general, children with disabilities are encouraged to be physically active. Of course, before exercising or trying a sport, you'll want to be sure that your child can safely participate in the activity. Talk with your child's medical and therapy team, so they can recommend appropriate activities, as well as ways to accommodate participation and the precautions you need to take.

Special sports programs

Children with special needs have more opportunities than ever to be active and involved. Most sports—even rock climbing and water skiing—have been adapted to accommodate people with disabilities. For example, specially designed saddles allow kids to participate in horseback riding programs that can improve balance and coordination. Goalball, introduced in the 1976 Paralympics, is specifically designed for people who have vision problems. The Special Olympics serves children with mental retardation, with cost-free, year-round training programs. (See page 202 for some useful addresses and websites.)

tips

How parents can make the difference

Try these ways to encourage your child with special needs to be physically active:
- Teach your child to try for his or her personal best—not someone else's.
- Help your child make contact with other children with disabilities or chronic conditions through your doctor, support groups, or special camps.
- Focus on fun, and send the message that just being active is the goal.
- Provide adaptive sports equipment, such as a sports wheelchair, so your child will enjoy exercise and keep on doing it.

Praise children for their effort and commitment to a sport or activity and take notice of their achievements, even if they seem small. If your child swims a lap a bit faster or works extra hard in a therapy session, let him or her know that you're proud of them. Give them the sense of accomplishment that comes from knowing they did their best.

"A coo win!"

The child athlete

Very active children who excel at sports may seem little cause for concern. But they need special attention, too, because of all that exercise they're getting during training and competition.

An athlete's special needs

Children and teens who are training for sports need more fluids and calories. In addition, they run the risk of getting hurt, so parents need to know how to guard against injuries. Child athletes also need the watchful eye of a parent who can spot when they're overscheduled, overdoing it, or taking health risks to improve performance (see pages 184–185).

Replacing fluids

Child athletes need to replace fluids before, during, and after sports participation. They are at increased risk of dehydration and may not drink enough to make up for what is lost during activity. Even mild dehydration can hurt performance,

endurance, and concentration. And more serious dehydration can lead to heat-related illnesses, including heat stroke, which needs immediate medical attention. (See page 67 for a list of signs of heat-related illness.)

Fluid requirements depend upon age, size, activity level, and climate. To be sure your child is getting enough:
- have him or her drink some water prior to game or practice time and every 15–20 minutes during activity;
- be sure the coach allows water breaks and that drinks are available during the practice or game;
- provide water bottles or sports bottles. If your child likes water ice cold, fill a plastic bottle and freeze it overnight. By afternoon practice, it will be thawed but still cold.

Although water is the best choice for keeping your child athlete hydrated, drinks with flavour may be more appealing. Avoid beverages that contain caffeine, such as cola or iced tea, and instead try a mixture of water and pure fruit juice or a sports drink. Both of these can be helpful during prolonged activity when children need to replenish energy supplies and electrolytes from salt losses through sweating, as well as fluid. Remember, though, that sports drinks contain sugar (and thus extra calories), so you may want to limit their consumption, particularly for a child who is overweight.

Food as fuel

The calorie needs of very active teenagers can be astounding. In general, male and female athletes who train more than 12 hours a week may need as much as 3,000–5,000 calories a day. Of course, needs will vary based on age, gender, size, and their stage of puberty.

It may be worthwhile to keep a closer eye on your child's nutrition when he or she is in training. One strategy involves keeping a food diary to look at total calories as well as how they are distributed among protein, carbohydrate, and fat. The proportions for an athlete are about the same as for a nonathlete. Some athletes, especially older teens who are strength-training, may need more protein; however, high-protein diets or protein supplements are not necessary, and may cause serious problems such as kidney damage. Calcium and iron also are very important (see below).

For those who need it, a nutritionist or sports medicine physician can help assess your child's diet. They can tell you if he or she is getting enough nutrients and also how to make adjustments during off-season times, if activity levels drop significantly then.

Regular meals are important

Athletes may skip breakfast and other meals because they're too tired or busy. Monitor whether they're skipping meals and put your foot down about it. Insist that your child eat breakfast every day. Yogourt with granola or a piece of toasted whole-grain bread with an egg are excellent choices for fueling up before activity.

The timing of meals and snacks is important to optimize performance. If your child is going to eat a full meal, serve it one and a half to three hours before game or practice time. During the practice or game, a snack may be needed, especially during all-day competitions. Prepare easy-to-eat snacks they can pack in their gym bag. Half a sandwich, some fresh or dried fruit, and nuts are all good choices.

After the game, let your child athlete replenish energy reserves with a balanced meal. Family dinners can go by the wayside when a child is busy with sports practices and competitions. When the evening is free, seize the opportunity to get the family together around the dinner table. At other times, consider having evening meals a little later to accommodate the athlete's schedule.

info

Calcium and iron requirements

Calcium builds strong bones, which are vitally important for athletes whose bodies endure increased stress and strain. Weakened bones are more likely to break.

Between the ages of nine and 18, children need 1,300mg of calcium a day. To add calcium to your child's diet, serve calcium-rich foods such as milk and other dairy products, dark green vegetables, and calcium-fortified orange juice.

Iron-deficiency anemia can hinder athletic performance and cause children to tire more easily.

One way child athletes lose iron is through sweating, so they need more to ensure peak performance and stamina. In addition, female athletes are at increased risk of iron deficiency due to the blood lost through menstruation.

Adolescent boys need at least 12mg of iron a day and adolescent girls need 15mg. The best way to get enough iron is to eat iron-rich foods, such as meat, eggs, and dried fruit. Give your child an iron supplement only if the child's doctor recommends it.

How can I tell if my child is using steroids?

A: These are some of the recognizable effects of steroid use/abuse:

- sudden increase in muscle size
- skin changes, including the appearance of stretch marks and worsening of acne
- excessive hair growth in females
- breast development in males
- male-pattern baldness (receding hairline at the sides of the forehead; loss of scalp hair at the crown, or top, of the head)
- violent behaviour and delusions

Preventing injuries

Many parents watching from the sidelines worry that their child athlete will be injured. Fortunately, there are some steps you can take to minimize the risk to your child. Choose a sports program that takes injury prevention seriously. Coaches should have first-aid training in cardiopulmonary resuscitation (CPR), and there should be procedures in place for handling emergencies.

It's also important to educate your child about sports safety. Make sure your child:

- warms up appropriately;
- knows the rules of the game and is playing with teammates of a similar skill level;
- wears the right protective equipment for every practice and competitive event;
- plays on surfaces that are properly maintained and designed for the sport;
- participates in a variety of activities, instead of focusing on one sport and performing the same repetitive motion over and over again.

Injuries do occur

Sometimes, despite taking precautions, a child is injured during practice or play. The three most common types of sports injuries in children are acute injuries, overuse injuries, and reinjuries.

- Acute injuries, such as bruises, sprains, and strains, occur suddenly. More severe acute injuries include broken bones, torn ligaments, and head injuries.
- Overuse injuries, which account for about half of sports injuries among middle school and high school athletes, occur when children perform repetitive actions that put too much stress on the musculoskeletal system. Such injuries are particularly problematic in childhood because

they can interfere with normal bone growth. Overuse injuries are most common in baseball, basketball, running, gymnastics, and swimming.
- Reinjuries are a risk when a child returns to a sport too soon. In addition, the still-recovering athlete may be compensating for pain and weakness, which can result in additional injuries.

Recuperation time will vary depending on the injury, but never allow your child to play through the pain. This may occur in professional sports, but it's not acceptable and often riskier for a child. Get medical attention for your child and follow the doctor's instructions about treatment as well as the advice about when it's safe for your child to resume participation in the sport.

Going to extremes

A child who is committed to a sport may start taking risks to improve his or her endurance and performance. Initially, these behaviours may be mild enough to go unnoticed by coaches and parents. But they can lead children to take increasing risks to stay on top of their chosen sport.

Losing weight

Wrestlers, gymnasts, ice skaters, and dancers may feel pressure to weigh less. Some teen wrestlers take extreme measures, such as fasting and trying to sweat off pounds so they can make their weight class. Gymnasts, ice skaters, and dancers may be at risk of eating disorders because of the emphasis placed on thinness. For girls, this can lead to a condition known as the female athlete triad, a combination of three interrelated medical problems (see opposite).

If your child is involved in wrestling, gymnastics (tumbling), ice skating, or dancing, be proactive by discussing weight issues with him or her. Watch for signs that your child is skipping meals, exercising excessively, or taking over-the-counter weight-loss products. Be sure your child knows that these practices are dangerous and that they may, in fact, worsen sports performance rather than improve it. (For more about eating disorders, see page 163.)

Bulking up

Sports like football value strength, prompting some young players to turn to questionable supplements as well as illegally obtained steroids to bulk up for the football season. Many people mistakenly believe sports supplements are harmless because they're widely available and are often labeled as "natural."

Common sports supplements include:
- megavitamins
- herbs, such as ephedra
- hormones, such as androstenedione ("andro") and dehydroepiandrosterone (DHEA).

Despite the claims on their labels, these supplements are often ineffective, a waste of money, and can be dangerous.

It's easy to understand why young athletes are interested in sports supplements. Creatine, used by some well-known professional athletes, has been found to increase strength in some circumstances. But supplements should be considered unsafe for children because they're not regulated and have not been adequately tested, and often the effects of long-term use are unknown.

Steroids, on the other hand, are illegal without a prescription and are known to cause health problems. Steroid use in children may stunt growth, change behaviour, cause infertility, and damage internal organs, including the liver and heart. Make sure your child understands the dangers of using steroids. Send a clear message that you disapprove and won't tolerate it. (See opposite for information about the signs of steroid use and abuse.)

Parental guidance

Everyone is looking for a magic pill, whether it's to lose weight or improve athletic performance. But such a miracle does not exist. Instead, parents need to teach their children that consistent training and healthy eating are the best and safest routes to excellence.

Many schools and sports teams ban steroids and performance-enhancing drugs, so using them could mean the end of your child's athletic career. If you're concerned that your child may be using steroids, taking sports supplements, or trying dangerous weight-loss tactics, talk with the child's doctor.

info

What is the female athlete triad?

A girl who feels pressure to stay small and slim for her chosen sport could be at risk for the female athlete triad, a combination of these medical problems:
- unhealthy eating pattern, ranging from dieting to a serious eating disorder
- loss of menstrual period
- weakened bones (osteoporosis)

Poor nutrition combined with excessive exercise causes hormonal changes that result in an interruption in regular menstrual cycles. The resulting low estrogen levels can affect the girl's ability to absorb calcium, which is needed for strong bones. A lack of adequate amounts of calcium in the girl's diet compounds the problem.

Female athlete triad is common among gymnasts, ice skaters, distance runners, and dancers, who may train and diet excessively to improve their performance.

Some young female athletes also may have a poor body image, which can be associated with a typical eating disorder. Because these problems occur while a girl is going through a key period for bone development, she may miss a critical opportunity to build strong bones. Even if the girl resumes her period and takes calcium supplements, her long-term bone health may be permanently affected.

Aside from missing menstrual periods, symptoms of the female athlete triad include fatigue, a decreased ability to concentrate, and an increased risk of bone fractures and muscle injuries. A girl who has the female athlete triad will need to cut back on her training and eat a healthier diet. To achieve this, she should work with her doctor and a variety of specialists, including a nutritionist and a psychologist.

HEALTHY**RECIPES**

When your **meals and snacks** are homemade, you **know what's in them**. Try these recipes if you'd like to bring **wholesome, healthful, and tasty** food to your family table.

"I love gram's cooking"

Good food for good health

You don't need culinary training to cook nutritious meals for your family. Whether you're an experienced cook or a novice, you can improve the way your family eats. They'll benefit from your efforts.

Fitting in some cooking

Cooking does take time—time to plan meals, shop for the ingredients, prepare the food, and clean up the mess. If you are in a pattern of eating out and heating up frozen foods, it may require some juggling for you to fit home cooking into your schedule. But regular, nutritious meals for your family are worth the effort—as the rates of overweight, heart disease, and diabetes climb, we're learning that a steady diet of take-out and convenience foods may be contributing to this public health crisis.

Feeding children is one of a parent's most important responsibilities. It is at once simple and complicated—as simple as making a peanut butter sandwich or as complicated as dealing with a child's weight problem.

The goals for every parent are to give kids nutritious foods and to foster healthy attitudes toward eating that will last a lifetime. Providing home-cooked family meals will go a long way to achieving these goals.

Plan meals in advance Having a weekly meal plan will save you from that awful feeling at the end of a long day, when everyone is hungry and you have no idea what to make for dinner. It may help to set aside time on the same day each week to draw up your menu plan. As you sketch it out, consider how you'll handle busy days when you and other members of the family have after-school or evening activities. Then, make a shopping list and decide on the time when you'll go to the market to stock up on the ingredients you'll need for the coming week.

Work ahead when you can If, for example, you know you want salad with tomorrow's dinner, wash the lettuce and cut the vegetables tonight. Or, buy pre-washed bags of salad. You also might marinate meats overnight, so they're already seasoned and ready for cooking. Saving that little bit of time can get dinner on the table with fewer last-minute hassles.

Make double batches for another day Soups and pasta sauces take considerable chopping and cooking, so why not make more than you need and freeze it? Then all you have to do later is thaw, heat, and eat! Or, if you prefer, wrap up the extra portion and keep it in the refrigerator, then eat the leftovers over the next few days.

The best choices

No matter how diligent you are, no family eats perfectly every day. Moderation is, of course, wise all the time, but one indulgent day or a week of vacation will not blot out many more days' or weeks' worth of healthy eating. Good nutrition is an average, and the aim is to improve how your family eats most of the time. Ask yourself these questions:

- What do you always have on hand for breakfast? For example, are the cereals loaded with additives or full of natural goodness?
- How do you cook foods? Do you often pan-fry or deep-fry or do you instead choose techniques that require little or no added fat? Do you boil vegetables in lots of water or steam them so they retain more of their nutrients?

- What kind of oil or fat do you use? Lean toward olive oil, peanut oil, and canola oil because other fats, such as butter, margarine, lard, or bacon grease, contain greater amounts of less healthy saturated and trans fats.
- How much fat do you use? Regardless of the type, be sparing with fat when preparing foods at home. You often can reduce the amount of oil or fat in a recipe without affecting the taste, especially if you use flavourful oils. (See page 26 for more ideas about lightening up favourite dishes.) And if you use nonstick pans and cooking spray when frying or baking, you'll find that you need much less cooking oil or fat.

Recipe for togetherness

Not only can home cooking improve nutrition, it can strengthen family bonds and create a comforting tradition in your home life. Eating meals together provides a chance to talk and spend more time with each other. Preparing meals together adds another dimension. Children welcome the opportunity to get their hands dirty and play an important role in the creation of a dish the family will eat together. They may even want to taste whatever they helped make.

On the following pages, you'll find recipes for breakfast, lunch, dinner, and snacks. All are uncomplicated and call for easy-to-find ingredients. These recipes provide a variety of nutrients, but we have noted when the dish has a significant amount of particular vitamins or minerals.

tips

Healthy cooking tips

- Leave skins on fruits and vegetables where appropriate, because much of their nutrient content is just under the skin and the skin offers valuable fibre.
- Prepare fruits and vegetables as close to eating or cooking as possible, to reduce vitamin loss. If not using immediately, cover and store in the refrigerator.
- When you cook vegetables in water some vitamins are released into the water; the longer you cook, the more nutrients are lost. So rather than boiling, poach

vegetables in the minimum of water, or steam them, for the shortest time possible.
- Poaching and steaming are great nonfat cooking methods for fish, as is cooking in the microwave.
- Little or no fat is needed when you stir-fry, cook on a ridged grill pan, broil, grill, or roast meat and poultry. Roasting or broiling on a rack lets fat drip away.
- Most of the fat in poultry is in the skin, so to reduce fat intake don't eat the skin (you can take it off before or after cooking).

"Hand-made Pancakes"

Breakfasts to start the day

Hearty Swiss cereal

Makes 12 servings

(½ cup/125mL each)

2 cups (160g) rolled oats

1 cup (150g) raisins

2 cups (500mL) 1% milk

1 cup (250mL) nonfat plain yogourt

2 teaspoons honey

1 teaspoon vanilla extract
(optional)

2 cups (340g) diced fresh fruit,
such as berries, apples, pears,
apricot, peaches, plums, melon

½ cup (65g) chopped walnuts,
sliced almonds, or chopped
pecans

● Combine the oats and raisins in a
bowl. Add the milk and stir, then let soak
for 30 to 40 minutes.

● Drain off excess milk, then add the
yogourt, honey, and optional vanilla.

● Add the fruit and nuts, and mix
together well.

● If not eating right away, this cereal will
keep in a covered container in the
refrigerator for three to four days. You
may prefer to add the fruit and nuts just
before serving.

● This traditional Swiss recipe is a nice
change from instant oatmeal or cold
cereal. Feel free to adapt it to suit your
child's taste by substituting different fruits
or omitting the nuts.

Nutritional analysis per serving	
calories	147
fat 1g (of which 0.5g is saturated)	
protein	5g
carbohydrate	25g
fibre	3g
minerals	iron, potassium, zinc
vitamins	A, folate

Food groups: grain products, milk
products, vegetables and fruit

Gingerbread muffins with fresh pears

Makes 12 muffins

2 eggs

½ cup (125mL) buttermilk or sour
    cream

½ cup (125mL) unsulfured molasses

½ cup or 1 stick (115g) unsalted
    butter, melted and cooled

½ cup (110g) firmly packed dark
    brown sugar

1 tablespoon grated or finely
    minced fresh ginger

1 ½ cups (190g) all-purpose flour

1 teaspoon baking soda

½ teaspoon ground cloves

¼ teaspoon grated nutmeg

¼ teaspoon salt

½ cup (60g) crystallized ginger,
    chopped into small pieces

Fresh pears for serving

● Preheat the oven to 180°C (350°F).
Lightly grease a muffin pan or use paper
liners in the muffin cups.

● Beat the eggs in a mixing bowl. Stir in
the buttermilk or sour cream, molasses,
butter, brown sugar, and grated ginger. Mix
until smooth.

● In another bowl, mix together the flour,
baking soda, cloves, nutmeg, and salt. Add
to the molasses mixture along with the
crystallized ginger. Mix well.

● Divide the batter among the cups of the
muffin pan. Bake for 20 minutes or until a
toothpick inserted into the center of a muffin
comes out clean.

● Serve the muffins warm with fresh pears,
cut into wedges (or into thin slices for
younger children).

Nutritional analysis per muffin with ½ pear	
calories	279
fat	10g (of which 5g is saturated)
protein	3g
carbohydrate	47g
fibre	3g
minerals	potassium
vitamins	A, B₁, B₂, niacin, B₆, folate

Food groups: grain products, milk products, vegetables and fruit

Blueberry pancakes

Makes 14 pancakes (4–5 servings)

1 ¼ cups + 2 tablespoons (170g)
    all-purpose flour

½ cup (60g) whole-wheat flour

2 tablespoons sugar

2 teaspoons baking powder

½ teaspoon salt

2 eggs

1 ½ cups (375mL) skim milk

2 tablespoons butter, melted

1 cup (145g) blueberries, rinsed

Butter to grease the pan

● Sift the all-purpose and whole-wheat
flours, sugar, baking powder, and salt into a
large bowl. Set aside.

● Crack the eggs into a medium-sized
bowl. Add the milk and melted butter, and
whisk until everything is well mixed.

● Add the flour mixture to the egg
mixture. Whisk until blended to make a
batter. Gently fold in the blueberries.

● Heat some extra butter in a frying pan
or skillet on medium heat. It is hot enough
when the butter starts to bubble.

● Use ½ cup (125mL) of batter for each
pancake. Pour the measured batter into the
pan; it will spread to make a pancake about
10cm in diameter. Cook three or four
pancakes at a time, depending on the size
of the pan. Cook until small bubbles appear
on the top of the pancakes.

● Lift them with a spatula to see if they
are light brown on the base. When they are,
flip them over and cook for another few
minutes until the pancakes are light brown
on the other side.

● Serve hot, with pancake syrup.

Nutritional analysis for 3 pancakes	
calories	295
fat	5g (of which 1g is saturated)
protein	11g
carbohydrate	51g
fibre	3g
minerals	calcium, potassium
vitamins	A, B₁, B₆, folate, C, D

Food groups: grain products, milk products, meat and alternatives, vegetables and fruit

"We always help mom in the kitchen"

Take time for lunch
Tortellini kabobs

Makes 4 kabobs (4 servings)

½ bunch of broccoli

12 medium to large frozen or dried
cheese-filled tortellini

½ red bell pepper

½ cucumber, peeled

8 cherry tomatoes

Herb sauce

Juice of 1 lemon

4 teaspoons extra virgin olive oil

1–2 tablespoons chopped fresh herb,
such as basil, thyme, oregano,
chives, mint, or cilantro

Salt and pepper

● Trim the thick stem from the broccoli
and separate the florets. Drop them into a
pan of boiling salted water and cook for
2 to 3 minutes or until just tender but still
firm. Drain and rinse with cold water, then
set aside.

● Cook the tortellini in boiling salted
water until al dente (not too soft, still a
little chewy). Drain and set aside to cool.

● Cut the red pepper and cucumber
into 2.5-cm pieces. Arrange the pepper,
cucumber, tortellini, broccoli, and
tomatoes on four wooden skewers that
are 10 to 15 cm long, alternating the
ingredients. Lay the kabobs on a tray or
large plate.

● To make the sauce, whisk together
the ingredients, seasoning to taste with
salt and pepper.

● Drizzle the sauce (or your child's
favourite salad dressing) over the kabobs.
Cover and refrigerate for 1 hour, turning
the kabobs occasionally. Serve chilled.

Nutritional analysis per kabob	
calories	134
fat 7g (of which 2g is saturated)	
protein	3g
carbohydrate	15g
fibre	3g
minerals	calcium, potassium
vitamins	A, C, E

Food groups: grain products, milk
products, vegetables and fruit

Pleasing pita pocket

Makes 1 pita pocket (1 serving)

2 tablespoons hummus (traditional or
  with roasted red pepper)

1 whole-wheat pita bread,
  cut in half

½ cup (30g) shredded lettuce

½ cup (90g) diced tomato

½ cup (75g) diced cucumber

● Using a knife, spread 1 tablespoon hummus inside each pita half, then add the lettuce, tomato, and cucumber.

● Serve as soon as possible, so the pita bread doesn't soften.

Nutritional analysis per pita pocket	
calories	242
fat	5g (of which .4g is saturated)
protein	9g
carbohydrate	45g
fibre	7g
minerals	iron, potassium
vitamins	A, B$_1$, B$_6$, C

Food groups: grain products, meat and alternatives, vegetables and fruit

Wild West wrap

Makes 2 servings

1 whole-wheat flour tortilla

120g cooked skinless, boneless
  chicken breast, cut in strips or
  pieces

30g Monterey Jack cheese,
  shredded

½ cup (30g) shredded lettuce

½ cup (90g) diced tomato

1 tablespoon chunky salsa

● Lay the tortilla on a clean preparation surface. Arrange the chicken, cheese, lettuce, and tomato evenly down the centre of the tortilla. Spoon the salsa over the filling ingredients.

● Fold in the tortilla over one end of the filling, then roll up the tortilla tightly.

● Cut in half and serve.

Nutritional analysis per serving	
calories	217
fat	9g (of which 3g is saturated)
protein	23g
carbohydrate	13g
fibre	1g
minerals	potassium
vitamins	A, B$_1$, B$_6$, C

Food groups: grain products, milk products, meat and alternatives, vegetables and fruit

Traditional quesadillas

Makes 4 quesadillas (4 servings)

Cooking spray

4 large flour tortillas

120g Cheddar or Monterey
  Jack cheese, shredded

½ cup (85g) drained cooked
  or canned black or pinto beans

½ cup (80g) cooked yellow corn
  kernels

Salsa

● Coat a skillet with cooking spray and set it over medium heat. Place a tortilla in the pan.

● Sprinkle one-fourth of the cheese on half of the tortilla. Add 2 tablespoons beans and 2 tablespoons corn.

● Fold the other half of the tortilla over the filling and press down gently. Cook for 1 minute on each side, until cheese melts.

● Remove the quesadilla from the pan and keep warm while you cook the rest.

● Serve the quesadillas cut in wedges, with salsa for dipping.

Nutritional analysis per quesadilla (without salsa)	
calories	299
fat	13g (of which 9g is saturated)
protein	14g
carbohydrate	33g
fibre	3g
minerals	calcium
vitamins	A, B$_1$, B$_6$

Food groups: grain products, milk products, meat and alternatives, vegetables and fruit

Crunchy baked fish with lemon

Makes 4 servings

1 teaspoon butter

4 fresh, white fish fillets, such as
    flounder, grouper, cod, halibut, or
    snapper, 80–90g each

Salt and pepper

1 teaspoon lemon juice

½ cup (125mL) light mayonnaise

1 cup (100g) Italian or plain
    bread crumbs

2 teaspoons olive oil

Lemon wedges for serving

● Preheat the oven to 180°C (350°F).
Use the butter to grease a baking sheet or
cookie sheet.

● Arrange the fish fillets on the baking
sheet. Season the fish with salt and pepper.
Drizzle a few drops of lemon juice over
each fillet. Thinly spread the mayonnaise
on top, then pat the bread crumbs onto
the mayonnaise. Finally, drizzle with the
olive oil.

● Bake for 10 to 12 minutes, depending
on the thickness of the fillets (test for
doneness with the tip of a knife: the fish
should flake easily).

● Serve hot, with lemon wedges.

Nutritional analysis per serving	
calories	305
fat 16g (of which 3g is saturated)	
protein	19g
carbohydrate	20g
fibre	0g
minerals	potassium
vitamins	B$_{12}$
Food groups: meat and alternatives	

Homemade chicken soup

Makes 10 servings

(¾ cup/185mL each)

1 whole chicken, weighing 1.4–1.8kg

Salt and pepper

1 teaspoon dried rosemary

2 bay leaves

2 teaspoons olive oil

1 onion, peeled and finely diced

3 carrots, peeled and finely diced

3 celery stalks, finely diced

4 garlic cloves, peeled and crushed

1 tomato, seeds removed and then
    diced

120g fettuccine, broken into
    5-cm pieces

Juice of ¼ lemon

Grated nutmeg

● Rinse the chicken in cold water, then
put it into a large pot. Cover with cold water
and add salt and pepper, the rosemary, and
bay leaves. Bring to a boil.

● Reduce the heat to medium so the
soup is simmering. Simmer for 40 minutes,
skimming off the foam from the surface.

● Remove the chicken to a plate. Strain
the broth and set aside.

● Wash the pot, then heat the olive oil
in it on high heat. Add the onion, carrots,
celery, garlic, and tomato. Stir the
vegetables for 3 to 4 minutes.

● Add the chicken broth. Bring to a boil
and simmer for 30 minutes.

● Meanwhile, take all the chicken meat
from the bones. Discard the skin, and cut
the meat into small pieces.

● Add the pieces of chicken and the
fettuccine pieces to the soup. Simmer for
10 to 15 minutes longer.

● Add the lemon juice and season with
salt, pepper, and nutmeg to taste. Serve
the soup hot.

● Homemade chicken soup can be kept
in the refrigerator for four days; it also
freezes well.

Nutritional analysis per serving	
calories	186
fat 6g (of which 2g is saturated)	
protein	18g
carbohydrate	13g
fibre	2g
minerals	potassium
vitamins	A, C
Food groups: meat and alternatives, vegetables and fruit	

Turkey meatloaf sandwiches

Make this meatloaf the night before for sandwiches the next day. The recipe also can be doubled, to serve hot for dinner one night and lunch the next day.

Makes 8 sandwiches (8 servings)

Olive oil cooking spray

½ onion, peeled and finely diced

1 carrot, peeled and finely diced

1 garlic clove, peeled and crushed

½ cup (25g) minced parsley

700g ground turkey

½ cup (125mL) canned tomato sauce

1 egg, lightly beaten

½ cup (25g) fresh bread crumbs

Salt and pepper

½ cup (125mL) ketchup

16 slices of whole-wheat bread
    for serving

● Preheat the oven to 180°C (350°F).

● Coat a skillet with cooking spray and place over medium heat. Add the onion, carrot, and garlic, and stir for 10 minutes until softened. Remove from the heat and let the vegetables cool.

● Add the parsley to the vegetables.

● In a large bowl, combine the ground turkey, vegetable mixture, tomato sauce, egg, and bread crumbs. Season with some salt and pepper. Mix well together. Pack firmly into a greased loaf pan and top with the ketchup.

● Bake for 50 minutes. Remove from the oven and cover with aluminum foil. If serving the meatloaf hot, let stand for 10 minutes before cutting into eight slices. For sandwiches, let the meatloaf cool completely before slicing.

Nutritional analysis per sandwich	
calories	324
fat 11g (of which 3g is saturated)	
protein	23g
carbohydrate	35g
fibre	5g
minerals	iron, potassium
vitamins	A, B$_1$, B$_6$, folate
Food groups: grain products, meat and alternatives, vegetables and fruit	

Crispy zucchini cake sandwiches

Makes 6 sandwiches (6 servings)

2 large zucchini, shredded

1 teaspoon salt

½ cup (115g) finely diced onion

1 cup (120g) finely diced bell
    peppers (half red, half green)

1 cup (200g) well-drained, thawed,
    frozen spinach

1 teaspoon chopped fresh basil

1½ cups (65g) fresh bread crumbs

1 egg

2 egg yolks

2 tablespoons light mayonnaise

Salt and pepper

Paprika

Lemon juice

4 teaspoons olive oil

6 whole-grain rolls, split open

● Place the shredded zucchini in a strainer and add the salt. Toss together, then let drain for 20 minutes. With your hands, squeeze any remaining water out of the zucchini.

● In a large bowl, combine the zucchini, onion, bell peppers, spinach, and basil. Add the bread crumbs.

● In a separate bowl, mix together the whole egg, egg yolks, and mayonnaise.

● Add the egg mixture to the zucchini mixture and toss together. Season with salt, pepper, paprika, and lemon juice. Form the mixture into small patties.

● Heat the olive oil in a skillet on medium heat. Cook the patties for 5 to 10 minutes on each side until crisp.

● Serve hot, on the whole-grain rolls or with a favourite dipping sauce.

Nutritional analysis per sandwich	
calories	275
fat 10g (of which 2g is saturated)	
protein	10g
carbohydrate	39g
fibre	5g
minerals	iron, potassium
vitamins	A, folate, B$_{12}$, C, E, K
Food groups: grain products, vegetables and fruit	

"Cooking is fun"

Sit down to dinner

Salad with pan-grilled chicken

Makes 4 servings

1 tablespoon chopped fresh rosemary
1 tablespoon chopped parsley
½ teaspoon garlic salt
4 chicken breast halves without skin, about 170g each
Cooking spray
½ cup (125g) chopped broccoli
½ cup (60g) chopped cauliflower
½ cup (65g) chopped zucchini
½ cup (60g) sliced carrots
½ cup (60g) sliced red onions
1 tomato, diced
4 cups (200g) mixed salad greens
2 tablespoons light dressing (optional)

● Sprinkle the rosemary, parsley, and garlic salt over the chicken breasts. Coat a ridged grill pan with cooking spray and heat it over medium-high heat. Pan-grill the chicken breasts until done, turning them over halfway through the cooking.

● Add the broccoli, cauliflower, zucchini, carrots, red onions, and tomato to the grill pan and cook for 2 minutes longer, stirring occasionally.

● Toss the salad greens with the dressing, if using, then pile on four plates. Top the greens with the chicken breasts and vegetables, and serve hot.

Nutritional analysis per serving (without dressing)	
calories	333
fat	7g (of which 2g is saturated)
protein	56g
carbohydrate	10g
fibre	2g
minerals	iron, potassium
vitamins	A, C, K

Food groups: meat and alternatives, vegetables and fruit

Mediterranean pasta soup

Makes 8 servings (1 cup/250mL each)

2 teaspoons olive oil

½ cup (80g) diced onion

1½ cups (375mL) water

2 cups (500mL) chicken broth

½ teaspoon ground cumin

¼ teaspoon ground cinnamon

¼ teaspoon ground black pepper

1 can (400g) chick peas, drained

1 can (400g) diced tomatoes

½ cup (80g) ditalini pasta (short tube-shaped macaroni)

2 teaspoons chopped parsley or cilantro

- Heat the olive oil in a large pot over medium heat. Add the onion and sauté until lightly browned.
- Add the water, chicken broth, cumin, cinnamon, pepper, chick peas, and canned tomatoes with their juice. Bring to a boil, then cover and reduce the heat. Simmer for 5 minutes.
- Add the pasta and stir, then cook for 10 minutes longer or until pasta is al dente (tender but still firm).
- Stir in the parsley or cilantro. Serve hot.

Nutritional analysis per serving	
calories	119
fat 2g (of which 0.4g is saturated)	
protein	5g
carbohydrate	22g
fibre	2g
minerals	iron, potassium
vitamins	folate, C
Food groups: meat and alternatives, vegetables and fruit	

Cheesy quiche

Quiche is a great way to serve eggs to children. You can add whatever you have available, such as ham, sausage, asparagus, broccoli, tomatoes, spinach, fresh herbs, or mushrooms, to the quiche filling. This recipe includes a pie crust recipe, but a store-bought, premade crust works just as well.

Makes 8 servings

Pie crust

1 cup (125g) all-purpose flour

½ cup or 1 stick (115g) butter

Pinch of salt

4 tablespoons cold water

Quiche filling

1 cup (250mL) milk

4 eggs

2 teaspoons all-purpose flour

2 cups (200g) shredded Cheddar or Swiss cheese

Pinch of paprika

Salt and pepper

- First make the pie crust: Sift the flour into a bowl and break in the butter by hand. Rub the butter with the flour until the mixture resembles crumbs.
- Dissolve the salt in the water. Gradually incorporate the water into the flour/butter mixture until it clumps together. Do not overwork the dough. Form it into a ball and wrap in wax paper. Let it rest for 30 minutes, or preferably overnight, in the refrigerator.
- Preheat the oven to 180°C (350°F). Roll out the dough and use to line a 15-cm pie pan.
- To make the filling, combine all the ingredients, including any vegetables or meats you'd like to add. Mix well and pour into the pie shell.
- Bake for 30 to 45 minutes or until the crust is golden brown and the filling is just set. Serve warm or cool. Cut into wedges for serving.

Nutritional analysis per serving	
calories	301
fat 24g (of which 15g is saturated)	
protein	12g
carbohydrate	9g
fibre	0g
minerals	calcium
vitamins	A, B_1, B_6, B_{12}, D, E
Food groups: grain products, milk products, meat and alternatives	

Pasta with fresh tomato sauce and basil

Makes 5 servings (²⁄₃ cup/150mL each)

450g pasta

Freshly grated Parmesan cheese
  (1 tablespoon each) for serving

Tomato sauce

3 tablespoons olive oil

2 garlic cloves, peeled and crushed

3 cups (540g) chopped fresh tomatoes,
  or 1 can (800g) tomatoes

Salt and pepper

¼ cup (10g) fresh basil leaves,
  shredded

● To make the tomato sauce, heat the oil in a large pot over medium heat. Add the garlic and cook for about 1 minute, stirring. Don't let it burn!

● Add the tomatoes and stir. Bring to a boil, then reduce the heat and simmer for about 10 minutes.

● Add salt and pepper to taste. Just before serving, stir the basil into the sauce and cook for 2 minutes.

● Cook the pasta in a large pot of boiling salted water until al dente (tender but still firm). Drain well. Pour the sauce over the pasta and toss together.

● Serve hot, with Parmesan cheese.

Nutritional analysis per serving	
calories	155
fat 3g (of which 0.1g is saturated)	
protein	5g
carbohydrate	25g
fibre	1g
minerals	–
vitamins	B₁, B₆, folate, C, E
Food groups: grain products, milk products, vegetables and fruit	

Vegetarian chili

Makes 9 servings (1 cup/250mL each)

2 tablespoons olive oil

1 onion, peeled and chopped

2 garlic cloves, peeled and minced

½ cup (55g) chopped carrot

½ cup (60g) chopped celery

½ cup (60g) chopped red bell
  pepper

1 teaspoon ground cumin

1 teaspoon chili powder

Hot pepper sauce or red pepper
  flakes (optional)

1 can (800g) crushed or
  diced tomatoes

2 cans (400g each) red
  kidney beans, drained and rinsed

1 cup (160g) frozen corn kernels
  (optional)

Salt and pepper

½ cup (50g) shredded Cheddar
  cheese

● Heat the oil in a Dutch oven. Add the onion and garlic, and cook for 2 minutes. Add the carrot, celery, and red pepper, and cook until just tender, stirring occasionally.

● Stir in the cumin, chili powder, and hot pepper sauce or flakes, if using. Add the tomatoes with their juice and stir to mix. Bring to a boil, then reduce the heat and simmer for 15 to 20 minutes.

● Add the beans along with the corn, if using. Continue simmering until the beans and corn are heated through.

● Season to taste with salt and pepper. Serve hot, sprinkled with the cheese.

● If your child is interested in a vegetarian diet, this is a great dish to try. Serve it with cornbread or over noodles or bulgur wheat.

Nutritional analysis per serving (without corn)	
calories	157
fat 4g (of which 1g is saturated)	
protein	7g
carbohydrate	24g
fibre	4g
minerals	potassium
vitamins	A, C, E
Food groups: meat and alternatives, vegetables and fruit	

Traditional meat sauce for pasta or gnocchi

This sauce tastes better if it is made in a big batch. It freezes well and also can be kept in the refrigerator for three to five days. It is great on spaghetti or any other kind of pasta, or on gnocchi.

Makes 12 servings
(¾ cup/185mL each)

900g ground beef (lean)
2 onions, peeled and diced
6 carrots, peeled and diced
1 celery root, peeled and diced,
    or 3 celery stalks, diced
1 cup (70g) sliced fresh mushrooms
4 fresh tomatoes, diced
6 garlic cloves, peeled and minced
120g tomato paste
1 teaspoon each dried oregano, dried
    thyme, dried basil, dried rosemary,
    and paprika
2 bay leaves

6 cups (1.5L) vegetable or beef
    broth
3 cups (750mL) water
Salt and pepper
Pasta or gnocchi for serving

● Put the ground beef into a large pot and brown over medium heat, stirring to break up lumps.

● Add the onions, carrots, celery root or celery, mushrooms, tomatoes, and garlic. Stir in the tomato paste, dried herbs, paprika, and bay leaves. Cook for 10 more minutes, stirring frequently.

● Add the broth and water, and bring to a boil. Reduce the heat, cover, and simmer gently for 2 to 3 hours.

● Season to taste with salt and pepper.

● Toss the sauce with pasta or gnocchi that has been cooked and drained.

Nutritional analysis per serving (without pasta or gnocchi)	
calories	257
fat	14g (of which 6g is saturated)
protein	21g
carbohydrate	11g
fibre	3g
minerals	iron, potassium
vitamins	A, B₁₂, C
Food groups: meat and alternatives, vegetables and fruit	

Salmon burgers

Makes 5 burgers (5 servings)

1 can (425g) salmon, drained
1 egg, lightly beaten
½ cup (60g) finely chopped green
    or red bell pepper
½ cup (20g) fresh, whole-wheat
    bread crumbs
1 teaspoon lemon juice
1 teaspoon grated lemon zest
½ teaspoon dried rosemary, crushed
Pinch each of salt and pepper
1 teaspoon olive oil

● Combine all the ingredients, except the olive oil, in a bowl and mix well. Form into five patties.

● Heat the olive oil in a nonstick skillet on medium heat. Fry the patties for 4 minutes on each side or until lightly browned.

● Serve the salmon burgers hot, on whole-grain buns or alone, with a favourite vegetable or salad.

Nutritional analysis per burger (without bun)	
calories	211
fat	11g (of which 1g is saturated)
protein	21g
carbohydrate	8g
fibre	0g
minerals	–
vitamins	C
Food groups: meat and alternatives	

Snacks and smoothies

Trail mix

Makes 7 servings (1/2 cup/125mL each)

1/2 cup (75g) golden or regular raisins

1/2 cup (70g) dried cranberries

1/2 cup (60g) dried apricots

1/4 cup (35g) unsalted peanuts

1/4 cup (35g) blanched, halved almonds

1/4 cup (40g) chocolate chips (optional)

1/4 cup (35g) sunflower seeds

1 cup (40g) crunchy wheat cereal or
   low-fat granola

● Combine all the ingredients in a container with a lid or in a bag. Trail Mix will keep, sealed, for about three weeks in a cool, dry place.

Nutritional analysis per serving (without chocolate chips)	
calories	208
fat	8g (of which 6g is saturated)
protein	6g
carbohydrate	36g
fibre	8g
minerals	potassium, zinc
vitamins	folate, B$_{12}$, E

Food groups: grain products, meat and alternatives

Healthy bean salsa

Makes 10 servings (1/2 cup/125mL each)

1 onion, peeled and finely chopped

4 tablespoons chopped fresh cilantro

1 can (425g) black beans,
   drained and rinsed

1 can (310g) white corn
   kernels, drained

1 can (400g) diced tomatoes

1 can (120g) diced chilies, drained

Juice of 1/2 lime

● Combine all the ingredients and serve with tortilla chips.

Nutritional analysis per serving	
calories	77
fat 0.4g (of which 0.1g is saturated)	
protein	3g
carbohydrate	16g
fibre	3g
minerals	potassium
vitamins	folate

Food groups: meat and alternatives, vegetables and fruit

Apple bars

Makes about 24 bars (1 serving each)

1/2 cup or 1 stick (115g) butter

1 cup (200g) sugar

1 egg, beaten

1 1/2 cups (190g) all-purpose flour

1/2 teaspoon baking soda

1/2 teaspoon grated nutmeg

2 cups (225g) sliced apples

Topping

1/4 cup (50g) brown sugar

1/2 cup (65g) chopped walnuts

1/2 teaspoon grated nutmeg

1/2 teaspoon ground cinnamon

● Preheat the oven to 350°F (180°C).
● Cream the butter (at room temperature) and sugar together. Add the egg and mix well.
● In another bowl, stir together the flour, baking soda, and nutmeg. Add to the creamed mixture and blend well. Mix in the apples. Spread the batter in a greased 23- by 33-cm baking pan.
● Combine the ingredients for the topping and scatter evenly over the batter in the pan.
● Bake for 30 minutes. Let cool in the pan before cutting into bars for serving.

Nutritional analysis per bar	
calories	130
fat	6g (of which 3g is saturated)
protein	1g
carbohydrate	19g
fibre	1g
minerals	zinc
vitamins	E

Food groups: grain products, vegetables and fruit

Strawberry-banana smoothie

Makes 2 servings

(1¼ cups/310mL each)

1 cup (250mL) 1% low-fat milk

½ cup (125mL) low-fat smooth tofu

½ cup (75g) sliced bananas

½ cup (125g) sliced fresh or frozen
    unsweetened strawberries

Coarsely crushed ice

- Put all the ingredients in a blender or food processor and blend until smooth and frothy. Serve immediately.
- Instead of low-fat milk, you can use nonfat milk or substitute soy or rice milk. Note, though, that soy milk contains considerably less calcium than cow's milk, and rice milk has less protein.

Nutritional analysis per serving	
calories	136
fat	5g (of which 1g is saturated)
protein	10g
carbohydrate	16g
fibre	2g
minerals	calcium, potassium
vitamins	B$_{12}$, C, D

Food groups: milk products, meat and alternatives, vegetables and fruit

Fruit-nutty smoothie

Makes 3 servings

(about 1½ cups/375mL each)

1 cup (250ml) nonfat plain yogourt

1 cup (250mL) 1% low-fat milk

1½ cups (380g) sliced fresh or
    frozen unsweetened strawberries

1 fresh peach, peeled and sliced, or
    ½ cup (125g) frozen
    unsweetened peach slices

2 teaspoons vanilla extract

For garnish

2 tablespoons chopped walnuts

Whole strawberries

- Put all the ingredients (except the garnish) in a blender or food processor and blend until smooth and frothy.
- Pour into glasses and garnish, then serve.

Nutritional analysis per serving	
calories	149
fat	4.5g (of which 1g is saturated)
protein	7g
carbohydrate	20g
fibre	2g
minerals	calcium, potassium
vitamins	A, B$_{12}$, C, D

Food groups: milk products, meat and alternatives, vegetables and fruit

Berry good smoothie

Makes 2 servings

(about 1½ cups/375mL each)

1 cup (250mL) 1% low-fat milk

½ cup (125mL) low-fat smooth tofu

⅓ cup (50g) fresh or frozen
    unsweetened blueberries

⅓ cup (40g) fresh or frozen
    unsweetened raspberries

⅓ cup (85g) sliced fresh or frozen
    unsweetened strawberries

Coarsely crushed ice

- Put all the ingredients in a blender or food processor and blend until smooth and frothy. Serve immediately.

Nutritional analysis per serving	
calories	129
fat	5g (of which 1g is saturated)
protein	9.5g
carbohydrate	15g
fibre	3g
minerals	calcium, potassium
vitamins	B$_{12}$, C, D

Food groups: milk products, meat and alternatives, vegetables and fruit

Recommended resources

Food and nutrition

5 to 10 a Day Campaign

This campaign encourages Canadians to consume at least five servings of vegetables and fruit and day as part of a healthy diet and healthy lifestyle.
http://www.5to10aday.com/eng/.index.htm

Breakfast for Learning, Canadian Living Foundation

Canada's only national, non-profit organization solely dedicated to supporting child nutrition.
(416) 218-3540/(800) 627-7922

Canadian Food Inspection Agency

Provides details about food safety and nutritional quality standards in Canada.
http://www.inspection.gc.ca

Canadian Institute of Child Health

Dedicated to promoting and protecting the health, well-being, and rights of all children and youth, through monitoring, education, and advocacy.
http://www.cich.ca

Canadian Paediatric Society

The website, designed specifically for parents, is a great source of information on feeding a vegetarian child, food allergies, fussy eaters, and vitamin supplements.
http://www.cps.ca

Canadian Produce Manufacturers' Association

This association provides consumer information on health, nutrition, and food safety, including consumer fact sheets on vegetables, fruit, and healthy eating.
http://www.cpma.ca/en/hnfs/hnfsconsumer.html

Club des petits déjeuners du Québec

The club provides nutritious breakfasts to children in need, to help them succeed both educationally and in life.
http://www.clubdejeuners.org

Dietitians of Canada

This association promotes health through food and nutrition and provides information about dietitians in Canada.
http://www.dietitians.ca

Health Canada – Food and Nutrition

The Food and Nutrition section of Health Canada's website includes Canada's Food Guide to Healthy Eating and information on topics such as food labeling and BMI.
http://www.hc-sc.gc.ca/english/lifestyles/food_nutr.html

Office of Nutrition Policy and Promotion

Provides detailed information on Canada's Food Guide to Healthy Eating.
http://www.hc-sc.gc.ca/hpfb-dgpsa/onpp-bppn/3

La Leche League of Canada

Help for breastfeeding, advice and support.
http://www.lalecheleaguecanada.ca

National Institute of Nutrition

Provides facts about food and offers information specifically about children and nutrition.
http://www.nin.ca

Physical activity and sports

Athletics Canada

The national sport governing body for track and field. They organize events across the country and encourage the participation of Canadians of all ages and abilities.
http://www.athleticscanada.com

Canadian Camping Association

The CCA offers information for parents on how to choose the right camp for every child and an online "Camp Search".
http://www.ccamping.org

Children's Safety Association of Canada

This non-profit organization offers tips on pool and playground safety, plus information on products and services.
http://www.safekid.org

Health Canada – Physical Activity

Provides national guidelines to help children and youth improve their health through regular physical activity:
Canada's Physical Activity Guides for Children/Youth
Teacher's Guide to Physical Activity for Children/Youth
Family Guide to Physical Activity for Children/Youth
GottaMove! Magazine for Children
Let's Get Active! Magazine for Youth
For copies, call 1-888-334-9769
All publications are available at: http://www.hc-sc.gc.ca/hppb/paguide/child_youth/index.html

Safe Kids Canada

This organization is dedicated to keeping children safe by providing information on how to prevent injuries.
http://www.safekidscanada.ca

Sport Canada

This government organization provides and supports sport programs across the country.
http://www.pch,gc.ca/sportcanada/

Associations for various sports and activities

Alpine Skiing http://www.canski.org
Baseball http://www.baseball.ca
Basketball http://www.basketball.ca
Cross-country skiing http://canada.x-c.com/
Curling http://www.curling.ca
Cycling http://www.canadiancycling.ca
Fencing http://www.fencing.ca
Figure skating http://www.skatecanada.ca
Geocaching http://www.geocaching.com
Golf http://www.cjga.com
Gymnastics http://www.gymcan.org
Hockey http://www.hockeycanada.ca
Judo http://www.judocanada.org
Sailing http://www.sailing.ca
Soccer http://www.canadasoccer.com
Speed skating http://www.speedskating.ca
Swimming http://www.swimming.ca
Tennis http://www.tenniscanada.ca
Volleyball http://www.volleyball.ca

Kids with special needs

Active Living Alliance for Canadians with a Disability (ALACD)

Advocates fitness and physical activity for Canadians with disabilities. Provides information on events.
http://www.ala.ca

Canadian Diabetes Association

The website provides information on managing diabetes.
http://www.diabetes.ca/Section_About/nutritionIndex.asp

Canadian Lung Association

This national organization is an advocate for people who have lung disorders, including asthma.
http://www.lung.ca

Canadian Paralympic Committee

CPC offers a broad range of programs and services for aspiring athletes with disabilities.
http://www.paralympic.ca

Heart and Stroke Foundation of Canada

HSFC's mission is to prevent and reduce disability and death from heart disease and stroke through research, health promotion, and advocacy. The website provides health information and resources, as well as recipes and lifestyle tips.
http://www.heartandstroke.ca

Juvenile Diabetes Foundation of Canada

Provides awareness, education, and support.
http://www.jdfc.ca

Learning Disabilities Association of Canada

This non-profit voluntary organization provides programs and support for Canadians living with learning disabilities.
http://www.ldac-taac.ca

Special Olympics Canada

This national non-profit organization is dedicated to enriching the lives of Canadians with a mental disability through sport.
http://www.canoe.ca/CanadianSpecialOlympics/

Index

A

activity log 60, 62

activity
  menu 60
  recommendations 63

adolescents 148–69
  dieting 162–3
  fitness 54, 164–9
  jobs 169
  nutrition 152–63

aerobic exercise 56

alcohol 155

allergies
  asthma 178–9
  food allergies 78, 79,
    174–5

allergists 173

amino acids 35

anaphylaxis 175

anorexia nervosa 147, 163

apple bars 200

archery 142

arm curl exercise 58

ascorbic acid 39

asthma 178–9

athletic children 136–7, 145,
  182–5

attention deficit hyperactivity
  disorder (ADHD) 120, 179

B

babies 68–91
  activity 54, 84–91
  burping 76
  feeding 70–1, 72–83
  night feeds 83
  overweight 71
  physical development 71,
    85
  play 88, 89, 91
  safety 86, 90

  self-feeding 82–3

baby carriers 87

baby food 80

banana smoothie 201

baseball 137
  safety gear 65

basketball 137
  safety gear 65

beans
  healthy bean salsa 200
  vegetarian chili 198

beef, traditional meat sauce
    for pasta or gnocchi 199

berry good smoothie 201

bicycling 137

binge eating 147, 163

blood sugar levels
  diabetes 151, 176, 177
  glycemic index 34

blueberry pancakes 191

bocce 142

Body Mass Index (BMI)
  18–19, 147

bones, calcium and 157

bottle-feeding see formula
  feeding

bowel movements, babies
  79

breakfast
  adolescents 153–4, 156,
    161
  preschool children 114
  recipes 190–1
  school-age children 130,
    133
  toddlers 97

breastfeeding 72, 74–6
  benefits of 74
  burping baby 76
  feeding schedule 73
  problems 74
  stopping 100

breathing problems
  asthma 178–9
  overweight children 22

bulimia nervosa 147, 163

burgers, salmon 199

burping babies 76

C

caffeine 116–17, 183

calcium 38, 39
  adolescent diet 156–7
  athletic children 183
  food labels 48
  preschoolers' diet 112
  school-age children's diet
    132
  toddlers' diet 96
  vegetarian diet 159

calf stretch exercise 57

calories 33
  adolescent diet 153, 156
  athletic children 183
  babies' needs 70
  food labels 48
  in pop 116
  preschoolers' diet 112
  school-age children's diet
    127, 132
  toddlers' diet 96

camps
  summer camps 141, 181
  weight-management
    camps 147

commercials, for food 29,
  115, 133

canned food 47

carbohydrates 34
  adolescent diet 153
  athletic children 183
  and diabetes 176
  food labels 48
  grains 40, 41

school-age children's diet
  127

cereal
  breakfast cereal 127, 154
  hearty Swiss cereal 190
  infant cereal 78–9

cheese
  cheesy quiche 197
  traditional quesadillas 193

chicken
  homemade chicken soup
    194
  salad with pan-grilled
    chicken 196
  Wild West wrap 193

child care 86, 107

chili, vegetarian 198

choking 83

cholesterol 36
  fibre and 34
  food labels 48

colleges 161

computer games 29, 62, 121

conflict at mealtimes 101–2

contracts, fitness 60, 167

convenience food 14, 42, 47

cooking 188–9
  involving children 45, 117,
    131

cooling-down exercises 64

coordination, baby's 88

crawling 91

croquet 142

cups, introducing 83, 100

curl-ups exercise 59, 63

curling 142

D

daily nutritional requirements
  32, 33, 48

dairy foods/milk products
  adolescent diet 157

Acknowledgments

KidsHealth

We would like to thank the following people:
Erica Blacksburg; Allison Brinkley, RD; Beth Dowshen;
Debra Duby; Randy B. Garber; Cathy Ginther;
Mary Lou Jay; Marissa Lippert; D'Arcy Lyness, PhD;
James M. Poole, MD; Eric Small, MD; Shaynee Snider;
Amy Sutton; Eve Tahmincioglu; and Laura Winchester.

Dorling Kindersley

We would like to thank Hilary Bird for the index; Jenn
Crake for the resources listings; Salima Hirani and
Kathryn Wilkinson for editorial assistance; Isabel de
Cordova, Sara Kimmins, Iona Hoyle, and Cath McKenzie
for design help.

Photography Janeanne Gilchrist, Unit Photographic